MANAGING SEVA (SELFLESS SERVICE) IN TIMES OF GREAT CHANGE

MANAGING SEVA (SELFLESS SERVICE) IN TIMES OF GREAT CHANGE

RAHUL M. JINDAL, MD, PH.D.

Professor, Department of Surgery and Division of Global Health at Uniformed Services University & the Walter Reed National Military Medical Center

Fulbright-Nehru Distinguished Chair to India, 2015-6

Commissioner, Governor's Office on Service and Volunteerism, Maryland

Commissioner, Montgomery County Office of Human Rights, Maryland

MANAGINGSEVA(SELFLESSSERVICE)INTIMESOFGREATCHANGE

Washington, DC, 2015

iUniverse books may be ordered through booksellers or by contacting:

iUniverse
1663 Liberty Drive
Bloomington, IN 47403
www.iuniverse.com
1-800-Authors (1-800-288-4677)

ISBN: 978-1-4917-8153-1 (sc)
ISBN: 978-1-4917-8154-8 (e)

Print information available on the last page.

iUniverse rev. date: 11/09/2015

Contents

.

FOREWORD

SEVA: THE SELFLESS COMMUNITY SERVICE

Seva is the spiritual practice of selfless service. *Seva*, a Sanskrit word[1], springs from two forms of yoga, Karma Yoga which is yoga of action and Bhakti Yoga, the yoga of worship inspired by divine love. Seva is one of the simplest and yet most profound and life changing ways that we can put our spiritual knowledge into action. Seva is asking *"How may I serve you?"* Or ask *"Can I help you?"* Another way of doing service is to roll up your sleeves and help where you notice that you are needed. We can share our resources and energy with those in need and respond positively when a person asks for help. "Being there as the need arises" is a simple definition of seva by Sri Ravi Shankar of the Art of Living Foundation[2]. When you consider work as divine service, you can do it anywhere, at any time. Doing seva is uplifting your own self, your own people and your world. Offering our seva is a way to make a significant contribution to the spiritual community of fellow beings on earth. It is a practice that feeds us spiritually and a spiritual discipline that awakens us to the greater truth of our own being. The concept of seva or selfless service has been with us in the East as well as in the Western countries since time immemorial. This was true since the time of Andrew Carnegie[3] and others and is now being seen in developing

---

[1] http://en.wikipedia.org/wiki/Seva (Accessed 08/10/2015)

[2] http://www.artofliving.org/us-en (Accessed 08/10/2015)

[3] http://library.columbia.edu/indiv/rbml/units/carnegie/andrew.html (Accessed 08/10/2015)

countries by the creation of new wealth. The proliferation of non-profits and non-governmental organizations (NGO) is a testament to this.

People also live longer and in their later years during retirement, they want to find a meaning to their lives – this is often expressed in volunteerism with a variety of local and national charity organizations. Many people do seva in their own little ways without formally joining a non-profit organization (NGO).

There is also a large and growing population of immigrants from the former developing countries who live in the West and wish to "give back" to their countries of birth. This seva is often by building schools and hospitals in their towns and villages.

Yet another form of seva is by carrying out medical missions to distant lands where there is an acute shortage of medical personnel and medications.

Despite the universal desire for seva, managing the process of seva is formidable and can create tensions and undo the desire to help the needy. There are frictions within the organization, either NGO or a non-formal group of people who wish to do seva. There are also personal rivalries and organizational issues which need to be navigated so that the end result is visible and tangible. Seva also has to comply with local, state, and national regulations, statutes and laws. Despite the concept of seva as selfless service, there is a need for adequate publicity to engage others who may have similar programs and to avoid duplication. Attracting funds is also a challenge. As programs become bigger, they create more paperwork and hierarchical systems which may impede progress and prevent funds going to the needy.

Introduction of new programs in a community give rise to a revolution of rising expectations[4]. Traditionally, the impact of "rising expectations" may lead to youth wanting and demanding more, quest for greater freedom, consumerism, education, desire for upward social

---

[4] http://www.icpd.org/development_theory/SocialDevTheory.htm (Accessed 08/10/2015)

mobility. This may in some cases lead to social unrest[5]. Frequently, both parties are disappointed and there may be a backlash towards the organizers of seva. We hope that our case studies will enable both the seva givers to better manage their seva programs. Our intention is not to discredit any government or officialdom, but merely to point out the problems we faced. There are of course, many dedicated government and non-government individuals who are honest and doing their job with dedication despite numerous challenges, many of which are inherent in any vast organization.

There are many models of government which may include a true democracy and autocracy and models in-between. Similarly, there are many forms and formats of seva. An ideal model may not exist. Recently, the erudite Thomas L. Friedman suggested that the ideal capitalist model may be a balanced *public-private* partnership — where government provided the institutions, rules, safety nets, education, research and infrastructure to empower the private sector to innovate, invest and take the risks that promote growth and jobs[6]. Perhaps, there lies a model of seva which may be close to ideal.

I was impressed by James Kofi Annan's lecture at Grinnell Young Innovators for Social Justice Prize Symposium[7] entitled "Passion, Commitment, and Innovation: The Critical Success Factors in Community Project Sustainability". James Kofi Annan, told of his own personal journey from being a child slave, a victim of child trafficking, and a survivor of child trafficking in the country of Ghana. He escaped from that institution and to become educated, from learning to read after the age of 13, to entering college, and then getting a master's degree in Ghana, and then working for Barclays Bank. But his commitment did not end with his own personal improvement. He then turned his passion for social justice, to helping other children who were in the same conditions he had once lived in himself, as anti-slavery activists

---

[5] http://www.icpd.org/employment/Rising%20Expectations,%20Demography,%20Aging_files/frame.htm (Accessed 08-24-2015)

[6] http://www.nytimes.com/2012/03/14/opinion/friedman-capitalism-version-2012.html?_r=1&hp (Accessed 08-24-2015)

[7] http://www.grinnell.edu/grinnellprize/winners/annan (Accessed 08-24-2015)

have done for many hundreds of years. James founded the organization Challenging Heights in 2003 to provide education and support for children who have emerged from human trafficking and to prevent children from being sold into slavery in the country of Ghana. As president, he provides for more than 500 children in a school as well as education and support for survivors who go through a reorientation process and are physically, literally saved from forced labor. I firmly believe that to sustain any project, there is a need for passion and commitment, and if there is no innovation, the project will wither away.

Paul Alofs, CEO at the fundraising efforts at Canada's leading cancer hospital, the Princess Margaret[8] has helped raise $550-million, and now he is leading a new quest for $1billion to finance research into personalized cancer treatments. Mr. Alofs is also about to launch a book, *Passion Capital*, offering his view on how institutions can harness workers' energy and intensity. The not-for-profit sector is served by volunteers. These are people who work for free and a lot of them report that this is the most fulfilling part of their week. We have found that harnessing the passion of volunteers, whether they are teachers in remote parts of India, volunteers in national blood donation drives in the USA or physicians in Guyana, was critical in our seva projects.

"To whom much is given, much is expected." The fact of life is that a lot has been given to us in the USA, while many in developing countries did not even have the opportunity to go to a primary school to acquire the most basic of education, primary health care lacks in many developing countries, before our medical mission in Guyana, there was no facility for kidney replacement services in Guyana, South America – a patient with kidney failure simply died. Our renal replacement program in Guyana[9] [10] and our blood and bone marrow donation[11] programs are in response to this need. This fact alone motivated us to do something – to give back to the community – the global community.

---

[8] http://m.theglobeandmail.com/report-on-business/careers/careers-leadership/at-the-top/trading-financial-profit-for-social-capital/article2417290 (Accessed 08/24/2015)
[9] http://sevakproject.org/ (Accessed 08/09/2015)
[10] http://bulletin.facs.org/2013/06/rrt-to-patients-in-guyana/ (Accessed 08/09/2015)
[11] http://hindusgiftoflife.org/ (Accessed 08/09/2015)

Participation in distance learning is another example which can help a large number of educators in developing countries who may lack resources in health psychology. The University of West London has initiated a Master's program in Global Health Psychology in which I have been involved since its inception. They have a special focus on developing countries and personnel who participate in humanitarian missions[12].

I have also participated as visiting faculty in the "Global Energy Parliament" which had its first conference in Kerala, India, in 2010[13]. Life for Total Consciousness (LTC) is espoused by Swami Isa who is also the patron of the Global Energy Parliament. There are many ashrams in India, some good, some commercial, but only a few achieve an international stature. Participation in this endeavor and introduction of vigorous evidence based clinical trial of mind-body medicine has been an eye opening experience.

This book details my personal experience of carrying our seva in the USA, India and Guyana, South America. I give case histories from my own experience and how I navigated the turbulent waters to deliver what we set out to accomplish. I hope that our team's work will motivate others to understand the difficulties and find solutions to fulfilling the goal of seva. At the end, we could not achieve anything without the help of dedicated team members many of whom gave up their vacations and willingly gave their money and energy to make a difference.

[12]   https://www.uwl.ac.uk/course/global-health-psychology/34348   (Accessed 08/09/2015)

[13] http://www.global-energy-parliament.net/ (Accessed 08/09/2015)

CHAPTER 1

Selection Of Country For Seva

Guyana and India are the two countries where the author of this book has managed the charity projects. I have been managing charity project of kidney transplants in Guyana and a mind-body research trial in Kerala, India, in addition to a national blood and bone marrow drive in the USA.

Seva projects of health care can definitely help the poor in the villages of India. In the case of Guyana, seva project took the form of a private-public partnership to provide dialysis and kidney transplant service which did not exist – patients with kidney failure simply died. Recently, we also initiated a survey and educational work in preventative care and sanitation in several villages of Guyana[14]. This would serve as a model for the rest of the country.

Over the last sixty years, India has developed in many ways, economically and socially. The country's large business community has expanded to become international in nature and importance. Major metropolitan cities in the country are bustling with resources that were once reserved for Western countries. The life in the villages, where over seventy percent of the population of India lives, has also developed, economically and partially socially. The majority of the population in India still remains poor, compared to any Western country. There are stark contrasts in all walks of life, ranging from the most modern and luxurious ways to the ways of the deprived people with meager resources.

Poor people do not have the luxury to go to the doctor or the hospital for checkup. They can hardly take care of their daily need for food. How can they pay for health care? Many of them do not even have the basic education. Lacking education, they do not even understand the importance of hygiene in routine and daily ways of life. We have seen the utterly unhealthy conditions in which the poor people live in India and Guyana. They do not have the facilities for daily functions, like a toilet and running water. Waste water runs in open drains next to the small sized cottages where they live, cook, eat and sleep. During

---

[14] www.sevakproject.org (Accessed 08/09/2015)

rainy season, pools of stagnant water can be seen all around their living quarters.

The dirty conditions all around the living environment are prone to all kinds of disease causing germs and bacteria. Fever from all kinds of infection is very common. Most of the poor people live through the fever, until it subsides naturally. They may go to the local medicine man, without any authorized qualification to practice medicine, who dispenses general medicines to the patients for all kinds of ailments. In most cases, the patients get better as a matter of chance, or by the grace of God, and with strong faith of the poor in God.

If Indians aren't charitable why should people from other countries help? A recent Satyamev Jayate[15] reaches 400 million viewers but so far has raised less than $305,000 for its recommended charities, half of which is in the form of a matching grant from the Reliance Foundation. That amounts to a tiny fraction of one cent per viewer. In fact, it's about 2 paise per viewer. It has been estimated that private charitable giving in India amounted to just 0.3-0.4% of gross domestic product. In the U.S., the figure was 2.2% in 2009, while in the U.K. in 2010 it was 1.3%[16].

The poor of India have shown strong resilience for paucity of resources. The poor have demonstrated the will to improve the lot of their children by working hard. They have begun to save their earnings so that their children may get good education. The poor spend most of their time to earn just enough to meet the bare minimum need to eat daily meals. They have no way to take care of other important needs, of education and health care. Seva projects can provide for these needs of the poor, namely education and health care. Due to basic economics, is probably the main reason that Indians might be reluctant to give to charity. But other reasons may well include a perceived lack of transparency and accountability among charities, tax laws that aren't favorable to charitable giving, and a lack of information about charities

[15] http://www.satyamevjayate.in/ (Accessed 08/24/2015)
[16] Why charity is different in India: http://blogs.wsj.com/indiarealtime/2012/07/11/economics-journal-why-charity-is-different-in-india/ (Accessed 08/24/2015)

to match the giving priorities of potential donors. Another factor could be that more ethnically diverse societies commit less to charity. A U.S. study[17] based on Canadian data found that diversity has a negative impact on charitable giving. In particular, the researchers found that a 10 percentage point increase in ethnic diversity caused charitable donations to fall by 14%. Likewise, a 10 percentage point increase in religious diversity caused charitable giving to fall by 10%. One reason suggested is that people tend to prefer giving to their own. As societies become more diverse, money given to a large charity tends to spill over into other ethnic or religious groups, and people might therefore be less willing to give.

Another reason may be the recent crackdown by the Federal Government in India in which their report specifically criticized the charities for organizing public protests against nuclear power plants, uranium mines, coal-fired power plants, genetically modified crops and electronic waste. A Federal official was quoted as "The negative impact on GDP growth is assessed to be 2-3 percent"[18]

Finally, there may be cultural differences in India, where people may prefer to give anonymously rather than making gigantic pledges, such as Bill Gates, Buffett, and other billionaires. I found resonance in the statement "While I commend [Buffett and Gates's] philanthropy, what remains amazingly inexplicable is their reason to 'sell' this idea to others," says Devdutt Pattanaik, chief belief officer of the Future Group, India's largest retail chain. "I guess it stems from their fear of mortality. To 'convert' is not an Indian thing. Those who are charitable are charitable, and those who don't want to be are not."

Pattanaik notes that all the publicity surrounding the Pledge[19] may well be changing Indian thinking. "In India, the idea is that anyone can be generous. In the epics, there are references to the poorest of the poor and even animals displaying acts of generosity. With the

---

[17] Diversity and donations: http://www.nber.org/papers/w17618.pdf?new_window=1 (Accessed 08/24/2015)
[18] India cracking down on foreign funded charities: http://www.mintpressnews.com/india-cracking-foreign-funded-charities/192732/ (Accessed 08/24/2015)
[19] The giving pledge: http://givingpledge.org/ (Accessed 08/24/2015)

Western discourse coming in, the idea is increasingly becoming that the 'rich have to be generous.' This notion that charity and generosity are functions of wealth, and not personal evolution, is the trend that is increasingly evident. There is a move to coerce people into being charitable. The focus is tragically behavioral, not belief-driven."

Negative views as expressed below can also discourage volunteers, an example is below.

"Volunteer Experience": Global Citizenship at Rural School, India
While I had been to India several times as a tourist since 2006, I never imagined that seven years after my first visit I would return as a volunteer to work in a rural school in northern India's Uttar Pradesh state. I was instantly drawn to this project when the director of an Indian rural school residing in the USA asked me if I would be interested in volunteering to coach village student children to become global citizens. Attributes to be considered included the villagers way of life; their value systems; the desire of parents wanting their children to speak, write, and read English fluently; aspects affecting their studying at home; the ambitions and goals of the students or their lack of them. My proposal was interacting with students to foster their involvement by facilitating their participation in extracurricular activities in the school and in their community. Student leaders were to be identified and trained to initiate a survey and to complete basic field work in their own village communities including demographics, life style, sanitation and monitoring blood sugar and blood pressure of villagers, similar to the SEVAK project successfully established in several villages in India and Guyana, South America by Dr. Jindal and Dr. Patel. These efforts would afford students not only to become proficient in English but also to become engaged in their communities as responsible globalized citizens from an early age. I was thrilled this endeavor would afford underserved village students, as future leaders of society, an opportunity to experience and develop crucial leadership skills while actively engaging in social and civic activities that would enhance the well-being of their own local community. There was only one thing holding me back, I did not know

Hindi at all! *"I will arrange someone to translate Hindi to English and vice versa, so that you may visit students, their parents at their homes, and other villagers, and collect whatever information you may need to write a report on the subject… I shall also be reaching the school either late in the night of February 5ᵗʰ or during the day on February 6ᵗʰ,"* said the school director. I was expected to arrive in Delhi on January 29ᵗʰ. It all began to come together, the project was very promising.

Upon my arrival at the Indira Gandhi International Airport in Delhi, I was happily surprised to be welcomed by Anuj and Gaurav, two of the student leaders in the school who were displaying a beautiful colorful poster they have made for me to identify them. The students and I had an almost instant rapport and that was very encouraging. Traveling from Delhi to the school, a car ride several hours long, gave us ample time to get familiar with each other; they were so excited telling me all they knew about the school and the surroundings they were familiar with. Once we reached the school, I retired and looked forward to begin with my assignment in the morning.

Early in the morning I met with students who arrived long before class time and who otherwise would be running freely all over the school facilities until assembly time. Once classes began and even during recess, it was hard to interact much with anyone before they went home. As the days passed, students would come looking for me every chance they had, gradually they felt more comfortable speaking in English, taking pictures of each other, running around the school, singing or catching ball. Most of the teaching staff did not speak English at all so it was quite difficult to communicate unless one of the two English speaking teachers was nearby. Although, the school principal could carry on simple conversations with limited English-proficiency, her husband, the school administrator could not. As promised by the school director before I accepted to volunteer in the school, I asked the principal who was the person he had arranged to translate Hindi to English and vice versa; she had no idea what I was talking about. Without access to an interpreter to communicate effectively and efficiently with the school professional staff was a critical issue; overcoming language barriers was a huge challenge. I remained confident; the school director was expected to arrive just a few days after my arrival.

I approached the principal to arrange meeting with students and teaching staff to begin training students who would conduct the health surveys in their respective villages and also to seek approval to hold events that would facilitate further interaction with students, teaching staff, and villagers in the area as soon as possible. The principal informed me that the school director was calling her and the administrator several times daily to discuss arrangements to organize the villagers to plan several functions to commemorate a school related anniversary within the next few days. He himself would be at that event and he had requested for those functions to take precedence over any other event to be held in the school. The principal and the administrator were very unhappy with the way the school director was constantly harassing them on the phone day and night, in the school and at home. Consequently, any conversation we engaged in those days ended up being an outpouring of their frustration and resentment towards the school director and a declaration of their desire to start a school of their own to opt out of their current posts.

Meanwhile, the school director demanded for me to submit a report and some photos which, with reservation, I sent him via email with a bcc to the principal and the administrator as per their own request. It was a report based on first impressions derived from a four-day observation of the daily routines in the school; no major developments had yet taken place regarding the global citizenship project; it had been a week of introduction and socialization mainly with students only. The principal and the administrator were stressed working out the logistics for the anniversary's event pressured by the school director's endless phone calls. Similarly, I kept receiving numerous messages from the school director, *"I am looking forward to your interim report, with more photographs, especially in village settings."* The event took place and the director did not show up. Messages continued to come *"You have now been at the school for about twelve days. Can you update your impressions, especially your impressions of the visits to the families in the villages? With some clear photographs, including yours with them?"* Clearly the school director was unaware of the tone and dynamics developing in the school. The principal and the administrator had repeatedly stated how unhappy they both were working in the school and their firm intention to start a school of their own; there was no designated interpreter or provisions to assign one; the director himself had postponed his arrival indefinitely with the possibility of not meeting with me at the school before my return to the USA. The resources he had originally promised to support this effort were simply not available to meet his own demands and expectations; his initial commitment was debatable and so it was the role of the principal and the administrator; they were displeased working in the school.

Inexplicably, right after my initial report was submitted and after the announcement of the indefinite postponement of the director's arrival, both, the principal and the administrator became unapproachable, negligent and unscrupulous. The principal canceled several of our set appointments at the last minute without an option to re-schedule during school hours resulting in fewer opportunities for me to gain collaboration from the teaching staff; she required her approval before I could approach any teacher in the school. They constantly harassed me for monetary funding and urged me not to return to the USA but to remain in India to support their plans to start a school of their own to compete with the school they were currently managing. When I questioned and condemned such unethical behavior, they repeatedly claimed to have royal lineage in their home town. Equally, other instances proved their qualifications as principal and administrator of a children school as less than undesirable. Upon informing the principal of an incident where a very young female student was brutally slapped by a member of the teaching staff, the principal responded "*she has done that before*" and when I asked her what action she was taking to remedy the situation and to prevent any other student from ever being subjected to this sort of abuse, the principal replied "*I'll ask her not to do it again.*" Neglecting critical issues like this and not taking any action to stop and/or prevent these practices from re-occurring account for the fact that students of all ages themselves vastly displayed the same type of violent practices hitting each other on the head or slapping each other on the face as a result of learning by example from their own teachers. The school was not a safe environment for children-- physical facilities deterioration, extreme poor maintenance of facilities and buses, and deplorable sanitation conditions posed a serious threat to the safety and well-being of all those who transited through the campus, including the children. For instance, obvious hazardous conditions were specifically pointed out to both the principal and the administrator and no efforts were made by either one to even attempt to correct such dangerous conditions so no one would get hurt, especially when students remained unsupervised for extended periods of time and they ran all over the school unaware of all the dangers they were exposed to. Principals set the tone in the school; they are responsible for the education each student receives under their care; they resolve staffing - student discipline issues, not ignore them. Administrators decisions must be made in terms of the best interests of the students not their own; they cannot allow their personal feelings or loyalties to cloud their judgment.

With my best interest at heart to conduct a study of the underprivileged children population in the rural school as per the school director's request, I was not only bullied but also practically forced to spend my own money to pay for various expenses such as shoes, shirts, skirts, blouses, pants and sweaters for the children; hotel expenses and meals for drivers; tolls; parking tickets; meals, movie and attraction tickets for staff and the principal's family members; groceries and even shawls for the principal, and a pair of pajamas for their driver. In addition, I was been asked to pay for a lunch for 50-52 staff members of the school in order to conduct an initiative to promote and advance the well-being of villagers in the local community with the help of selected trained students to perform a science based survey and demonstrate their newly acquired skills monitoring blood sugar and blood pressure of villagers, including members of their own families. During my stay at the school, I paid for telephone and internet charges myself and I also paid for medical instruments and office supplies which were kept by the school administration. All of this was totally unacceptable and unethical behavior on their part. As a visiting volunteer, I should have never been put in a situation to have to spend money out of my own pocket to cover for such expenses, much less to be subjected to such an abusive treatment in an attempt to blackmail me to recover fictitious expenses, allegedly incurred by the school.

As a dedicated volunteer who sacrificed and donated my own personal time and who took the risk to visit a rural school in India with my best interest at heart to conduct a study of the underprivileged children population in a remote area as per the school director's request, I was extremely distraught over this unfortunate experience due to the unscrupulous behavior of the principal and the administrator who managed the school on behalf of the family who owns the school. Not only have they tried to ruin my reputation by fabricating an alleged incident and by conveniently trying to hush up the whole situation, and with the school director's approval, but they also obtained false declarations from their staff and unsuccessfully tried to lure me into taking inappropriate photos inside the room I stayed in at the school with one of the teaching staff members shortly before I left the school to return home. What was more shocking to me is the fact that the same individual who had asked me to go to the school he directs in India to coach students to become global citizens and who had specifically requested for me to consider attributes such as their "value systems" was the same individual who have shamelessly approved of an ill-fabricated incident by attempting to hush up the whole situation without conducting a full investigation. How can he, a school director, maintain and protect the integrity of an educational institution when he himself lacks transparency, ethical values, and objectivity in judgment.

I thank Dr. Jindal who supported and counseled me professionally through this devastating volunteer experience I was subjected to by individuals whose best interest at heart was their own not that of the underprivileged students attending the rural school they managed. Dr. Jindal took time out of his busy schedule to contact me and listen to my side of the story to document and state the facts accurately and impartially. The members of the board of directors of this rural school in India were duly and formally informed; they offered their apologies and regretted this whole incident ever happened.

CONCLUSION

Knowledge of the poor's suffering causes pain in the rich person's mind. When the rich donate their extra resources to help alleviate the suffering of the poor, charity happens. Not all donations would qualify to be called charity. Only when the donation truly helps alleviate the suffering of the needy, the act of donation qualifies as charity. The true needs of the poor should be fulfilled by genuine seva, or charity projects[20].

Charity happens when part of the self is donated to the truly needy person, to alleviate his/her suffering. True charity becomes synonymous with the act of sacrifice. In India, sacrifice has been hailed as the most purifying spiritual practice prescribed in the scriptures. The country where one practices seva is not important, each country has ups and downs, good and the bad, seva should not discriminate and be "offering an important part of the self" to the needy in the community. *Sacrifice is seva.*

---

20 Bhagavad Gita, Chapter 17, V.20

CHAPTER 2

The Public Private Partnership Model To Provide Humanitarian Services In Developing Countries

The regional Combatant Commands in the United States are reaching out to allied countries and their military forces to create mutual security. One way to create such partnerships is through health programs, which are often perceived as unthreatening to the host nation. Some of these partnership activities involve direct provision of healthcare by US military medical personnel, but the trend is away from that unsustainable, Cold War model. Increasingly, the facilitation of health programs to build capacity can be done by non-governmental organizations (NGOs) as the model. NGOs often remain in a country continuously for many years, developing a host nation capacity in ways that a short-term military mission could not. Interventions by NGO's that are intermittent but long-term can also encourage the host nation to take ownership and sustain the health service capacity on their own.

We describe a Public-Private Partnership (PPP) model for a variety of humanitarian services in Guyana and in India by medical professionals in uniform, retired military officers, and US Federal employees. Public-private partnerships can be formal, with specific memoranda of agreement delineation of duties and deliverables, or can take a less structured form that suits all parties. In Guyana, the work was specific, based on the local needs for renal replacement therapy (RRT), corneal transplantation, and a village-based public health effort, the SEVAK[21] program. These services were provided to bring the best available medical expertise from the U.S to a developing country at no cost to patients, in partnership with a philanthropist from the USA local governments and health care personnel in Guyana and in India. Such a PPP does not rely on direct funding by any US governmental agency and may be a model which could be replicated in other countries. Our work continues to undergo modifications as we learn from our five years of experience.

As the US military continues its efforts in global health engagement, there will be opportunities to facilitate or implement PPPs to enhance

---

[21] Sanitation and Health, Education in Village communities through improved Awareness and Knowledge of Prevention/Management of Diseases and Health Promotion

mutual security. Out of the activities of PPPs and NGOs may be some best practices that can be adapted to the needs of the health and security challenges of developing countries.

RRT PROGRAM IN GUYANA, SOUTH AMERICA

Our work has been possible because of an intricate partnership between private and public sectors. The initial idea and funding for the project came from a Guyanese philanthropist, living in the U.S., who saw a dire need for RRT and corneal transplantation in his country of origin (Guyana) and sought to help those in despair. In a developing country like Guyana, very few patients could afford the cost of RRT and related services. The transplant team, led by Dr. Jindal, consists of other transplant surgeons, a nephrologist, an operating room nurse, a dialysis nurse, and an anesthesiologist. Most of the team members are from the US, and the exact participants for each visit depend upon availability. Trips are scheduled a few months apart, to allow the recipients to stabilize before new surgery is performed. The Ministry of Health of the Guyanese government plays a significant role in facilitating hospital space, some of the hospital services, and free of cost medications (generic, imported from India), while the local medical staff identify patients and provide pre- and post-operative follow-up care. US providers also bring documentation of their credentials for examination and certification by the government of Guyana.

Since its commencement in 2008, our PPP has carried out 26 living kidney transplants and numerous peritoneal dialysis catheter placements and vascular access procedures for hemodialysis. This service was not available in the country before the US team arrived. Host nation providers have participated in the surgery and care of these patients, learning new skills and gaining confidence to work independently. We also can biopsy the native kidneys, which are read by U.S. pathologists, ex gratis. We have also delivered lectures and held press conferences to make local doctors and patients aware of the program, and helped change the government's health policy[1][2]. Our work has also led to a number of professional journal publications, which may assist physicians in other developing countries to develop a renal replacement program[3][4].

Post-operative and some unstable pre-operative patients are closely followed via Skype™ videoconferences and e-mails with the local physicians. A primer of transplantation and immunosuppression, taking into account the local availability and cost of medications, has been developed. This educational process is crucial for the sustainability of the RRT program in Guyana, and it is an ongoing process.

A local urologist, anesthesiologist, internist, and operating room nurse are now well trained to manage dialysis and transplant patients, so the visiting team is smaller and over the next few years our role will mainly be support via tele-medicine. Creating a capacity solely within the host nation is the ultimate goal of the program. The Department of Defense has limited RRT capability, but being able to provide some of these services in a forward-deployed scenario and utilizing teleconference consultation is realistic. Lessons learned from efforts in Guyana can inform planners and medical leaders about best practices in this field. Further, the Southern Command can benefit from positive publicity brought to our nation, and from the access and influence it provides. Several national newspapers in Guyana have reported positively on the outcomes of the kidney transplant program[5][6].

CORNEAL TRANSPLANT PROGRAM IN GUYANA, SOUTH AMERICA

In the developing world, the restoration of sight can also be a powerful tool for creating positive publicity and restoring the ability of recipient patients to contribute to local economic activity. Dr Waller, our surgeon was part of an Air Force team that performed such surgery in Nicaragua in the late 1990's, when the US did not have a military-to-military relationship. The cornea transplant surgery was featured on national TV and in the Managua newspapers[7], and helped open the door to a better military relationship with the host country. That short-term mission was not designed, however, to bring independent corneal transplant capability to Nicaragua, as the work in Guyana is focused on achieving.

The inception of a successful, sustainable corneal transplant program in a developing country like Guyana takes substantial, long-term efforts and involves partnership with government agencies, sponsorship to help with incurring costs and building surgical capacity, establishing an infrastructure for an eye bank, identification of appropriate patients, and reliable follow up. Eye banks in the U.S. must be certified by Eye Bank Association of America (EBAA) and the Food and Drug Administration (FDA). Eye banks in Latin America and the Caribbean basin should be certified by the Pan American Association of Eye Banks (APABO). The certification requirements include adequate space and equipment; 24-hour telephone service; certified technicians; a medical director, who is an ophthalmologist with expertise in cornea transplantation; and acceptance by the national association of ophthalmology and ministry of health in the host country. The medical director is responsible for ensuring application of medical standards, education of health care personnel, release and distribution of corneal tissue for transplant, and oversight of the waiting list. A separate administrative director is responsible for public awareness and quality control, and interaction with accreditation agencies (APABO, host nation ministry of health, and the national association of ophthalmology. An eye bank will also require at least one certified technician. The role of the eye bank technician involves consent of family, medical history review, physical examination of donor, ability to evaluate the eye and determine appropriateness of tissue for transplantation, ability to retrieve tissue by following standard operating procedures (SOPs) of the eye bank, and responsibility for obtaining serologic testing of the donor. The technician must ensure that there are no specific contraindications for donation, such as positive HIV status, hepatitis status, and injectable drug abuser profile, or active infection of the eye. The medical director oversees all these tasks by the technician, and ensures an equitable system for transplant waiting list with priority to younger patients and those with bilateral blindness.

An independent eye bank must establish medical standards (to protect the recipient and the technician), uniform evaluation procedures, recipient and donor data collection, quality assurance procedures, outcome analysis and accountability. The EBAA is the national accrediting organization for eye banks in the U.S., along with the FDA. Due to the efficient framework established by the EBAA and high rates of eye donation, there is an increasing trend of donations of corneas in the US, and often there are high quality corneas available gratis for humanitarian use. Dr Waller has utilized this resource in over a dozen countries, never paying for the donor corneas, nor charging the host nation recipients. A similar program in the developing world is at the National Eye Bank of Sri Lanka, which is a shining example of corneal donation and international export of corneas in Asia, and serves as a role model for both developed and developing countries.

In Guyana, the PPP corneal transplant mission in 2014 began first with an educational visit, including talks with host nation ministry of health and hospital leaders, and a city-wide lecture to the ophthalmologists on corneal transplantation[8]. Patients were examined together with a host nation ophthalmologist to determine suitability for subsequent corneal transplantation, and a waiting list was created. The conversation continued after the US team departed, as host nation surgeons obtained the necessary equipment for surgery. Six successful transplants of gratis US corneas were performed by the Guyanese surgeon, under supervision of Dr. Waller, during a second mission a few months later. All patients had substantial improvement in their vision post operatively. Further missions are planned as more patients are placed on the waiting list for corneal transplants in Guyana, and to continue the capacity-building that is required to independently sustain an eye bank and corneal transplantation services[9]. There is no firm timeline on establishing the eye bank in Guyana, but each visit by the PPP team improves local capacity, and all parties are focused on an effort that the host nation can sustain on its own.

SEVAK PROGRAM IN INDIA AND GUYANA

SEVAK Project[22] began in July, 2010, in India. It empowers a local lay person look after some of the basic health care needs of the people in their own village. The acronym SEVAK stands for "**S**anitation and Health **E**ducation in **V**illage communities through improved **A**wareness and **K**nowledge of Prevention/Management of Diseases and Health Promotion"[10]. The inspiration for this project came from the long-standing and successful Independent Duty Corpsman (IDC) program in the US Navy. Thakor G. Patel, CAPT MC USN (Ret), former Director of Surface Medicine for the US Navy, designed the SEVAK program and modeled it after the IDC program. The idea is that young people when empowered with training and practice can provide basic health care services in a culturally acceptable manner and at local standards.

Independent Duty Corpsmen are high school graduates that are given 12 months of intensive Navy medical training and then assigned to Marine Corps units or Navy ships. They are often fondly referred to as the "doc". IDCs provide primary and preventive care, evaluate trauma, and manage disasters, along with conducting environmental checks, such as humidity, temperature and sanitation. In global health terms, they are community health workers trained in a consistent fashion to provide health services and monitoring for a specific population. SEVAK training emphasizes lifestyle intervention and health screening for diabetes, hypertension, obesity, immunizations, and chronic diseases. SEVAK volunteers also received basic training in sanitation, environmental health, water purification, infectious diseases, and how to build toilets and smokeless cooking stoves. The project started in July 2010 in the Indian state of Gujarat and was approved by the Prime Minister Narendra Modi, then Chief Minister of Gujarat. It is the basis of Modi's current national program to improve sanitation in the entire

---

[22] www.sevakproject.org (Accessed 08/09/2015)

country of India[23]. The SEVAK volunteers are trained for two and half months vice one year for IDC.

Left to right: Prime Minister Narendra Modi with Dr. TG Patel and the local SEVAK coordinator.

The SEVAK project was extended to Guyana, South America in 2013. One SEVAK volunteer per village in each of 27 districts in Gujarat, India, and 8 rural villages in Guyana were chosen to screen the residents for diabetes, hypertension, and obesity and to monitor those with chronic diseases. Coordinating with the villages and identifying bright, enthusiastic individuals with medical and or non-medical backgrounds (one per a village of 1000-1500 population) leads to the selection of individuals to be SEVAK volunteers. Training includes techniques for good sanitation practices, safe drinking water, smoking cessation and malaria prevention. SEVAKs are also trained for monitoring of blood pressure, blood sugar, observing for fluid in the legs (common in hypertension and vascular disease), lifestyle modification education, and dietary practices. Day-to-day supervision of SEVAKs in Guyana is done by local high school biology teachers. Pre- and post- evaluation of the SEVAK training is done by the authors via internet and personal visits to Guyana. During these visits, we accompany the SEVAKS in the field

---

[23] http://www.narendramodi.in/pm-modis-sanitation-campaign-gets-lauded-by-united-nations/ (Accessed 08/09/2015)

and monitor their work. Particular effort is made to visit the patients diagnosed with hypertension and diabetes to confirm the findings of the Sevaks. Our preliminary observations are that such a program can become self-sustaining as the SEVAKs live in the village and are able to continue the screening, delivery of care, and health education.

SEVAK collecting data from house to house in an Indian village.

The SEVAK Project in Guyana received approval from the Government of Guyana. The major difference between the Indian model and the Guyanese model is that the Sevaks in Guyana are still in high school and they work in their villages only during the weekends, while SEVAKs in India are full time workers and are paid a salary.

SEVAKs maintain a database on the medical problems of the villagers and target the high-risk groups for detailed health education and monitoring. They also act as liaison between the patients and their physician and help ensure that patients on TB, HIV, and malaria treatment are adherent with their medicines, and that patients with diabetes and hypertension come for regular checkups and attend health classes. Pregnant women are screened for gestational diabetes and encouraged to deliver their baby in a safe environment to decrease maternal mortality.

Using open well for daily water needs (in many villages in India and Guyana) causes diarrheal diseases. SEVAK Program is building closed wells with electric pumps and water filters.

SEVAK providing lifestyle modification training in a village in India.

Future plans for the SEVAK project are to advocate for the program with Governments of India and Guyana to obtain host nation health care funds, and to extend the concept of SEVAK to other regions of both India and Guyana.

CONCLUSION

Public-private partnerships are a method for US strategic leaders to improve mutual security, and increase access and influence in strategic international situations. Our PPP team has shown that specialized services such as dialysis, kidney transplantation, management of immunosuppression and follow up of transplanted patients is feasible in a developing country. We have also shown that corneal transplantation can be successfully performed in a developing country using gratis corneas from the US that are in excess supply, in hopes of establishing autonomous eye bank capacity in the future. The IDC concept that has been successful for many decades in the US Navy has been modified to form the SEVAK program in India and subsequently in Guyana. Preliminary results on these programs from stakeholders in both the countries have been encouraging. Some of our foreign aid could be used to create SEVAK or other PPP projects in key developing countries, which could help in ground level work for disaster response and humanitarian crises. The PPP strategy is a win-win for both the USA and the host nation, and the PPP model could be adopted by a variety of US agencies with minimal costs to the taxpayer.

CHAPTER 3

Manage Funding And Professionals For Seva Projects

INVESTMENTS FOR A SEVA PROJECT[24]

The monies required to start seva projects can range from a few thousand dollars to large sums amounting to millions of dollars. The following figures of a typical educational and health care facility in India may provide some guidance to anyone wanting to start a new project:

**Typical financial figures of a high school for
900 students, with 12 grades of classes**

HIGH SCHOOL	12 GRADES OF CLASSES		12 GRADES OF CLASSES
Budget	75 Students/ Class		75 Students/ Class
	Avg. 350 Rs/ Monthly Fee		Avg. 7 $/ Monthly Fee
	110 Rs/ Monthly Bus Fee		2.20 $/ Monthly Bus Fee
	20 Teachers		20 Teachers
	20 Non-teachers		20 Non-teachers
INCOME	MONTHLY -RUPEES-	10-MONTH YEAR -RUPEES-	10-MONTH YEAR -DOLLARS-
• Education fees	315,000	3,150,000	63,000
• Bus fees	99,000	990,000	19,800
TOTAL	**414,000**	**4,140,000**	**82,800**
EXPENSES			

[24] Seva to realize self, by MC Mangalick, Hamilton Books, 2014 (ISBN-10: 0761863702)

Salary			
• Teachers	80,000	800,000	16,000
• Non Teachers	80,000	800,000	16,000
Sub-total	**160,000**	**1,600,000**	**32,000**
Bus Expenses			
• Repair & Maintenance	40,000	400,000	8,000
• Diesel	40,000	400,000	8,000
Sub-total	**80,000**	**800,000**	**16,000**
Other Expenses	**100,000**	**1,000,000**	**20,000**
TOTAL	**340,000**	**3,400,000**	**68,000**
PROFIT (LOSS)	**74,000**	**740,000**	**14,800**

The above table shows a typical operating financial statement. The school runs smoothly in this example, with 20 teaching and 20 non-teaching staff. Six buses transport the students to the school and back to their homes.

Breakdown of investment required to install the above high school

HIGH SCHOOL, 900 STUDENTS		
INVESTMENT REQUIRED	RUPEES	DOLLARS
Working Capital: Three-month Expenses	1,120,000	22,400
Cash	**1,120,000**	**22,400**
• Land-2 Acres, 50,00,000 Rs/Acre	10,000,000	200,000
• Buildings, 20,000 sq. ft. x 1,000 Rs/sq. ft.	20,000,000	400,000
1 with 20 Classrooms, 25x30 ft. each		
2 with 6 Classrooms, 5,000 sq. ft. total		

Sub-total	30,000,000	600,000
• Furniture and Fixtures	5,000,000	100,000
• Labs and Computers	2,000,000	40,000
• Generators	5,000,000	100,000
• Buses, 6 @ 2,500,000 Rs. per bus	15,000,000	300,000
Sub-total	27,000,000	540,000
TOTAL INVESTMENT	**58,120,000**	**1,162,400**

A total investment of $1,162,400 is not too difficult to arrange, especially if the philanthropist puts up a major part of this sum. The land and buildings in the above example amount to $600,000. The requirement for land and buildings can be much less if the high school is planned in outlying areas away from the city. The need for a seva project is mostly in the outlying villages around the cities anyway. The building costs continue to increase. However, even in today's economic environment, the building costs may be less than half of what is shown in the above example, especially if the high school is planned in lower-index-of-living areas.

It is not difficult to find selfless dedicated professionals to work for the seva project, in India, Guyana or in the US. The success of the seva projects run and managed by selfless monks strongly indicates that only when the seva is done with selfless and true spirits to help the poor and needy, the project succeeds.

Typical financial statements of a charity hospital

50-BEDS HOSPITAL ANNUAL PROFIT/LOSS ESTIMATE			
ITEM	NUMBER	RS, LACS	DOLLARS
EXPENSES			
• Medical Staff	20	100	200,000
• Non-medical Staff	100	50	100,000

• Other Expenses, Utilities, etc.		100	200,000
TOTAL EXPENSES		**250**	**500,000**
REVENUE			
• Indoor Patients = 45*1000*360		162	324,000
• Outdoor Patients = 100*50*360		18	36,000
• Labs and Diagnostics Revenue		70	140,000
TOTAL REVENUE		**250**	**500,000**

Typical investment required for a 50-bed hospital

50-BED HOSPITAL INVESTMENT REQUIRED	RUPEES	DOLLARS
Working Capital: 3-month Expenses	6,250,000	125,000
Cash	**6,250,000**	**125,000**
• Land- 2 Acres, 50,00,000 Rs/Acre	10,000,000	200,000
• Buildings- 20,000 sq. ft. x 1,000 Rs/sq. ft.	20,000,000	400,000
Sub-total	**30,000,000**	**600,000**
• Medical Equipment and Fixtures	10,000,000	200,000
• Labs and Computers	10,000,000	200,000
• Generators	5,000,000	100,000
• Ambulances (2) and other vehicles	5,000,000	100,000
Sub-total	**30,000,000**	**600,000**
TOTAL	**66,250,000**	**1,325,000**

Once again, the land and buildings costs may be lower, especially if the hospital is planned in outlying areas, where the land and construction costs are lower. These figures only provide broad guidelines.

CHAPTER 4

Case History 1: Kidney Transplants And Dialysis, Guyana, South America

SEVA BEGINS WITH A SIMPLE FLYER ASKING FOR HELP

We describe how a simple flyer led to Guyana's first kidney transplant and the subsequent development of a full dialysis program, introduction of peritoneal dialysis and development of health policy for renal replacement therapy in developing countries. It also led to the commitment of the government of Guyana for supply of expensive anti-rejection medications for life – a unique development, as this is not done even in developed countries. Kidney failure was considered to be a "death sentence" in Guyana, but is now a manageable disease.

George Subraj is a man of action and of few words, owner of Zara Realty[25] is an American of Guyanese origin, having left Guyana when he was eighteen years old to make a living in the new world and escape the political oppression in Guyana at that time. George Subraj is at the top of his game. His company is based in Queens, one of the most vibrant and culturally diverse communities in New York, and the neighboring suburb of Nassau County, Long Island.

He finds this flyer being circulated amongst the Guyanese community.

Friday, January 4, 2008

Mom Pleads for Kidney Transplant to Save Son's Life[26]

Below is a story I noticed this evening in the Guyana Chronicle about a young man with "end stage renal failure" and his mother's plea for help. The single mother is giving her kidney to her son, but needs monetary help to pay for his kidney transplant. This story struck a personal chord with me because my grandmother passed away more than a year ago from complications related to kidney failure and she underwent painful

---

[25] www.zararealty.com (Accessed 08/09/2015)
[26] http://www.caribvoice.org/Pop%20Ups/help.html (Accessed 08/09/2015)

dialysis prior to her death. Believe me, it's a hellish experience for a family to go through. Fortunately, she lived a long life, but this young man won't if he doesn't get help soon. I hope there's a doctor out there reading this story who can sponsor this surgery.

LEELKUMARIE Mangal, 41, of Lot 119 Lusignan Pasture, East Coast Demerara, is appealing to the business community and the general public to help her son get a kidney transplant in India and dialysis treatment here. She said her son, Munesh Mangal, 18, was diagnosed with 'end stage renal failure' in August last year, after he became ill and was a patient for two months at Georgetown Public Hospital Corporation (GPHC).

The woman told the Guyana Chronicle yesterday that he currently receives haemodialysis treatment at 5G Dialysis Centre, Lots 235-236 Baramita and Aubrey Barker Streets, South Ruimveldt, Georgetown, at a cost of G$100,000 weekly.

"I cannot afford to meet that amount so often and this is why I am asking for help to raise the funds," she appealed.

It is very difficult for him to cope and is often overwhelmed with pain and the burden of long-term dialysis treatment would be impossible for her to meet as a single parent, his mother said.

She said she is willing to donate one of her kidneys for the operation in India but has to raise US$36,000 for expenses.

Munesh said he was forced to leave the private school he attended when he took sick suddenly.

His mother, a vendor of green vegetables, said she approached the Ministry of Health and was assisted with the payment for 10 dialysis treatments which he has already received.

She can be reached on telephone numbers 220----, 646----, and 653----. (Michel Outridge)

We flew to Georgetown, Guyana, to check out the story of the kid who cried for help! George and his friends, Jaskaran Persaud, Lakeram Persaud and I will spend a few thousand dollars to check out the story which George found on a flyer on Hillside Avenue, Queens, New York City.

EXPLORATORY VISIT TO GEORGETOWN, GUYANA

George, Jaskaran, Lakeram and I set out to Georgetown to investigate the story of a young man who is dying of kidney failure and his mother is desperate to send him to India for a kidney transplant. She herself is the potential kidney donor, but she does not even know if she can medically donate a kidney, she may well have diabetes, hypertension or many conditions which may preclude her from undergoing surgery. And of course, she has very little money to enable her son to get a kidney transplant.

All we know is that she is a vendor of green vegetables at the local market and on many days, she does not even sell enough to recoup her bus fare to the market. She is also a single mother, her husband left her for the US when he could not cope with his son's illness. We have no knowledge of his whereabouts and Munesh has not heard from his dad for over four years.

We take the flight from the John F. Kennedy Airport to Georgetown. Caribbean Airways has a direct flight to Georgetown with a brief halt in Trinidad. We land early in the morning on March 22nd, 2008.

DR. LESLIE RAMSAMMY, THE HONORABLE MINISTER OF HEALTH

We had a poolside conference with Dr. Leslie Ramsammy, the Honorable Minister of Health in the Guyana Federal Government. Dr. Ramsammy heard through the grapevine that a group from New York was in town to investigate the story of a young man who was suffering from kidney failure. In a small country news travels fast. I was taken aback that the minister himself would come to talk to us informally at our hotel.

Dr. Leslie Ramsammy earned his PhD at St. John's University in Queens, New York. After receiving postdoctoral fellowships in neurochemistry and nephrology, he became a professor of medicine at the State University of New York at Stony Brook. Dr. Ramsammy returned to Guyana in 1994 and was chosen as the health minister seven years later. Most recently, Minister Ramsammy was elected President of the World Health Assembly. He grew up in an impoverished community in Guyana. Dr. Ramsammy says he was always driven by a sense of service to others. As a young man, he hoped to be a journalist but ended up studying microbiology in the USA. Enjoying and excelling in his studies, he returned to Guyana during a time of political transition where he says he got "caught up in the development". And there he has remained until now, serving in a wide range of public office positions culminating in the post of Minister of Health in 2001.

Dr. Ramsammy believes that global health must be driven by Member States and that countries must be clear about what they want. "We are too conservative in our global health standards," he says in an interview. "A child born in Tanzania should have the same chance of survival and for living a healthy life as a child born in a developed country[27]."

He also cautions the health sector not to wait for perfect programs, techniques and interventions while people suffer. We must be practical

---

[27] http://www.who.int/mediacentre/events/2008/wha61/ramasammy/en/index.html (Accessed 08/09/2015)

and pragmatic about health interventions for communities, he emphasizes. That's why he came to meet us. Knowing well that Guyana does not have the infrastructure for a kidney transplant program and there were only four hemodialysis chairs for the entire country Minister Ramsammy was open to doing something about patients suffering from kidney failure.

Ramsammy "Most patients in kidney failure die or try to fund a transplant in India."

"Why India?"

Ramsammy "In India, it costs 10 percent of what it costs in the United States."

"What about the travel and family support?"

Ramsammy "The family has to go with the patient and they have to stay there for at least three months for follow up as most acute rejections occur within the first three months."

"Of course, you can't send the patient alone without family."

"And who does the follow up, making changes in medications, monitoring for rejection, drug toxicity and potential surgical complications?"

Ramsammy "I don't know, patients perhaps return to India or communicate to the physicians in India by e-mails or telephone calls."

"Are there any local physicians who can follow up the transplant patients in Guyana?"

Ramsammy "I don't know. I assume some of the recently hired physicians from India may have had exposure to kidney transplantation."

"But, Guyanese traveling to India may become victims of fraud. In Toronto, a refugee who paid for a transplant in India ended up in Zaltzman's office with poor kidney function. Despite a six-inch scar on his abdomen, an ultrasound revealed there was no transplanted kidney and he was the victim of a con" Probably more such cases of fraud may have gone unreported.

"Further, who is going to guarantee the quality of hospitals where the transplants take place? I know that donors have died in some hospitals in India, and there is no quality control outside of major hospitals[28]."

"Even more important is that the government of India has proposed a total ban on the donation of organs to foreigners by Indians, which may make it virtually impossible for Guyanese getting kidney transplants in legitimate hospitals in India[29]."

"What about doing kidney transplant here in Guyana?"

Ramsammy "Never thought of that angle, you think it is possible?"

"We shall have to see."

"We shall see if we can do the transplant surgery right here in Guyana."

The next few days were spent visiting Georgetown Public Hospital Corporation[30], meeting the physicians, laboratory staff, operating room personnel and ward nurses.

SURPRISE VISIT TO THE MANGAL'S HOME

Although we had already spent two days in Georgetown meeting the Minister of Health, seeing the hospital, and visiting with the local physicians to gauge the possibility of carrying out the operation in Guyana, we still had to meet Munesh Mangal and his mother. In fact we had an appointment to see Munesh and his mother in the surgical ward of the hospital with their Nephrologist. So when we showed upon the ward at 10 AM, the appointed time, there was no one there to meet us. As we were leaving, George noticed a young man with his mother standing near the stairs to the ward. George likes to chat to people he meets here and there even if they don't know him.

[28] Bansal RK. Donors do die in kidney transplantation in India. Indian J Med Sci [serial online] 2003 [cited 2008 Nov 17]; 57:320. Available from: http://www.indianjmedsci.org/text.asp?2003/57/7/320/11941 (Accessed 08-24-2015)

[29] http://timesofindia.indiatimes.com/India/New_transplant_policy_to_curb_rackets/articleshow/3718196.cms (Accessed 08-24-2015)

[30] https://www.facebook.com/pages/Georgetown-Public-Hospital-Corporation-GPHC/1509032579346095? (Accessed 08-24-2015)

> George "What are you doing here in the sun, it's hot."
>
> Munesh "Waiting for some doctors from the United States."
>
> George "That's us!"
>
> With that, George escorted Munesh and his mother to the ward.

Munesh is shy and hardly ever talks; he wears a towel over his shoulders to hide the dialysis catheter hanging from the right side of his chest. The catheter is used to access his blood stream for dialysis.

In the United States, we use a fistula or a graft connecting the artery and vein in the arm or forearm to puncture the fistula for dialysis[31]; clothing can hide this. However, in many countries where dialysis is just starting, physicians use a catheter as it gives easier access to the blood stream—cosmetically, it is not attractive, besides the fact that a catheter gets clogged up frequently and it has to be changed. We found that as patients could afford only short periods of hemodialysis and eventually died soon thereafter, there was no real indication for placing a permanent vascular access for hemodialysis. In Guyana or other developing countries, the possibility of long-term dialysis does not exist as it is too expensive and patients simply die unless they can afford to obtain a kidney transplant.

We examined both the son and his mother thoroughly, and talked with them extensively to make sure they understood that a kidney transplant has never been done before in Guyana, and they would be kind of pioneers. Fortunately, the mother is extremely motivated and she understood the implications and potential complications of a surgery and its side-effects. Munesh understood the possibility of the transplant kidney not working, taking medications and life-long compliance with medications, and follow up care. He raised questions about the cost of medications, between US$8,000 and US$10,000, certainly prohibitive

---

[31] Ryan JJ, Sajjad I, Jindal RM. ABC of vascular access for hemodialysis. Federal Practitioner 2005; 22:53-62.

even for the well insured in the United States. We assured them that we would talk to the Department of Health about it.

We spent over two hours talking with them.

"What do you want to do after you get the transplant?"

Munesh "Go back to school and hang out with my friends."

"What do you want to do when you finish school?"

Munesh "Become the best car spray painter in the whole of Guyana."

"Why do you want to become a spray painter?"

At this point, the ward nurse overheard our conversation "His dad was a car spray painter and he left the family, so he wants to become a spray painter and show his dad how good he is."

Certainly, Munesh was determined to be the best car spray painter in Guyana, and why not?

At that point, our minds were made up.

However, there is always the nagging doubt that we may be made victims of fraud and they may not be really genuine cases of charity. So that evening, we drove twenty-five miles or so outside Georgetown to Lot 119 Lusignan Pasture, East Coast Demerara to see for ourselves how the Mangal family lived.

We went there unannounced and were taken aback by the poverty of the area and the condition of their house. The Mangal's have a single room with no inside bathroom. The shack is made of wood, and the only running water is from the tap outside which also serves as a bathroom. The front yard is full of junk, and materials from a car that his dad left behind. And there were also rusting cans of car paint in the front yard, a legacy of Munesh's dad who left them to seek his fortune in the United States. The family does not know of the whereabouts of Munesh's dad and he had made no attempt to contact the family for a couple of years. For all practical purposes, the dad may have been dead.

The Mangal's were surprised to see us; however, they were very gracious and showed us around their home—a single room. The Mangal's house is in Lusignan; a village that is comprised of mainly indo-Guyanese and is sustained by subsistence farming. The community was brought to international attention following what has become known as the Lusignan Massacre[32]; a terrible event that left eleven persons, including five children, dead, after a group of heavily armed gunmen led by Rondell "Fineman" Rawlins stormed the village. All the eleven murders took place on the same street where the Mangals live. We visited one of the houses, four houses down from the Mangal's where both the husband and wife were killed. Rooplall Seecharan, fifty-six; his daughter, Raywattie Ramsingh, eleven; and his wife, Dhanrajie, called Sister, fifty-two, were killed in a hail of bullets[33]. We spoke at length to their son and daughter, who were still grieving at their loss. Guyana is still a country torn by inter-racial strife and violence—and we saw first-hand what it was by talking to some of the victims[34].

SOCIAL NETWORK ANALYSIS OF THE GUYANESE KIDNEY TRANSPLANT

The kidney transplant required the coming together of four communities: Guyanese-American, Guyanese Ministry of Health, the United States transplant professionals and a team of Guyana-based doctors. The networks were linked by loose ties[35]. The networks that came together to help Munesh were evenly balanced in terms of power, skill base and support. The American-Guyanese business community had undertaken many goodwill health initiatives to their native Guyana in the past. Therefore, they were familiar with the socio-economic and political infrastructure of the country. The United States medical team, led by Dr. Jindal, had the medical skills to adapt to less sophisticated medical environments such as the operating facilities that they would encounter in Guyana. The medical team on the ground in Guyana, although lacking the skills needed to perform the transplant, was familiar with the patient's social networks and medical history. The

---

[32] http://en.wikipedia.org/wiki/Lusignan,_Guyana (Accessed 08/09/2015)
[33] http://www.guyana.org/massacre_lusignan.html (Accessed 08-24-2015)
[34] http://news.bbc.co.uk/2/hi/americas/4270299.stm (Accessed 08-24-2015)
[35] The Struggle for Life: A psychological perspective of kidney disease and transplantation, by LS Baines and RM Jindal. Publisher: Praeger, Westport, CT, USA, 2003. ISBN: 0-86569-323-4

Minister of Health and his team were ready to facilitate the teams and give an undertaking to provide free medications for at least three years (one year of anti-rejection medications costs about US$8,000).

Dr. Jindal and the United States medical team started to cultivate a working relationship via e-mail and telephone with the local Guyanese doctors as they worked up the patient. The flow of information between the medical teams supplied vital information for the sponsor (Mr. George Subraj) who was able to formulate their budget and manpower needs. It also provided George Subraj with positive reinforcement and motivation to pursue the mission.

The medical team in Guyana formed a professional network based upon a shared opportunity to fulfill a medical need within their country. The network was required to be highly flexible, in terms of making a number of timely transitions with regards to the role they played in the whole operation. In the early work up stages, they assumed a heightened role. However, once the United States-based team arrived in Guyana their role became both supportive by playing host to the visiting team helping them negotiate the logistics of hospital life. The Guyanese-based medical team was also privy to relational idiosyncrasies and external points of influence, such as the social networks in which the donor and recipient were embedded.

Dr. Jindal was clearly the 'star' or point of centrality that pulled together all four social networks. His centralized positioning meant that all information flowed through him and he was therefore in a position to influence the outcome of the transplant. Dr. Jindal used his position to ensure cohesiveness of the group and firm up inter-dependencies, minimize differences and prevent isolation between the four networks. He actualized this by ensuring that there were inter-connecting paths of communication between all four networks. This eliminated the potential for rigid boundaries and ensuring a balanced and harmonized network.

Dr. Jindal used his position of centrality to override any potential dysfunction.

KIDNEY TRANSPLANT IS BIG NEWS IN GUYANA

The news that Guyana will carry out its first kidney transplantation was covered in all the national newspapers. This put us under the microscope and intense pressure. Here are some of the news reports:

Lusignan Teen to Access Kidney Transplant at GPHC in July

-To be conducted six times annually—Ramsammy

By Melanie Allicock

A medical feat is expected to be performed at the Georgetown Public Hospital Corporation (GPHC) on July 12 when a 17-year-old boy from Lusignan on the East Coast of Demerara undergoes a kidney transplant. And, if all goes according to plan, the hospital will facilitate this surgery six times per year. The life-changing medical intervention will be led by two teams of more than 60 surgeons, nurses and other support staff from New York, and will be aided by local medical staff.

The US doctors will be volunteering their services as part of an arrangement with the Health Ministry to bring relief to the hundreds of Guyanese presently suffering from chronic renal failure. The cost of this initial venture will be not be borne by the patient or government, since a group of concerned US-based Guyanese have mobilized resources to cover the expenses that will be incurred by the medical team. He however disclosed government's plans of covering some of the expenses for future ventures of this kind.

A Stitch in Time

This intervention into the public health system could not have been timelier. Renal diseases contribute a major public health problem in Guyana, mainly because of the high incidences of diabetes and hypertension that exist. Guyana sees about 10,000 new hypertension and 8,000 new diabetes patients each year. These two conditions mainly result in kidney failure and account for a considerable portion of the more than 200 Guyanese in need of Dialysis treatment at the moment. As the prevalence of these two conditions continue to rise, more and more renal failure patients have surfaced, pleading for financial assistance through almost every medium available.

Guyana has struggled for a long time with dealing with the high incidence of kidney disease. Those who could afford to leave Guyana for dialysis treatment got temporary relief, but many of the less fortunate became very ill and died. In its bid to assist the situation, the Health Ministry offered a monetary assistance of US $5,000 to every patient, but for a person accessing dialysis care in Guyana at approximately US$200 per treatment, twice weekly, that money did not last long.

US-Based Help

Minister Ramsammy said these persons were pleasantly surprised at what they found.

"They came to Guyana with the perception that Guyana's health system was extremely weak and backward but they were pleasantly surprised that this was not the case and noted that with just a few adjustments, the GPHC could be made ready to facilitate kidney transplants without investing any money."

"We need to do that because to take out a healthy organ and leave an unhealthy one will accomplish nothing." However, there are challenges in carrying out the organ compatibility studies needed prior to transplants.

PREPARATIONS BEGIN FOR THE KIDNEY TRANSPLANT

After returning from Guyana, we set about the tasks of coordinating the "work-up" of Munesh and his mother for the transplant; getting the medical team ready, and getting their licenses and travel plans; as well as preparing the local team in terms of the Operating Room, anesthesia, Intensive Care Unit, laboratory facilities, and nursing staff.

Some of the tests such as tissue typing and cross-match were not done in Guyana; we obtained blood samples to perform the tests in the Immunology Laboratory of Walter Reed Army Medical Center, Washington, DC. The staff of both hospitals was very gracious in donating their time and expertise.

A total of 300 e-mails were exchanged and over one hundred telephonic calls were made by me, George Subraj and other players to Guyana to coordinate this effort.

There was some suspicion and apprehension amongst the staff in both places, but a continuous flow of e-mails, this was gradually overcome and trust was built between the teams; the medical team from Walter Reed, George Subraj and his team; medical, nursing and laboratory staff at GHPC and the Minister of Health, Dr. Leslie Ramssamy and his officials. In short, a social network was established to ensure the smooth and successful completion of kidney transplant.

KIDNEY TRANSPLANT SUCCESSFUL

The press release from the Ministry of Health summarizes the first kidney transplant, I have re-produced it verbatim:

41

Sunday, July 13, 2008

Landmark kidney transplant operation a resounding success

The first local kidney transplant was successfully completed ahead of the scheduled time yesterday, thanks to the hard work and dedication of the medical team which undertook the task. The surgery to transplant a kidney from 41-year-old Leelkumarie Nirananjan Managal of Lusignan, East Coast Demerara, to her son, 18-year-old Munesh Mangal began at 7.30 am and was completed just after 2 pm.

Lead Transplant Surgeon at Walter Reed Army Medical Center in DC and Attending General Surgeon at the Brookdale University Hospital, Indian-born Dr. Rahul Jindal, said that the surgery was without complication and that both the recipient and donor are awake and recovering at the Intensive Care Unit, at the Georgetown Public Hospital (GPHC). He made this disclosure at a press conference yesterday at GPHC after successfully completing the operation. He explained that the mother is expected to remain at the ICU for another day, after which she will be transferred to the ward and then discharged. While her son will remain at ICU for about three days and once he is stable, will be sent to the ward for monitoring for another week.

"His kidney is making urine. We don't expect any problems later on," Dr. Jindal said, but noted that there is always the possibility that the lad's body might reject the new kidney. He however, noted that adequate medication would be provided to minimize the possibility of rejection and the next 48 hours remain a critical period for the recipient.

"It is a difficult operation. You only have one chance because if you fail and the kidney is dead, others are not easily available," stated Dr. Jindal.

"This is a truly historic day in our country it is a celebration of partnership and a milestone for the Georgetown Hospital and the country. We celebrate the local and international professionals who came together to truly achieve what is a miracle. This means so much to the health sector and to our country. We have worked successful to complete the first kidney transplant in our country," asserted the minister.

Dr. Jindal expressed gratitude for the confidence placed in him by local authorities and the family to do the surgery and noted that his involvement was prompted when he learnt of the family's financial difficulties in providing treatment and care for the sick child.

Munesh suffered renal failure years ago because of hypertension. He has been ill for most of his childhood, but in 1995 he began experiencing chest pains and was suffering from shortness of breath.

In March this year, Dr. Jindal was introduced to the local health sector and arrangements were put in place. Kidney transplant is a surgical procedure involving heterotopic placement of the donor kidney into the iliac fossa of the recipient. It has emerged as the preferred means of renal replacement therapy for patients with End-Stage Renal Disease of any etiology.

Dr. Ramsammy said at present there are about 200 Guyanese who should be on dialysis for renal failure and a portion of them would require transplant. Meanwhile, the Chief Executive Officer of GPHC, Mr. Michael Khan expressed his appreciation with the overseas team in performing the surgery free of cost and is looking forward to future collaboration with the group. He said the exercise will benefit the local doctors tremendously and it is hoped that very soon they will be able to perform such surgeries with little or no outside assistance.

The team will be staging a clinic at GPHC for other patients with similar conditions during their stay in Guyana. The team includes businessman George Subraj and his son, Tony; Lakeram Persaud, Jas Persaud and Kewan Totaram, as well as Caribbean Airlines, which sponsored the tickets for the visiting persons. And, according to Mr Subraj, yesterday's undertaking could be regarded as the beginning of an ongoing programme of assistance, even as he estimated that he would probably be able to bring the team back a few more times to conduct about five more operations. The medial team has already examined about six patients, two of whom may be eligible for surgery, according to Dr. Jindal.

In addition to the undertaking being a partnership of expertise, the minister said that yesterday's operation also shows how the Diaspora can help in development. "The Diaspora has been an important component in Guyana's development for over a decade now. Many of our programmes are tied to this contribution…"

Source: The Guyana Chronicle

July 15, 2008

Team awarded for successful kidney transplant

… Momentous occasion in Guyana—Ramkarran

After conducting a successful kidney transplant for the first time here in Guyana, the team of doctors which made the operation a success was last evening presented with awards, indicating Munesh Mangal's (the kidney patient) appreciation for giving him another chance to live.

Caribbean Airlines, Buddy's International Hotel and the Neal and Massy Group were also awarded for their participation in making the surgery a successful one. All told, those who received awards were Dr. Melanie Guerrero, Dr. Edward Falta, Dr. Arthur Womble, Dr. Rahul Jindal, Nurse Laura Owen, Jas Persaud, and General Manager for Caribbean Airlines, Carlton Defour, Mr. Sanders also of Caribbean Airlines, Neal and Massy representative, Shameer Hoosein, and Om Prakash Shivraj.

Special mention was also given to Tony Yassin, Health Minister Dr. Leslie Ramsammy, and Publisher of Kaieteur News, Glenn Lall among others for their contribution toward making the surgery a success. The initiative to have the operation done in Guyana was spearheaded by New York-based Guyanese, Mr. George Subraj, after he saw a flyer that was being circulated for financial assistance for the kidney patient. The awards ceremony, which was held last evening at Buddy's International Hotel in Providence, East Bank Demerara, attracted Chief Executive Officer of the Georgetown Public Hospital Corporation, Michael Khan and Speaker of the National Assembly, Ralph Ramkarran. Mr. Ramkarran noted that the success of the kidney transplant is a momentous occasion for Guyana and he thanked the surgeon, Dr. Rahul Jindal, for giving life to Munesh Mangal. "When I heard about the project two months ago, I became immediately sympathetic. I understand the trauma of finding money every week for dialysis treatment," Mr Ramkarran said. In a case like this, the doctors and the supporting team dedicated their willingness, time, energy and resources to make it a success, Mr Ramkarran said. The man who put together the entire project, George Subraj, said the venture was not an easy one, as there were a lot of stumbling blocks. He, however, noted that more such transplants will be conducted here in Guyana, as he committed to facilitate at least five more kidney transplants. By Knews[36]

THE WORK EXPANDS TO INITIATING OF PERITONEAL DIALYSIS

Pertinent to this chapter is the feasibility of providing renal replacement therapy in developing countries where the issues of infectious diseases and infrastructure issues are a major problem. Renal failure affects a relatively small proportion of population, so it could be argued that the government with limited resources cannot provide free renal replacement therapy. Twenty million Americans suffer from chronic kidney disease (CKD), and twenty million more are at elevated risk; soon, one in nine Americans will have CKD. Control of co-morbidities may slow its progression, and two are critical—type 2 diabetes and hypertension[37]. The employers are only now beginning to understand the effect of this on their financing systems.

A key factor influencing the cost of dialysis care is the timing of referral to a Nephrologist[38]. When patients are either referred late to a Nephrologist's care or must urgently initiate dialysis without a planned access, they are generally sicker, require longer hospitalization and are nearly always started on HD. Early referral and planned start result in cost savings and improved survival. Patients who are referred earlier to a Nephrologist have an extended time prior to starting dialysis during

---

[36] http://www.kaieteurnewsonline.com/2008/07/15/team-awarded-for-successful-kidney-transplant/ (Accessed 08-24-1025)

[37] Sullivan S. Employer challenges with the chronic kidney disease population. J Manag Care Pharm 2007; 13(9 Suppl D): S19.

[38] Wavamunno MD, Harris DC. The need for early nephrology referral. Kidney Int Suppl 2005;94: S128.

which access may be planned and placed, and patients may be objectively educated about their treatment choices. This approach has usually been found to result in fewer inpatient hospital days, thereby reducing the total cost of dialysis by the creation of vascular access or PD and taking steps to improve nutrition and treating infectious problems.

Horl et al. compared access to End Stage Renal Disease (ESRD) treatment modalities was made with reference to the healthcare provider structure in a range of industrial countries[39]. The countries were grouped into 'public' (Beveridge model), 'mixed' (Bismarck model) and 'private' (Private Insurance model). In 'public' provider countries, 20-52 percent of dialysis patients are treated with home therapies (haemodialysis and peritoneal dialysis), and the number of patients with renal transplants is 45-81percent of all ESRD patients. In 'mixed' provider countries, only 9-17 percent of all dialysis patients are treated with home therapies, and 20-48 percent of ESRD patients have renal transplants. In 'private' provider countries, 17 percent of the United States, and 6 percent of the Japanese dialysis patients are treated with home therapies. Japan has 0.3 percent and the United States has 26 percent of ESRD patients who receive renal transplants. It thus seems that provider structure influences access to and choice of ESRD treatment.

For Guyana to develop a renal replacement therapy as a national program, it would have to allocate resources for dialysis therapy and decide the preferred modality, HD versus PD. Should Guyana be influenced by the experience in the United States or other developing countries? Compared with countries worldwide, the United States has one of the lowest PD populations as compared with its HD population. Approximately 12 percent of the total dialysis population in the United State is on PD[40]. There have been arguments for and against each modality of therapy in the context of a developing country, but the

---

[39] Horl WH, de Alvaro F, Williams PF. Healthcare systems and end-stage renal disease (ESRD) therapies--an international review: access to ESRD treatments. Nephrol Dial Transplant. 1999; 14 [Suppl 6]:10-5.

[40] Gadallah MF, Ramdeen G, Torres-Rivera C, et al. Changing the trend: a prospective study on factors contributing to the growth rate of peritoneal dialysis programs. Adv Perit Dial 2001; 17:122-6.

preponderance of evidence is in favor of PD in developing countries. In a seminal paper, Just et al[41] made an argument for providing PD, which may be more cost effective. The costs of dialysis around the world can vary widely according to many local market conditions, including local production and distribution factors, import duties, the presence or absence of local suppliers and purchasing power. HD cost is driven largely by the fixed costs of facility space and staff. HD machines typically cost ~ $18,000 to $30,000 each, but the machines have a five to ten year life cycle, and, in a weekly schedule, three to six patients can be treated on one machine. The cost of dialyzers for HD ranges from $1,000 to $5,000 per year. Other items that factor into the cost of HD are additional facility costs such as maintenance and utilities, and the costs of transportation to and from the HD facility. They further argue that the economics of PD are driven primarily by variable or 'disposable' costs, such as the costs of solutions and dialysis tubing, and PD exhibits a near constant economy of scale. A review of the literature determined that the cost of PD materials ranges from $5,000 to $25,000 annually. The use of automated cyclers generally adds to the cost of PD. The machines cost $3,000 to $10,000 each when purchased outright. However, they may be leased or provided, in which case their actual cost is bundled into the cost of solutions and materials purchased through the same company.

A North American literature review concluded that PD is less expensive than HD and that the difference in cost is dramatic when the PD program is relatively large and well run. Lee et al. reported their cost analysis for care for in-center, satellite, and home/self-care HD and PD were US $51,252, $47,680, $42,057, $29,961, and $26,959, respectively (P < 0.001). After adjustment for the effect of other important predictors of cost, such as co-morbidity, these differences persisted. They suggested that dialysis programs should encourage the use of home/self-care HD

---

[41] Just PM, de Charro FT, Tschosik EA, Noe LL, Bhattacharyya SK, Riella MC. Reimbursement and economic factors influencing dialysis modality choice around the world. Nephrol Dial Transplant 2008; 23:2365-73.

and PD[42]. In general, reports from Western Europe are in agreement with the North American findings. A review of the literature found that in-centre HD was about twice the cost of PD in France and 30 percent more expensive than PD in Italy and the United Kingdom. The majority of the countries in South Asia lack government healthcare system for reimbursing renal replacement therapy. The largest utilization of chronic PD is in India, with nearly 6500 patients on this treatment by the end of 2006. A large majority of patients are doing two L exchanges three times per day, using glucose-based dialysis solution manufactured in India[43]. A recent conference of academic Nephrologists and government officials from China, Hong Kong, India, Indonesia, Japan, Macau, Malaysia, Philippines, Singapore, Taiwan, Thailand, and Vietnam proposed the "peritoneal dialysis first" policy model, incentive programs, nongovernmental organizations providing PD, and PD reimbursement in a developing economy[44].

Very little research exists on the economics of dialysis in developed Asian countries[45]. A multi-national survey of Asian Nephrologists conducted in 2001 suggests that HD is generally more expensive than PD in the developed Asian economies of Hong Kong, Singapore, Taiwan and Japan. However, the extent of cost savings with PD varies by region.

According to the survey results, the ratio of costs for HD compared to PD ranged from a low of 0.99-1.09 in Japan to a high of 1.42-2.39 in Hong Kong. The economics of dialysis in the developing world differ from advanced nations. PD requires less technology than HD, so it would seem particularly well suited for developing nations. In

[42] Lee H, Manns B, Taub K, Ghali WA, Dean S, Johnson D, Donaldson C. Cost analysis of ongoing care of patients with end-stage renal disease: the impact of dialysis modality and dialysis access. Am J Kidney Dis 2002; 40:611.

[43] Abraham G, Pratap B, Sankarasubbaiyan S, et al. Chronic peritoneal dialysis in South Asia - challenges and future. Perit Dial Int 2008; 28:13.

[44] Li PK, Lui SL, Leung CB, et al. Increased utilization of peritoneal dialysis to cope with mounting demand for renal replacement therapy--perspectives from Asian countries. Perit Dial Int 2007; 27 Suppl 2: S59.

[45] Li PK, Chow KM. The cost barrier to peritoneal dialysis in the developing world--an Asian perspective. Perit Dial Int 2001; 21 [Suppl 3]: S307.

poorer countries, though, labor is relatively inexpensive, while the cost of imported equipment and solutions is high. Costs are often considered as related only to supplies rather than assessed as a total therapy. Therefore, there is often a perception that PD is more expensive than HD in developing countries. To reduce costs, patients may be placed on outdated straight-line systems and sometimes transfer sets may be reused. However, high peritonitis rates increase the cost of PD treatment even further, and dropout rates are high.

Vikrant et al[46] review their experience of PD in the Indian context and may be applicable to Guyana. They investigated the feasibility of PD in hilly, remote state of India with predominant rural population with a population of 6 million involved 25 patients who were initiated on PD between October 2002 and December 2006 and who survived and/or had more than 6 months follow up on this treatment with last follow up till June 30, 2007. The total duration on PD treatment was 541.1 patient-months with a mean duration of 21.6 ± 12.2 months and median duration of nineteen patient-months (range: 6-56.3 patient-months). No patient had exit-site infection. There were twenty-six episodes of peritonitis. The rate of peritonitis was one episode per twenty-one patient-months or 0.6 per patient-year during the treatment period. The main cause of death was cardiovascular complications. Patient and technique survival at one, two, and three years was 80, 36 and 12 percent, respectively. They concluded that PD was a safe and viable mode of renal replacement in remote and rural places.

In a study by Neil et al[47] the relative advantages of HD and PD was discussed to estimate the country specific, five year financial implications on total dialysis costs assuming utilization shifts from HD to PD in two high-income (United Kingdom, Singapore), three upper-middle-income (Mexico, Chile, Romania), and three lower-middle-income (Thailand, China, Colombia) countries. They found that PD was a

---

[46] Vikrant S. Continuous ambulatory peritoneal dialysis: A viable modality of renal replacement therapy in a hilly state of India. Indian J Nephrol 2007;17:165 http://www.indianjnephrol.org/text.asp?2007/17/4/165/39171 (Accessed 08-24-2015)

[47] Neil N, Walker DR, Sesso R, et al. Gaining Efficiencies: Resources and Demand for Dialysis around the Globe. Value Health. 2008

clinically effective dialysis option that can be significantly cost saving compared to HD, even in developing countries.

In developing countries, infections are the leading causes of morbidity and the second commonest cause of mortality in the dialysis population. Tuberculosis is endemic in several developing countries and impaired cell-mediated immunity increases the susceptibility among the dialysis population. The reported incidence of tuberculosis in dialysis patients varies from 10 to 15 percent in India. Further, the infection rate is higher in government-funded hospitals that cater to patients from the lower socioeconomic groups. The principal causes of death are cardiovascular (40-51percent) and infections (15-23 percent).

MORE KIDNEY TRANSPLANTS FOLLOW

What started as one transplant deal ended up since program inception in 2008; we have performed 25 living kidney transplants, 17 PD catheters and 20 vascular access procedures. To date, approximately 450 patients with various stages of CKD have been screened. This program has provided them with appropriate medical therapy including kidney biopsies, which have been read in the US by Renal Pathologists. Critical tests, such as HLA tissue typing and cross match, are done gratis by US-based laboratories. An education program was launched to sensitize the population on the importance of organ donation and prevention of diabetes and hypertension by holding regular press conferences. The medical–surgical-logistical-educational team goes to Guyana 3-4 times a year, each trip lasting from 6 to 9 days. Video-conferences via Skype have been instituted to provide patient monitoring and consultation with the local health care providers and selected patients.

We are gearing up to get other transplant programs in the US involved as one team from Walter Reed cannot be expected to go to Guyana 4- 5 times a year. We are also involving the Department of Pathology, Drexel University, Philadelphia, to process and read pathology specimens from patients in Guyana.

Eventually, we hope that eventually, we will have Guyanese physicians visit transplant programs in the US to gain first-hand experience of transplantation surgery and medicine. This is going to take some time as obtaining US visa is a difficult task, given that the local sponsoring hospital and the government of Guyana have to give an undertaking that the physician will return to the country of origin. Obviously, complex and politically challenging issue of "brain-drain" from developing countries will have to be tackled.

PROMOTING TRANSPLANTATION AND PREVENTION BY USING MEDIA

We frequently use the media to promote awareness of kidney transplantation and prevention of diabetes and hypertension. Many of our patients come from the capital area, Georgetown, but our message has still not reached the hinterland. A news report in the highest circulating newspaper in Guyana is an example of how we promote this.

Renowned physician highlights benefits of kidney transplant

May 30, 2011 | By KNews | Filed Under News.

"The age does not matter, what matters is the patient's physiological state; how physically fit the patient is matters," said Dr. Rahul Jindal as he addressed the importance of kidney transplants in Guyana. He alluded to the high cost of dialysis which patients are required to undergo indefinitely if they are not afforded a transplant operation.

In Guyana the cost per dialysis session is about US$200, a process which must be undertaken at least three times per week. This process must also be complemented by necessary but costly medication. "Dialysis is very expensive and persons have to find the money for dialysis …this whole process is lifelong and there is no way that an ordinary person can afford to go on like this, and on top of this it will affect the quality of life….

They are tied to a machine five to six hours every other day and they have all of the other problems related to dialysis."

In addition persons who are forced to undergo regular dialysis will undoubtedly be subjected to a reduced life-span which could be equivalent to one third of the life-span of a normal, healthy person, Dr Jindal revealed. As such, he noted, that when an individual suffering from renal failure is able to undergo a transplant operation, whereby a bad kidney is replaced with a good one, the life-span is likely to become normal again.

Dr Jindal was ably assisted by a team of about nine acclaimed professionals including a nephrologist, anesthesiologist and other surgeons as well as staff from the Balwant Singh hospital. The renal failure patients were both males in their 50s who had received the crucial organs from family members. As at the weekend both patients as well as the donors were alert and recovering well.

The move was regarded as the start of a public/private partnership which saw another transplant operation being undertaken in the following year.

Then it was 47-year-old Winston George, an army officer who was forced to retire because of his ailing condition caused by his kidney condition. Two more operations were reportedly done through the collaboration.

MOVING TRANSPLANTS TO A PRIVATE HOSPITAL

Ongoing problems at the public hospital forced us to move transplant surgery to a private hospital with the support of the government, creating a public-private partnership. We suggest that seva givers need to have the flexibility to change locations and partners to provide the best possible use of resources. There should be plans for all eventualities if there are insurmountable problems. In our case, we were unable to get the public hospital change a culture which was embedded in the workforce. We were unable to overcome this cultural barrier.

Some things are just not right at GPHC[48]

July 20, 2008, By Knews

Within recent times, there have been many complaints about the operations of the Georgetown Public Hospital. The most recent complaint was leveled by a woman who gave birth to a baby that was said to have been stillborn.

This woman claimed that she never saw her baby because she was under an anesthetic. She said that when she recovered no one could tell her anything about the baby. Weeks later, after the woman went to the press and her predicament became public knowledge, the hospital duly went public with the fact that the baby was in the mortuary of the hospital. If this is the case, then something had to be wrong. The woman must have been visited by relatives who would have asked about the baby. Certainly, the persons who asked must have not got any response, and being simple people, they would have muttered and moved on.

The child's mother said that she took her daughter to the hospital with pains, and after a brief period of observation the hospital gave the girl some medication and sent her home. A few days later, the child was rushed back to the hospital, and again there was nothing more to be had than some tablets. By the time the hospital recognized that something was seriously wrong, the girl was dead. She had succumbed to a ruptured appendix. A week ago, there was this former officer of

---

[48] http://www.kaieteurnews.com/2008/07/20/some-things-are-just-not-right-at-gphc/

the Customs Anti-Narcotics Unit who was discharged from the hospital having been taken there suffering from hypertension. The man died a few hours later at home.

We have had people who went to the hospital for hysterectomy and died, some hemorrhaging because the surgeons could not stop the bleeding. And in one case a woman died because she was given aspirin although she was allergic.

The problem seems to be the shortage of skilled medical practitioners at a time when the administration is boasting about providing a vastly improved service. The hospital is performing a series of new surgeries, the most recent being a kidney transplant. The hospital is also supposed to be doing hip replacements and heart surgeries. Any facility that can do such things should be able to diagnose ailments. Indeed, many ailments could present the same symptoms, so that further investigation is necessary. This seems not to be the case at the Georgetown Public Hospital. But for all this, the hospital has scored many successes largely because visiting doctors are coming home to share their skills and, as some say, to give back to the society. Some crucial surgeries have been performed, and the locals have had a chance to work with these visiting experts.

PROBLEMS IN COMMUNICATION

There needs to be clear lines of communication and understanding that some commercial agencies have different regulations in countries outside the US. An example is given below whereby critical blood samples from Guyana to US failed to reach Dr. Jindal's laboratory in Washington, DC. All transplant patients and their donors need tissue typing and cross-match before the procedure (to check compatibility).

These sophisticated tests cost about 3000 USD per patient. Guyana does not have the capability to perform these tests and to establish a laboratory and to hire personnel trained for this would be prohibitively expensive.

Dear Dr. Jindal,

The samples were sent today via FEDEX, tracking number 876342463485

Thanks,

Ivorine De Franca

Dr. Balwant Singh's Hospital Inc.

314 East Street, South Cummingsburg

Georgetown, Guyana.

South America.

Tel# 592-226-

Fax# 592-227-

However, the samples were stuck in Memphis, TN, which is the central hub for customs clearance. I sent an e-mail to Dr. Singh asking why the "commercial invoice" was not filled.

Dear Dr Madhu Singh

Nisha or someone forgot to send the custom clearance forms/invoice with the FEDEX box. The box is now stuck in customs in MEMPHIS. I just faxed them the form.

This is a serious issue as the samples may be useless due to the delay. Please urge the nurse or Nisha to take this seriously as each processing of each sample is US $ 3000 (each patient). If the samples are spoiled, we have to start all over again.

Please let the nurses know that this type of incident should NEVER occur again.

Thanks

Rahul

Here is Dr. Singh's reply:

Dear Dr. Jindal,

The Customs clearance form is filled up by the FEDEX agents and not at the Hospital. I have spoken to the FEDEX office here and they are looking into what may have happened.

Dr. Madhu Singh

After some acrimonious e-mail exchanges later, Dr. Singh acknowledges that the clearance form indeed was filled but not sent with the parcel.

Dear Dr Singh

I spoke to the head of FEDEX in DC and he told me that the "commercial invoice" should have been filled out at the hospital. FEDEX does not fill these out.

FEDEX also traced previous packets from your hospital and found that this was true for all samples so far (form was filled up by someone at the hospital).

I have now filled out the invoice and faxed it to Memphis. FEDEX is not sure if I will get the samples tomorrow because of the delay. I will let you know.

Thanks

Rahul

Dr Singh continued to defend the staff at her hospital. Her response:

Dear Dr. Jindal,

I have spoken to Fedex here for the third time today and they have assured me that they fill out a Commercial invoice at the time of shipping. According to them this was done for this shipment and they have faxed a copy of this also to Memphis. I have asked to see a copy of this and they have promised to fax it to me. As soon as I have it I will scan it and send it to you so that you can see it for yourself.

Dr. Madhu Singh

Finally, Dr Singh accepted the error and her response:

Dear Dr. Jindal,

It has been confirmed that the commercial invoice was sent with the samples, I have attached the invoice which was indeed signed by our office assistant.

FEDEX in MEMPHIS is asking if they should store the Samples in the refrigerator or dry ice.

Dr Madhu Singh

It is important to have a root cause analysis so that such incidents are not repeated in the future.

Dear Dr Singh

You should investigate why there was a problem and why the invoice was not send with the box. If the invoice was sent with the box, why and where it was lost. This will prevent future incidents like this.

If FEDEX is responsible, then you should ask for compensation.

I wasted 6 hours yesterday on the phone trying to get the packet released.

Thanks

Rahul

If the correct procedures had been followed, a lot of time, energy and resources could have been saved. The samples reached late and were useless. Another batch of samples had to be sent leading to delay, anxiety for the patients, and of course, additional expenses in packaging and shipping which could have been used for direct patient care.

SEVA OR SOCIAL ENGINEERING?

This is an article which appeared after our 10th kidney transplant in Guyana. The West Indian newspaper is widely read in the Caribbean communities in the US. It is our belief that the mission has to be clearly defined and we have to be careful not to take sides in countries or communities where there is a racial or ethnic divide.

"This is a compelling story that transcends ethnicity and fear and it took place in one of the most beautiful countries of the world, Guyana, South America".

Here are the players: Grand Sponsor Mr George Subraj and Team Coordinator Mr. Lackram Persaud, Guyanese-born, US citizens; Dr. Rahul Jindal is an Indian-born, Washington-based, US Citizen; Drs Edward Falta, Arthur Womble, Alden Doyle and Stephen Guy are Americans; most surprisingly here are two Indo-Guyanese financial donors who wish to remain anonymous; while at the centre of it, is the life of a charming young lady of Afro-Guyanese ancestry – 22-year-old Diana Williams.

But why the emphasis on race? It is so because this splendid event took place just two weeks ago by this diverse group of business and medical professionals in Guyana, as post-elections drama mostly along racial lines, threatened to usurp the lives of thousands of Guyanese. But most depressing for this group was the fear and suspension of normal life in Georgetown which was going to prolong the agony of a desperate Diana. The unfortunate post-election situation in Guyana was definitely going to influence Diana's chances of survival, as she was quickly losing her battle with irreversible kidney disease. But was the group going to listen to the negative reports out of Guyana and protect themselves by staying away and abandon the once sprightly Diana; or follow their conscience and march into the unknown?

This then is how the 11th Medical Mission of this team began: A plot which reveals that true kindness and love transcends the color of one's skin! "Let me add, Guyana is special country. While we may experience these embarrassing hurdles from time to time, because of racial divide, we are a people known to be the most hospitable. That is why I knew we would be able to cross the ethnic boundary and get to Diana on time. I feel that someday soon Guyanese would all be able to look beyond the color of each their skin and help each other as one!" said George. But what was so urgent that this team was prepared to go in harm's way during the holiday season rather than postpone their trip?

Diana Willams of New Amsterdam, Berbice, began 2011 experiencing severe shortness of breath. She also became very weak, dizzy and noticed that several parts of her body were swelling. Just into her twenties,

Diana was perturbed. Very few doctors locally knew what was wrong, but her condition deteriorated. She was then transferred to Georgetown Public Hospital Corporation where further tests revealed that her kidneys had completely failed. Diana's world collapsed. In her weakened state, Diana was driven to depression. She was going to die, she thought. Her mother had passed away when she was just eleven years old and this news was just as shocking.

Luckily, tests conducted in Guyana and USA showed that her sister Paula was a compatible donor. Now Diana, whose funds were exhausted, still had to find the cash for her hospital bills. As her illness was, draining and tiring, finding the required sum for hospital expenses was just as demanding. The population becomes more polarized and Diana's optimism was on the wane again! Making a final push, Diana made a public appeal for $3 (G) million through the media.

USING SKYPE[49] TO CONDUCT LIVE CLINICS FROM USA

We conducted a number of live clinics from the USA in which we talked to patients who have received a kidney transplant and modified their medications. Using Skype, we also spoke to patients on dialysis who had potential donors. It was a good exercise as patients and their donors could actually interact with us. It instilled confidence in both, the local physicians and the patients as well. In particular, donors who were unsure got a chance to talk to us and clear their misconceptions.

---

[49] http://www.skype.com/en/

Rahul M. Jindal, MD, Ph.D.

Dr. Jindal conducting a Live Clinic from the USA via Skype.

DEVELOPING HEALTH POLICY FOR TREATING RENAL FAILURE IN DEVELOPING COUNTRIES

In an ideal situation, the government should provide free care to all its citizens in some sort of a national service as in the United Kingdom or Canada. This is of course a matter of much debate and controversy[50]. This is not the place to discuss the pros and cons of different systems of health care which may range from[51]insurance-based as in the United States or a National Health System (NHS) in the United Kingdom or a mixed form as in India[52], where the government will provide only the basic health care in the country side with a few tertiary centers which provide very highly specialized forms of health care. In developing countries such as India, the management of end-stage renal disease is

[50] Moore R, Marriott N. Cost and price in the NHS: the importance of monetary value in the decision-making framework--the case of purchasing renal replacement therapy. Health Serv Manage Res 1999;12:1.
[51] Lameire N, Joffe P, Wiedemann M. Healthcare systems--an international review: an overview. Nephrol Dial Transplant 1999;14 [Suppl 6]:3.
[52] Bhowmik D, Pandav CS, Tiwari SC. Public health strategies to stem the tide of chronic kidney disease in India. Indian J Public Health 2008;52:224.

largely guided by economic considerations. In the absence of health insurance plans, only 5-10 percent of all patients with End Stage Renal Disease (ESRD) in India obtain some form of renal replacement therapy.

It is necessary to learn from the experiences of other developing countries in setting up a health policy for Guyana. Due to the population mix of Guyana, where approximately half the population is of Indian descent and the other half of African descent, analyses from India and other Caribbean countries may be particularly relevant.

Experience of Jamaica: Trisolini et al.[53] from makers develop health policy for renal failure. The results of this analysis could be useful for Guyana and developing countries, where both resources and data may be limited. Their analysis included eight issues: (1) a review of currently available clinical and scientific understanding regarding ESRD; (2) a review of country-specific socioeconomic and clinical issues relevant to ESRD in Jamaica; (3) estimates of the magnitude of the need for treatment in the Jamaican population; (4) comparison of the need with available treatment capacity; (5) cost analysis related to options for expansion of treatment capacity; (6) comparison of costs to government budget resources and other potential sources of financing; (7) development of policy options; and (8) sensitivity testing of policy scenarios and trade-offs with competing priorities. They reached a conclusion that rationing available treatment capacity may be the best option, which although politically challenging. In addition, cost saving strategies such as peritoneal dialysis, pre-emptive kidney transplantation, preventative measures and public education should be undertaken. They calculated that if all renal failure patients in Jamaica were to be treated with hemodialysis, the recurrent costs could reach 68 percent of the total Ministry of Health budget, a situation which would be unacceptable. This is interesting as Guyana has approximately 40 percent population of African descent, and these figures could be applied to Guyana. Boston, United States, collaborated with the physicians, governmental officials and health care payers in Jamaica to help decision.

---

[53] Trisolini M, Ashley D, Harik V, Bicknell W. Policy analysis for end-stage renal disease in Jamaica. Soc Sci Med 1999; 49:905.

Experience of India: In India, Jha[54] has succinctly summarized the state of treatment options for renal failure. The high cost of hemodialysis puts it beyond the reach of all but the very rich and maintenance hemodialysis is the exclusively preserve of private hospitals. Government-run hospitals concentrate on renal transplantation, as this is glamorous and also is the best option for a majority of patients. India does not have state-funded or private health insurance schemes and patients have to raise finances; however this may change due to the recent introduction of employer-based health care systems. Physicians in India have empirically tried to reduce costs by cutting down the frequency of dialysis, use of cheaper cellulosic dialyzers, dialyzer reuse and non-utilization of erythropoietin. There is no organized cadaver donation program and an overwhelming majority of transplants are performed using living donors. They concluded that the financial burden of renal replacement therapy in developing nations impacts on the lifestyle and future of entire families, and extracts a cost far higher than the actual amount of money spent on treatment.

Experience of Guatemala: Of relevance may be the experience in Guatemala[55], a country in Central America, where the health issues may be similar to that in Guyana. It is estimated that only 35 percent of Guatemalan patients with end stage renal disease would be diagnosed and treated, and unlike many developed countries, the age of presentation in 60 percent of the patients is before the forth decade. Therefore, the cost of death and disability due to a chronic renal failure in this young population is particularly profound, resulting in reduced productivity and economic growth of the country. It is also estimated that 400 pediatric cases develop progressive kidney disorder (neurogenic bladder, reflux nephropathy, chronic glomerulonephritis) annually, which, if left untreated, could result in ESRD in adulthood.

---

[54] Jha V. End-stage renal care in developing countries: the India experience. Ren Fail 2004; 26:201.

[55] Lou-Meda R. ESRD in Guatemala and a model for preventive strategies: outlook of the Guatemalan Foundation for Children with Kidney Diseases. Ren Fail 2006; 28:689.

Experience of Pakistan: Pakistan is fairly representative of a developing country. It has a population of 140 million, with two-thirds of the people living in rural areas. The per capita income is less than US$500 and health expenditure by the government is 0.9 percent of gross national product (GNP). Overall, 33 percent people live below the poverty line with only $1 a day for sustenance. Life expectancy is sixty-one years for males and sixty-three for females.

Rizvi et al.[56] from Sindh Institute of Urology and Transplantation (SIUT), Dow Medical College, Karachi, Pakistan, have developed a unique community-government partnership, which has been successful over 15-18 years. They carry out 110 transplants a year, with free after care and immunosuppressive drugs. According to their estimates, in Pakistan the prevalence of ESRD is 100 pmp. For a population of 140 million there are 150 dialysis centers, mostly in the private sector where dialysis costs US$25 per session. Of the fifteen transplant-centers, ten are in the private sector where a transplant costs between US$6 to 10,000, which is exorbitant for the vast majority of the population. The "free" transplantation costs to SIUT are $1,640 for transplant surgery and $300 per month for immunosuppressive drugs. SIUT spends $1.6 million each year only on transplantation. They have consistently reported excellent results; of the more than 1000 transplants have been performed with one and five-year graft survival of 92 percent and 75 percent and one and five-year patient survival of 94 percent and 81 percent, respectively. However, the problem of post-transplant infections continues to be a major issue; with 15 percent developing tuberculosis, 30 percent cytomegalovirus, and nearly 50 percent bacterial infections.

Experience of Thailand: Prakongsai et al.[57] explored the policy options renal replacement therapy for end-stage renal disease patients under universal coverage in Thailand. They investigated various options, efficiency in utilization of government health resources and equity in

---

[56] Rizvi SAH, Naqvi SAA, Hussain Z, et al. Prevention and Treatment of Renal Disease. Kidney Int 2003; 63: S96.

[57] http://papers.ssrn.com/sol3/papers.cfm?abstract_id=1072047 (Accessed 08-24-2015)

access to health care. They found that although neither hemodialysis nor peritoneal dialysis was cost-effective due to its expensive costs per life year saved, but a wider societal concern of protecting households against financial catastrophe justified public funding treatment of renal failure, and to be feasible, rationing is unavoidable. They proposed that prevention of renal failure and provision of renal replacement therapy to every patient, up to an age cut-off, or to every patient with a defined number of renal replacement years by providing more years to the younger patients. These two options were financially feasible and achieve ethical principles of providing an equal chance to all patients, while the other two alternatives which provide life-time medical services to all or select some, would become relatively less possible. However, they recommended significant improvement in health services for preventative strategies and a centralized system of purchasing key medications such as peritoneal dialysis solution and erythropoietin injection, and finally there should be a mandatory report of all ESRD patients on newly created "Thailand Registry of Renal Replacement Therapies."

Experience of Bangladesh: Rashid et al.[58] describe their experience of managing patients with renal failure and kidney transplant in their country of 128 million people, 75 percent live in rural areas and the annual per capita GNP is $380, which is less than many developing countries discussed in this book. As expected, treatment of ESRD has low priority in. As seen in other countries, including India, less than 10 percent of ESRD patients are able to maintain dialysis in private hospitals. The majority of patients present late in the course of their disease. More than 80 percent of patients presenting with ESRD are usually unaware of their disease. Therefore, most of them either dialyze by temporary access like Jugular or femoral catheterization. Peritoneal dialysis is done if hemodialysis is not available. The survival rates for the patients on three times per week dialysis schedule were 77 percent and 57 percent at three and five years, whereas those on twice per week dialysis had survival rates of 55 percent and 40 percent at three and

---

[58] http://www.sjkdt.org/text.asp?2004/15/2/185/32905 (Accessed on 08-24-2015)

at five years, respectively. Renal transplantation is not as expensive as dialysis and is less costly in the university hospital than in private hospitals, in particular pre-emptive kidney transplant. There is one kidney transplant center in the university hospital and another in the private sector. A total of 458 renal transplant patients were registered between 1981 and 2001. All patients usually receive cyclosporine, azathioprine and prednisolone for three to six months then cyclosporine is withdrawn within six months to one year due to financial reasons. The graft survival in their report was 90 percent and 80 percent at one and five years, respectively. The mean age of transplant patients was thirty-six years, whereas the mean donors' age is forty years. The donors included parents; especially mothers, siblings; usually sisters, spouses; mostly wives and second- degree relatives; uncles and aunts. It is not known if commercial renal transplantation is performed in Bangladesh. The annual cost of hemodialysis at private hospitals can vary between US$4000-5500 for twice weekly or thrice weekly dialysis, an exorbitant amount of money in a developing country.

SUMMARY

Numerous developing countries are grappling with the issue of health care funding for renal failure. In a recent review, Barsoum[59] collaborated with leading Nephrologists in ten developing countries in filling a 103-item questionnaire addressing epidemiology, etiology, and management of renal failure in their respective countries on the basis of integrating available data from different sources. Through this joint effort, it was possible to identify a number of important trends. These include the expected high prevalence of renal failure, despite the limited access to renal replacement therapy, and the dependence of prevalence on wealth. Glomerulonephritis, rather than diabetes, remains as the main cause of chronic renal disease with significant geographical variations in the prevailing histopathological types. The implementation of different modalities of renal replacement therapy was inhibited by the lack of funding, although governments, insurance companies, and donations usually constitute the major sponsors. Hemodialysis is the preferred modality in most countries with the exception of Mexico where chronic ambulatory peritoneal dialysis takes the lead. In several other countries, dialysis is available only for those on the transplant waiting list. Dialysis is associated with a high frequency of complications particularly HBV and HCV infections. Data on HIV are lacking. Aluminum intoxication remains as a major problem in a number of countries. Treatment withdrawal is common for socioeconomic reasons. Transplantation is offered to an average of 4 per million population (pmp).

A great deal more needs to be done; economic deprivation in developing countries and the meager expenditure on health care translates into poor transplantation activity, with a rate of less than 10 pmp in contrast to the developed world at 45 to 50 pmp. With an estimated world incidence of ESRD between 80 and 110 pmp, developed countries fulfill 30 to 35 percent of their needs as compared to 1 to 2 percent of the developing world.

---

[59] Barsoum RS. Overview: end-stage renal disease in the developing world. Artif Organs 2002; 26:737.

CHAPTER 5

National Blood And Bone Marrow Donation Campaign By Indian-Americans, USA

Rahul M. Jindal, MD, Ph.D.

USA-- ONLY 5% OF ELIGIBLE ASIANS DONATE BLOOD IN THE UNITED STATES

"Why don't Indian-Americans donate blood at the same rate as native-born Americans?" Someone asked me at a social gathering.

Although, I am a Transplant Surgeon, and I am used to routinely order blood products for my patients, I did not know the underlying reason.

- Was it apathy?
- Was it lack of information?
- Or was it just mistrust of the system?

Giving it more consideration on my way back home, I thought that it was probably a combination of all. Looking up the American Red Cross web site I made some startling discovery. Only, 5% of eligible Asians donate blood while 40% of native born Caucasian Americans donate blood[60]. Wow – that's a huge gap!

- There is a lot of information on the web and most Indian-Americans are net savvy and have good high paying jobs – in fact Indian-Americans have one of the highest incomes[61] – but why the gap in blood donation statistics?
- Should something be done about the gap and who is going to do it?
- Indian-Americans are disproportionately represented in the medical field[62], but why is no one taking the challenge of motivating Indian-Americans to donate blood?

---

[60] http://www.redcrossblood.org/info/pennjersey/asian-community-outreach-program (Accessed 08/09/2015)
[61] http://www.nritoday.net/national-affairs/475-indian-americans-the-fastest-growing-and-the-highest-income-group (Accessed 08/09/2015)
[62] http://blogs.wsj.com/source/2011/07/17/five-reasons-why-we-should-embrace-migrants/ (Accessed 08/09/2015)

Apart from the need for blood products, the act of giving blood (or bone marrow or organs after death) is one of the highest altruistic acts and this may be a good way to show that as a model minority, Indian-Americans are very much part of the wider American community.

WHY DON'T INDIAN-AMERICANS GIVE BLOOD?

Some Indian-American organizations are indeed doing their bit by conducting blood donation drives – but it is probably too little. The venerable Hindu service organization, popularly known as the BAPS[63], which has 65-70 temples across North America organizes blood donation camps in their temples once a year. According to their web site[64], they collected less than 1000 units a year – a miniscule amount to the requirement and to the growing Indian-American population in the US.

I raised this question with Dr. Suresh C. Gupta, MD, a well-known and influential physician in Greater DC area. Dr. Gupta is an icon in the Indian-American community having being the Chairman of the Board of Medicine, Maryland, and President of the medical association of Montgomery County Hospital. Dr. Gupta is also a well-known supporter of the Democratic Party and its causes. What is not well known is that Dr. Gupta is also an ardent supporter of Hindu causes and is the founding member of the Durga Mandir[65], Fairfax, VA, and the Hindu Mandir Executive Committee (HMEC)[66].

Dr. Gupta was not sure why Indian-Americans don't donate blood; maybe *"Indian-Americans are too busy making money"*
"Perhaps, too busy raising children and living the American dream"
"But, living the American dream also means, giving back to the community"
"Perhaps, too much misinformation on the logistics of giving blood"

---

[63] http://www.baps.org/ (Accessed 08-24-2015)
[64] http://www.bapscharities.org/usa/activity-categories/events/ (Accessed 08-09-2015)
[65] http://www.durgatemple.org/ (Accessed 08-24-2015)
[66] http://mandirsangam.vhp-america.org/ (Accessed 08-24-2015)

"Maybe some think that Indian-Americans are not eligible to give blood"
"Only, partially true, visit to India within the past one year makes one ineligible to give blood"
"Malaria is rampant in India and the malarial parasites live in the liver cells for a year, so there is a danger of transmitting to the patient receiving contaminated blood"
"What about visitors who take anti-malarial prophylactic medications before and during their visit to India"
"The American Red Cross still will not allow anyone visiting India in the past year to donate blood"

A lot of interesting statistics, but the question bothering me was still unanswered. Why the huge gap between Indian-Americans and native-Americans in their rate of donating blood?

WELL, WHO IS GOING TO BRIDGE THE GAP

I called the American Red Cross office in Washington, DC, and spoke to their outreach office. She gave me a great deal of statistics and what they were doing to increase blood donation amongst Asians, such as setting up web sites and public service announcements. However, there has not been an appreciable increase in blood donation over the year.

- "Does setting up web sites deal to positive results?"
- "Who monitors the outcomes of such initiatives?"

The answer I got was there was no mechanism to do so. So what is the solution?

I came to the realization that the solution has to come from within the ethnic community. Clearly, public sector announcements can go so far and no more.

My thoughts were that someone with influence within the Asian community has to step forward and do something about this issue. However, it is easier said than done – the Asian community is made up of many different ethnic people, ranging from Indians, Chinese, Far East and so on. Even within the ethnic Indian community is a huge range of diversity; North Indians, South Indians, East and West and to add to this are Indians who have migrated to the US from the Caribbean, Guyana, Fiji, and even from the UK, Canada, and so on.

- "Where do we even begin with the massive diversity that is the Asian community?"
- "Why not begin with Indian – Hindus and then take the message to other denominations in the Indian Diaspora"

But how does one reach the Indian – Hindus across the vast country as is the US?

I started bouncing this concept to my friends at a number of social gatherings, where I reached a conclusion that the Hindu temple (mandir) may be the starting point. The Indian immigrant community has built a number of small and big mandirs across this vast nation. Some of these have become symbolic of the growing economic and political clout of the increasing Hindu – Indians in the US. These are mostly in New Jersey, but now also in Atlanta, Toronto and Chicago. Other Hindu mandirs are relatively small and being converted from shut down factories or shops. Another fascinating feature I found was that even 8th generation Indians emigrating from the Caribbean countries have built beautiful Hindu mandirs in bustling areas of Queens, New York, and other large cities.

Clearly, then, the starting point would be the Hindu mandirs and then the message could be taken to Sikh Gurudwaras, Jain Derasars and later to Indian Christian churches and mosques (masjids). This is certainly going to be a work of a life time, if not a life time, certainly a full time job which will consume many days and weekends for the next few years.

I did not think that bouncing these concepts and ideas would ultimately lead me to become the national spokesperson for the Hindu national blood donation drive and would consume every weekend that I was not on call for my hospital.

NETWORKING STARTS WITH A VISIT TO HOUSTON FOR THE HMEC NATIONAL CONFERENCE

At one of the social gatherings, I ran into another influential Indian-American, who lives in Virginia and is the President of Durga Mandir in Fairfax, VA. Sant Gupta is a distinguished looking gentleman with a deliberate manner and a kindly face and a huge smile. I asked him the same question "Why don't Asians donate blood at the same rate as native born Caucasians?" Sant Gupta was smarter than many others I had spoken to. Instead of giving me a lot of vague answers and theoretical reasons why Asians don't donate blood, he came straight to the point "We will give you a platform to talk to the wider audience"

"Where might this be, Sant ji (as he is affectionately called)?"

"I am the co-chair of the HMEC which is meeting in Houston. I will give you a speaking spot at the convention where you could bounce off your ideas and get a feedback"

I had never heard of the HMEC.

Sant ji "Hindu Mandir Executives' Conference (HMEC) is an annual initiative seeking development of network between the executives of all Hindu mandirs of America. You, as a mandir executive are the natural leader of Hindu society by virtue of your intense motivation, deep experience, and selfless service. You understand Hindu-American needs and challenges. At HMEC-2010 you will deliberate on ways of ensuring the sustenance of Hindu Dharma in North America. A key component to this deliberation would be to explore ways of anchoring Hindu Dharma's sanaatan values in the hearts of coming generations and roles which mandirs can play to make that happen. The Conference will also be a place where you could offer your wisdom in specific areas, for everyone else's benefit. The conferees would also explore avenues of expanding mandirs' roles to meet the ever changing needs of the N. American Hindu. Finally, this annual Conference would be a place of formal recognition of your efforts".

"Sant ji, how come, I never heard of this organization?"

Sant ji "That's the whole point; the HMEC is a very young organization with the aim of uniting American Hindus via mandirs"

"Who is going to pay for my trip to Houston"

Sant ji "There is no sponsorship, everyone pays their own way, the hotel is subsidized"

I made up my mind to take a chance and as I was not working on the weekend of October 22-24, 2010. I went to Houston, Texas, to present my idea of blood donation at Hindu mandirs.

ALLIANCE WITH MUSLIMS YIELDS RESULTS

Re: Final Report Muslims for Life

From: Waseem Sayed (wsayed@...)

Sent: Mon 10/31/11 3:23 PM

To: Rahul M. Jindal (jindalr@...)

Dear Dr Sahib: Good afternoon and greetings of peace!

Thank you for your best wishes. The video was very informative and I pray God blesses your campaign with extra-ordinary success. Your aims are lofty and will surely lead to many lives being saved.

May God bless you and all involved in this great work.

Was-salam - and peace!

Waseem A. Sayed, PhD

On Mon, Oct 31, 2011 at 12:11 PM, Rahul M. Jindal <jindalr@... > wrote:

Dear Dr Syed

Congratulations on your great achievement. The Hindu Mandir's blood donation campaign is ongoing into the month of November as many mandirs and Indian-American student unions could not participate on 9/11 for logistic reasons. We recently produced a short video to mark this historic event.

http://www.youtube.com/watch?v=dSP7tSOw9
p0&feature=youtube

Many of the mandirs participated for the first time and will continue to do so yearly.

Regards,

Rahul M. Jindal, MD, PhD, MBA

From: wsayed@...

Date: Mon, 31 Oct 2011 09:25:59 -0700

Subject: Final Report Muslims for Life

Dear All: Good morning and greetings of peace!

Here is our final summary report:

October 27, 2011: We have now closed the Nationwide Muslims for Life Blood Drive Campaign. All data on blood drives conducted has been posted on our website: www.MuslimsForLife.org Please note that data from many multi-day blood drives has been presented as just one entry.

Blood drives were conducted in 168 cities across this great nation of ours and a total of 11,803 pints of blood has been collected. The collaboration of many faith groups, communities and organizations went into making all this possible and we are eternally grateful to them all and pray that God bless them for their help and assistance. We have endeavored to list every one of these helpers on our website but if we have missed anyone we ask to be informed so we can make amends and recognize their contribution.

Allah has blessed us immensely and the goal has been met - we had intended to try and collect at least 10,000 pints of blood to help save as many as 30,000 lives and we have been blessed to collect some 1,800 pints more than our goal!

Alhamdolillah! Hallelujah! God be praised!

I humbly request prayers for all who worked to make these results possible. May Allah bless each and everyone in abundance and always keep them under His special care and envelop them with His Love and Mercy and Grace. Amen!

Waseem A. Sayed, PhD

National Co-coordinator

Muslims for Life

THE CONCEPT OF BLOOD DRIVES SPREADS TO APARTMENT BLOCKS

George Subraj is a man of action and of few words, owner of Zara Realty[67], and known as a humanitarian and always willing to help the unfortunate and the needy (a phrase he uses very often). George as is known to be flamboyant, always in a suit, tie and a hat—reminds you of a long-gone British era. George is an American of Guyanese origin, having left Guyana when he was eighteen years old to make a living in the new world and escape the political oppression in Guyana at that time.

George Subraj is at the top of his game. His company is based in Queens, one of the most vibrant and culturally diverse communities in New York, and the neighboring suburb of Nassau County, Long Island. A competitively priced real estate and rental market, coupled with transport orientated development, in the form of Jamaica Station, expedient subway access to Manhattan, two major international airports, JFK adjacent to Jamaica Bay and LaGuardia by the East River, has helped Queens emerge as a bustling heart of commerce, trade and community living. The development of corporate space continues at a

---

[67] www.zararealty.com (Accessed 08/09/2015)

rapid pace as does the necessary supportive infrastructure for corporate visitors, the academic community from centers of excellence such as CUNY Law School and tourists on the ancestral trails of jazz icons such as, Louis Armstrong and Ella Fitzgerald, or the Kaufman studios in Astoria, Shea Stadium and much more. Major hotel chains such as Ramada and Comfort Inn recently opened their doors along with white tablecloth restaurants. While the development of a lush new Green Gateway at downtown Jamaica's western entrance is imminent and the Jamaica pathways provide green, safe links for pedestrians between parking and commercial areas.

George and I have worked together in Guyana for the last 3 years setting up their kidney transplant and dialysis program. I was now trying to convince him of an experiment in human behavior that I wished to carry out. The national blood donation drive which I was spearheading was limited to Hindu mandirs; I now wanted to expand it to commercial apartment blocks.

"Let's do an experiment in human behavior" I said to George.

"Let's arrange a blood donation drive in your apartment block to see if people would be motivated to come and donate blood"

George "It's not going to succeed, people are always in a hurry to catch the subway or going to work or shopping, it just won't work"

It took 6 months to convince George to let us do this experiment in human behavior. We first set up a booth with literature on the need for blood donation right at the entrance of the largest block of apartment complex in Hempstead, Long Island, New York. We were present to explain to the people who walked in and out of the building and were able to register 46 potential donors. We took their telephone and addresses so that we could remind them a few days prior to the drive.

Barbara Foote, the coordinator of the blood donation center of Queen's Hospital, was not convinced it would work. "It has never worked, what's different this time?"

"We have done a lot of education and given our literature and personally manned the booth to distribute flyers and explain the process of blood donation"

Barbara "We shall see"

So now we have 2 skeptical players, George Subraj, the President of Zara Realty and Barbara Foote who is the coordinator of the blood bank. Only, Luz Rodriguez and I are optimistic. We both firmly believed that there is goodness in every human being – and we can draw this out if the process and problem is presented clearly and passionately.

The big day arrives – 25th February 2012. I drove down from Washington, DC, while Luz Rodriguez came in from Queens. The blood donation mobile and the crew including Barbara Foote arrive on time at 9 AM to set up the mobile. It is a cold and windy day, not a good sign that people will come and donate blood, even though over 40 people had signed up. We, of course, cannot force anyone to give blood even if they signed up in advance – the process is completely voluntary.

The Subraj family was the first to donate, his daughter, Jasmine, followed by myself, Luz and Gloria – George's wife. Gradually, people trickled in and by the end of the 4 hours, we had 32 volunteers. Very encouraging was that many of these were new immigrants and first time blood donors. Overwhelmingly, all donors felt a great sense of joy and satisfaction in "giving back" to the community in which they live.

The following press release on the West Indian – a local Queens, New York, newspaper, captures the essence of our work with the national blood donation drive. It shows how George, President of Zara Realty, who was initially skeptical became a convert to the cause and is now spearheading a blood donation drive in his 33 other apartment blocks!

Initiated by Dr. Rahul M. Jindal to commemorate 9/11 nationally

Great start to ZARA-sponsored Blood Drive at Long Island

NEXT DRIVE SLATED FOR APRIL 14, ZARA's NEW HAVEN PLACE, 166-07 HILLSIDE AVENUE.

By R.B.Mahase

SEVERAL units of blood were collected in just a few hours to launch the North American Hindu Temples National Blood Donation Campaign, at Zara's New Haven Place, 451 Fulton Ave, Hempstead, Long Island, New York, Saturday, February 25, 2012.

In collaboration with the Vishwa Hindu Parishad of America and coordinated by Dr. Rahul M. Jindal, Transplant Surgeon at Walter Reed Army Medical Center, the concept of a national blood drive was to commemorate the tenth anniversary of the tragedy of the World Trade Center (9/11). "We are now in the second year of this drive as there always a shortage of blood," said Dr. Jindal, who is also an author of 2 books, Transplant Surgeon at Walter Reed Army Medical Center and Clinical Professor of Surgery at George Washington University, Washington, DC.

"Each unit of blood saves three lives- you have the red cells, plasma and platelets', so eventually three patients benefit from each unit of donated blood. There is an ongoing demand of blood across the country, especially in major trauma centers such as here in Queens, New York, and in Chicago and other major urban centers. So we are trying to see how we can get the communities involved in this practice of donating and assisting the blood banks," said the Indian-born surgeon.

Barbara Foote, a Blood Donor Recruiter, New York Hospital, Queens, Jamaica, said, "There is always a shortage of blood, especially in the winter months. That's a constant need, so having blood drives during these months is essential."

Asked if as a recruiter she was looking for a particular blood type Barbara said, "We are always looking for O Negative and O Positive but all types are welcome.

Once we bring in the emergency cases we give them O Negative and cross match them, then type their blood with a similar blood type so that all blood types are important."

"I am making a further appeal here," said George. "Today is only the beginning of a process which we would like to see continue and expand in our community. We are sort of examining the logistics of the entire process and hope to have more residents come forward at our next drive on April 14, 2012, at our 166-07 Hillside Avenue, address."

George's wife, Gloria; children, Tony and Jasmine; and brother Jay Sobhraj, Senior Vice-President of Zara; and several members of staff, also donated their blood. Gloria said that she was happy to be giving; and Jay commented that, "Forty years ago I was in a similar situation. I needed blood and some else was there for me. So giving today gives me nice feeling but it's also my way of saying 'thanks'."

Coordinator of the first-ever Zara Realty Blood Drive, Ms. Luz Rodriguez said that, "It was the brain child of Dr. Jindal, who initiated this blood drive last year and it has been very successful".

"There are no real dangers in donating blood as the red blood cells form back in the body within 48 hours," said Dr. Jindal. "Once you are 17 and above, do not have hepatitis, HIV, recent infections, not on blood thinners you can donate. The immediate pre-screening involves checking for anemia and your 'vitals'. Anyone barring those circumstances can donate every 56 days. The blood forms very quickly.

"You don't have to take a day off. It could be done at your place of work, temples churches," said Dr. Jindal who declared his 2011 launch as a Hindu Seva (service)

Day and got the participation of 79 Hindu temples (mandirs). This was followed by students from Rutgers, several other college student unions from New Jersey participating in this national program.

In concluding, Dr. Rahul Jindal said, "This is the first time, to my knowledge, that a commercial apartment block has sponsored a blood drive. Because of the enthusiasm and energy of Mr. George Subraj it was successful launch. We will be at one of his Hillside, Queens address next, and are hoping to make this a regular event."

BONE MARROW DRIVE ACHIEVED SPECTULAR RESULTS

Hi Dr. Jindal,

I hope you're doing well! I wanted to update you on my friend Amit. He found a match on 10/10 categories and will be having his bone marrow transplant within the next week! While we obviously don't know who the match is, they very well could have been at one of the drives you helped us organize. Just wanted to let you know and thank you again!

Take care,

Charu

THE CONCEPT OF BLOOD DRIVE SPREADS TO INDIAN STUDENT UNIONS IN UNIVERSITIES

Dr. Jindal

I am updating the Middlesex County College blood drive information. We got a huge success at Middlesex County College.

There were 42 donors signed up for the blood drive and 27 complete blood donation. The result came out much better than I expected. Blood Drive was started at 11:30 am and ended at 3:00 pm. The event was very successful without any accident and all donors were in good condition. I am mentioning couple of volunteers who helped me a lot for this event. Sonali Patel who is an undergraduate student majoring in Biology. She helped me to post flyer all over the campus and one of the blood donor for this blood drive. Dr. Virender Kanwal who is professor of Anatomy and Physiology at Middlesex County College. She received the Central Jersey Blood Bank staff in the morning and provided all necessary assistant. Professor Naresh Dhanda computer science department who was at the event whole day and promoted everyone to donate blood. At the end, everyone was happy and achieved a successful community service. Thanks to everyone.

Sonali Patel: spatel1391@...

Dr. Kanwal : VKanwal@...

Naresh Dhanda: NDhanda@...

Sincerely,

Mayur Patel

Rutgers, The State University of New Jersey

Public Health Class of 2013

Bloustein Public Service Association

Vice President

mhp67@...

(732) 979---

Re: Rutgers

From: Mayur Patel (mayur2843@...)

Sent: Wed 11/09/11 7:28 PM

To: Rahul M. Jindal (jindalr@...)

Hi Dr. Rahul

Rutgers University blood drive went excellent. We finally reached more than our target. I was curious when we started blood drive but after time went it was huge turn out from donors. At 2:30 we reached our goal and started wrapped up everything I was the last donor for this blood drive. I am sending you more details with pictures, videos, and article because I want to make nice documentary and write an article about Rutgers University Blood Drive Campaign that is a successful example for Universities.

There are 52 donors registered for blood drive and we got 38 successful donations, 12 donors rejected to donate blood, and 3 donors changed their mind. We had been doing very well since we started blood drive in the morning. We got support from volunteers and especially Central Jersey Blood Bank crew. Sharllet Ragan from Central Jersey Blood is very happy with our great work and would be willing to happy work with us in the future.

I would give my special thank to you because I got success in this blood drive based on your motivation. I already started looking future dates with CBNJ so we can set more blood drive in the Rutgers University.

Sincerely,

Mayur Patel

Rutgers, The State University of New Jersey

Public Health Class of 2013

mhp67@...

(732) 979---

On Wed, Nov 9, 2011 at 5:41 PM, Rahul M. Jindal <jindalr@.. > wrote:

How did the blood donation drive go? Raritan mandir is doing their drive on Dec 11, they will need your help. We still have openings for the other dates.

Sincerely,

Rahul

The purpose of organizing a blood drive is to support 9/11 cause and save someone's life. The first blood drive that I organized was at Shree Swaminarayan Temple, Somerset and there I met Dr. Rahul M. Jindal (Transplant Surgeon and Clinical Professor, Walter Reed AMC, Washington, DC). He shared some information about the National Blood Donation Campaign and how that increases the awareness of blood donation to support 9/11 cause. After a long conversation with him I was motivated to organize blood drive at Colleges, Universities, and religious places like temples, churches, etc.

During my blood donation camp at Shree Swaminarayan Temple, Vadtal Dham, Somerset, I followed certain steps to organize blood drive. Firstly, I contacted The Central Jersey Blood Donation for incoming dates availability for the blood drive. The date I preferred was one that had special occasion on that day which allowed me to make lots of announcements in our temple. There are approximately five hundred family members that visit every Saturday at our Vadtal Dham Temple. The marketing for blood drive would be a main component because that motivates blood donors to donate blood for good cause. I made blood drive flyers, posted them on the notice board, announced every week in Sabha on Saturdays, and each week email was sent to general list serve. The prior requirement from blood bank was to at least get 20 donors sign up in a week. On the day of blood drive, the donors were separated according to the different timing based on their availability to avoid delay and make it easier for blood bank crew. We had 17 donations and blood drive lasted for 4 hours and due to bad weather we wrapped up half an hour early.

The second project I did was hosting a blood drive at Rutgers, The State University of New Jersey New Brunswick Campus. I was totally thankful to Dr. Jindal because he gave me an idea to organize blood donation camp at Rutgers University. Rutgers University is divided into four different campuses Livingston, Busch, College Avenue, and Cook-Douglas. The first major concern was how can I enlighten about this blood donation campaign at Rutgers University? The goal was to advertise blood drive words among 56,000 students in all four major campuses at Rutgers University. I followed certain necessary steps in order to make this blood drive successful in this widely diverse institution. At first I contacted the Central Jersey Blood Bank and chose flexible date that everyone can participate. I talked to the blood bank coordinator about giving gifts to the students that donate blood. I gave them an idea about giving out blood bank offered t-shirt, but then realized that students wear t-shirt only once and then throw it in the cupboard. Finally, I convinced them to give $5 dollars Dunkin Donut gift card to all blood donors. As soon as, blood bank coordinator sent me reply, I was excited to host blood drive at Rutgers University. This was the main key to promote more donors in the blood drive. I followed the simple mechanism "Give and Take" for this blood drive because student at least use this Dunkin Donut Gift Card and buy coffee. They should organize fundraising event and use those money to buy gift for donors. I started preparation including choosing appropriate location and room reservation, creating flyers, face book group, promotional email, and inform all faculty about blood drive one and half month ago. We chose college avenue campus location because it is central hub for Rutgers University. The Blood Drive was held in Multi-purpose room that is located near cafeteria and especially we selected lunch time from 11:00 am to 3:00 p.m. We created face book events for blood drive that was foremost social media source. As soon as, we created face book event, we got huge response from blood donors. I distributed blood drive in to six groups all over the university. Each member of our organization was only responsible for posting one or two buildings. We had contacted individual faculty and students via generating promotional email and we sent them five times before blood drive. I reached 2 hour early at blood drive location and setup tables and chair before blood drive crew. We received 52 blood donors signed up, and 39 completed donations in the whole day. All donors were in good condition without any injury end of the day. Rutgers University Blood Drive was one of the most successful achievements for me and Dr. Rahul Jindal.

I hosted third blood drive at Middlesex County College where I finished two year college. This blood drive seemed challenging task for me because I did not know most of the students. My each step were more challenging toward hosting blood drive because I was hoping blood donors based on the marketing, unexpected volume, and visitor donors. I first started generated professional email with purpose of this blood donation drive and sent couple of professors that I knew them at Middlesex County College. Association of Indian Students organization supported this blood drive and I was a former president of this student club. I contacted the advisors of this organization and convinced them to host blood drive. I applied same developmental and marketing steps that I created for Rutgers University Blood Drive. The Central Jersey Blood Bank offered same $5 dollars Dunkin Donut Gift Card to all blood donors. I used to visit Middlesex County College twice a week with maintaining academics at Rutgers University. The social media source was most effective source for blood drive because I included all necessary information for blood donors. We had received so many questions and responses regarding blood donation eligibilities. I posted flyers all over the campus and sent an email to all faculties to make an announcement in their classroom. Some faculties were excited for this blood drive and made this event as extra credit assignment. I requested to the marketing department and they posted blood drive announcement on the college website. I had a class on the day of blood drive, so I found the volunteer who received blood bank crew and helped them to set up room. We received so many unexpected and visitor blood donors because this was the first blood drive hosted all over the campus. The Association of Indian Students Organization also called college newspaper and advisors gave interview couple of minutes. We had received unexpected 40 blood donors signed up, and 27 completed blood donations from 11:00 am to 3:00 p.m. All donors were in good condition without any injury and illness. Middlesex County College blood drive was most exciting experience for me because blood drive success was depended on publicity and marketing.

It is my honor to host blood drive for National Blood Donation Campaign. I will continue promote awareness to support this blood donation campaign and host more blood drive for 9/11 cause.

PRESS IS VERY HELPFUL IN SPREADING THE MESSAGE

Re: National blood donation drive on 9/11-India Abroad newspaper

From: George Joseph (gjoseph12@...)

Sent: Sun 9/11/11 3:10 PM

To: Rahul M. Jindal (jindalr@...)

Please send some info now. If possible a picture.

On Sun, Sep 11, 2011 at 3:07 PM, Rahul M. Jindal <jindalr@.. > wrote:

Hello

Sorry for the delay as I was helping with the blood donation drive. I will send you the press release and pictures in due course.

Thanks

Rahul

Date: Sat, 10 Sep 2011 20:33:16 -0400

Subject: Re: National blood donation drive on 9/11-India Abroad newspaper

From: gjoseph12@...

To: jindalr@...

Any location in Manhattan?

In case we could not make it tomorrow, Pl take photos and send a write up about the program at the earliest.

Regards,

George Joseph

On Thu, Jul 21, 2011 at 11:29 AM, George Joseph <gjoseph12@... > wrote:

Thanks. We will come to cover the event.

Regards,

George Joseph

On Thu, Jul 21, 2011 at 8:22 AM, Rahul M. Jindal <jindalr@... > wrote:

Dear Mr Joseph

Thank you for your note and interest in the National Blood Donation Drive sponsored by the HMEC. Here are my responses. Please feel free to call me in my office before 5 PM and on my cell after that.

Can you please send a quote about the program?

Hindu-Americans across North America will mark the 10th anniversary of 9/11 by donating blood. This will be first time ever that such an ambitious project is held at the many Hindu mandirs (temples) in North America. This effort is being coordinated by the HMEC (Hindu Mandirs Executive Conference (www.myhmec.org), an apex body of approximately 600 temples in North America, and agencies such as the American Red Cross will collect the blood. The HMEC and leaders of the

Indian-American community are making an appeal to the temples to come forward and join this movement.

So far what is the response to the program?

It has been excellent even though this is the first time we are attempting something like this. Out target are 100 temples. We have a solid base and everyday more and more temples and organizations are joining the movement.

Why HMEC took such a decision?

Donating blood is sharing the gift of life. Potentially, each one of us is a blood donation recipient. No one knows whose life may be saved with a blood donation; it could be yours, friends, relatives or neighbors. The Hindu citizens of this country decided to collectively mark 9/11 as a Day of Giving by being a blood donor, volunteer, coordinator in remembrance of all the victims of 9/11. Hindus are a diverse community originally from India and many other countries around the world. They form the majority of approximately 3 million Indian-Americans in the USA.

How many volunteers will work for the success of the program?

Literally hundreds are involved in planning and executing this across the country through the Hindu Temples.

Kind regards,

Rahul

Date: Wed, 20 Jul 2011 11:19:07 -0400

Subject: Re: National blood donation drive on 9/11-India Abroad newspaper

From: gjoseph12@...

To: jindalr@...

Dear Doctor,

Can you please send a quote about the program?

So far what is the response to the program?

Why HMEC took such a decision? How many volunteers will work for the success of the program?

Regards

George Joseph

Deputy Managing Editor

India Abroad

On Thu, Jun 30, 2011 at 8:45 PM, Rahul M. Jindal <jindalr@.. > wrote:

Dear Sir

I enclose the press release for the national blood donation drive on 9/11 organized by the HMEC as part of the Hindu Seva Divas.

Sincerely,

Rahul

Even the press in India reports the national blood donation drive in a big way. The 2 largest newspapers in India report this as follows:

US Hindus to donate blood on 9/11 anniversary

The writer has posted comments on this article IANS |Jul 11, 2011, 03.04PM IST

WASHINGTON: Hindus in the US plan to donate blood to commemorate the 10th anniversary of 9/11 this year.

The Hindu Mandirs Executive Conference (HMEC), an apex body of about 600 temples in the US, has appealed to the Hindus who form majority of the approximately three million Indian-Americans in the US to join the effort.

The initiative is expected to benefit patients of Asian descent who require a closer blood match than that provided by ABO positive/ negative blood typing.

The HMEC, which is coordinating the initiative with agencies such as the American Red Cross, said it is extremely important to increase the number of available blood donors from the Asian communities.

This is for the first time that such an event will be held at temples across North America, the organizers said.

Just five percent of the total eligible population in the US gives blood, however less than one percent of the Asian community donates blood, HMEC said in a statement Friday.

According to the US National Institutes of Health, nearly 14 million units of whole blood and red cells are required every year.

Rahul M. Jindal, transplant surgeon at Walter Reed AMC and national coordinator for the event, has urged Hindus and Indian-Americans to donate blood on 9/11 or around that time.

About 3,000 people were killed September 11, 2001, in the US when Al Qaeda terrorists crashed hijacked commercial jets into the twin towers of the Word Trade Centre, the Pentagon and in a field.

Dinesh G. Patel, chief of arthroscopic surgery, Harvard, said: "Our karma (action) is to follow our dharma (duty) and that is to perform our prescribed duty without anticipating any fruits.

"What better because to do than donates our blood where our spirit of giving is flowing and do without thinking about race, religion, gender or age?"

The article was followed by a spirited debate in the newspapers, some of the comments were completely irrelevant to the topic – just to show that even a good cause will attract criticism; perhaps this reflects the open society that is India!

satyadev (India)

14 Jul, 2011 11:45 AM

"Donating blood is a noble cause. Why add religion to that? You are human being and you are donating blood. Fair why call it by religions? God never manufactured souls keeping all these silly classifications which man invented him. Don't try to spoil the purpose of the noble act."

What is the scoop? (Earth)

14 Jul, 2011 02:47 AM

"Would Hindus do something for nothing? Shrewd business minds always seek "what is in it for them", behind the scene. Biggest business, rather killers and virtual too, that scapegoat others to be visible wrong doers. Watch it folks!"

Kundi (Auzi)

13 Jul, 2011 02:23 AM

"Oh god.....now the Americans will start saving money and buying gold if they get the Indian blood....oh nooooo."

Desi (US)

12 Jul, 2011 07:55 PM

"I am still trying to read, Where is RSS written? Morons stick to the article and its underlying message of peace and goodness."

Sid (USA)

12 Jul, 2011 03:40 PM

"Hindus should not give blood that will go into the impure bodies of Christians! Christianity is a cult, a scam and Hindus should not protect any follower of this fraud."

Nitin (Patna, Bihar)

12 Jul, 2011 01:57 PM

"I am proud that Hindus have taken this step. This is what defines Hinduism and not the preaching of RSS. Believing in every religion, respecting mankind and giving behavior is what Hinduism all about. Now weather American-Indians qualify for the donation or not that is a separate thing but showing your willingness to donate is what makes them great. Love u all for taking this step. Jai Hind!"

Prenesh (india)

12 Jul, 2011 01:11 PM

"Indiana Jones, is the best example .... If you except their wish... u'll be among them, and if not, they'll expel you from their community - That's why they are called LUST - devotee...!!!"

Yay! (India) replies to Sid

12 Jul, 2011 05:40 PM

"Spoken like as true anti-Hindu moron! As Hindus, we have to be tolerant of people, regardless of who or what they believe in, even idiots like you. Blood gives life. Any Hindu that gives life will receive a major bump in his/her Karma."

Nor (now at Cochin)

12 Jul, 2011 01:00 PM

"is American will donated blood for Indian or they will take blood from Indian ???? one example master mind 26/11 is from American yet they not handover India. Pls donate for Indian"

Hindu (thane) replies to Nitin

13 Jul, 2011 08:08 AM

"RSS never preached anything other than Hinduism by the way where is RSS in this? Hinduism along with teaches to stand up against injustice and that is exactly what RSS does that too peacefully."

S.jang (Noida) replies to Nitin

13 Jul, 2011 01:15 AM

"Abe is me RSS kahan se aa gaya.. First get to know well about the RSS then open your mouth...They are doing very good in helping the downtrodden and latest they were present at the Kalka mail crash site to help.. samjhe bhaiyaa"

DB (SG)

12 Jul, 2011 09:25 AM

"Way to go, Hindus....Serve Humanity, be educated, rise professionally and donate a part of your earnings to poor and needy Hindus....This is the Dharma..."

Deepak Gowda (Chicago)

11 Jul, 2011 05:19 PM

"I doubt much will be collected even if there are hordes of people ready to donate blood. The rules here for blood donation include a 1 year moratorium on blood donation for anyone who has visited a tropical country, including India. So, only those who have not visited India for the past 1 year only will be allowed to donate blood. How many do you think would even qualify this requirement (apart from health and BMI requirements?"

JN Nambiar (India)

11 Jul, 2011 04:09 PM

"RSS does not represent Hindus. If so, BJP would always rule Hindu dominated India. You can associate RSS with Hindus if Al-Qaida represents all the Muslims all over the world."

Indiana Jones (India)

11 Jul, 2011 03:58 PM

"The heading must read as "RSS supporters in US plan to donate blood"."

General (Chicago) replies to Deepak Gowda

12 Jul, 2011 05:38 AM

"Even if they qualify who how much you think a malnourished Guju can donate before he collapses? Really just look at these Guju's here in US, they seems didn't eat for days. No wonder India is on top of Hunger chart in the world, because all these banya mentality people die for money."

Sree (USA) replies to Deepak Gowda

12 Jul, 2011 03:03 AM

"I had a similar issue when I went to American Red cross to donate blood. They said I should not have visited any of the Asian countries in the last 3 years"

Kiran (Mumbai) replies to Deepak Gowda

11 Jul, 2011 11:40 PM

"I don't think all Indians visit India every year. Besides you think they haven't checked all the requirements before organizing such a thing? I bet majority of them are doctors for crying out loud. How come you're the only smart one left among the entire desi crowd?"

sean (Italy)

11 Jul, 2011 03:58 PM

"While in India, the Muslims give odes to Osama bin laden in mosques, while there in the US, we are donating our blood for society. Difference between Hindus and Muslims."

menz (Delhi) replies to JN Nambiar

12 Jul, 2011 10:44 PM

"Associating RSS with Al Qaida is really terrible judgment. RSS is a nationalist organization. Problem is that if you are too Nationalist you look like communal."

Thakur pratap singh (Noida) replies to Indiana Janes

13 Jul, 2011 01:19 AM

"Why you are always afraid of RSS?? because you can't fight with them on spiritual ground or intellectual ground... hahahah shame on you..... Missionaries know that if they were unable to convert when English ruled for 200 years how you can do that when strong and committed organization like RSS is working for Hindu awakening..."

jayshree (WORLD)

12 Jul, 2011 02:47 PM

"is it a crime to be a Hindu !!! Kindly note....you all were Hindus before your forefathers were looted, raped, murdered or bribed to change your religion. Pls check your family history..."

Tejas (Mumbai) replies to Indiana James

12 Jul, 2011 03:51 AM

"I am a Hindu and I don't support the RSS. Come back when you grow a brain."

Ravi (India) replies to Indiana James

11 Jul, 2011 11:56 PM

"Yes we are RSS supporters donating blood. But you Islamic terrorists suck the blood of innocents all over the world. Btw Mr Paki please use your own name and your country name while making a comment. Inshallah !!!! lol"

Bharat (bengaluru) replies to Indiana James

11 Jul, 2011 10:43 PM

"Your Religion teaches you hatred. Come to Hinduism, it will preach u to respect everybody. Universal Brotherhood - Vasudaiva kutumbam."

Madan Malviya (Mumbai) replies to Inidiana James

11 Jul, 2011 04:10 PM

"you must be feeling very ashamed, don't u? That your community cant join in to help people. Because u guys r nothing but third class Porki beggars. Learn something from them and help all people irrespective of your brainwashed prejudices."

gama (London) replies to sean

13 Jul, 2011 06:27 AM

"so when Hindus are gone donate their daughter for US troops for peace and fun?"

Hindu (thane) replies to gama

13 Jul, 2011 08:13 AM

"who knows it better than giving their daughters to Arabs"

CARIBBEAN HINDU MANDIRS ALSO JOIN THE NATIONAL BLOOD DONATION DRIVE

To Rahul M. Jindal, Caribbean Hindus

From: Patanjali Rambrich (prambrich@...)

Sent: Sat 9/10/11 11:53 AM

To: Rahul M. Jindal (jindlr@...); Caribbean Hindus (caribbeanHundus@...)

Namaste/Jai Shri Raam

I like to congratulate the spiritual leader of the Surya Narayan Mandir, Pt. Ram Hardowar, for organizing a Blood Drive in remembrance of the 10th anniversary of the 9/11 World Trade attack on America. The Blood Drive was coordinated by Dr. Anand Hardowar. On his own initiative, Dr. Anand contacted Dr. Rahul M. Jindal, Transplant Surgeon, Walter Reed Army Medical Hospital and Clinical Professor, the National Coordinator for the Hindu Mandirs Executive Conference (HMEC) 9/11 Blood Drive Campaign. Dr. Jindal, is no stranger to the Caribbean community due to his many medical outreach trips to Guyana Dr. Jindal was the surgeon who performed the first kidney transplant in Guyana. Dr. Jindal had set a very ambitious national goal of donating 5000 pints of Blood to Americans in remembrance of the 10th Anniversary of 9/11.

Dr. Anand accepted the challenge and moved quickly to host the only HMEC Blood Drive among the large Caribbean Hindu community in New York. Surya Narayan Seva Outreach Sang volunteers included Dr. K. Ramkissoon, Shankar Ramkissoon, Rohan, Vishal and a few other volunteers.

This blood donation event organized by the Surya Narayan's Mandir is reminiscent of the largest ever blood donation event spearheaded by Swami Aksharananda in Guyana where 240 units of blood was donated in a single Saturday in 2009, setting a new record in Guyana and the English-speaking Caribbean. We hope this positive trend will continue as it sets a very good example for the Caribbean Hindu community.

The Surya Narayan Mandir's Blood Drive exceeded the projection of the NY Blood Center. The NY Blood Center had projected to receive only 25 pints of blood, 34 pints were collected. The equipment staffs arrived at 8:00 AM and the nurses arrived at 10:00 AM. The registration room was flooded with devotees from the Mandir, other Hindu volunteers and even two African Americans who saw the signs for a blood drive outside the Mandir and rushed to donate blood. Approximately 58 individuals registered to donate blood. However, a few were rejected due to their recent visit to foreign nations and not meeting the required weight or pulse rate. However, 34 individuals were approved and allowed to donate blood. This was a great achievement. Although the nurses were over worked due to the flood of volunteers, everyone was very happy to contribute their part to save a life in America. The age group of the blood donors range from 16 years old to a grandmother in her 60s. The entire process took between

30 minutes to one hour with most of the time spent waiting to complete the screening process and availability of beds. The Blood Center six staffs and other Surya Narayan volunteers were at the Mandir after 5:30 PM. They were very exhausted but were happy that they had exceeded the goal and proud of making a contribution to our great nation.

The objective of the 9/11 Memorial Blood Dive Campaign was to support our nation by making a difference in the minds of the larger American society that Hindus are giving back to America in many ways. Many Hindus are going Seva in America.

The Blood Center provided snacks and drinks to all volunteers. It also gave a 9/11 Commemoration Coin, that was enclosed in a glass case, to all blood donors. Special 9/11 envelope with a drop of blood immersed in the twin towers was provided to all.

The Surya Narayan Mandir presented a T-shirt to all who registered for the blood drive and other volunteers. The Mandir staff also provided a delicious meal which included a mouth-watering dessert.

On Behalf of the Vishva Hindu Parishad America New York Chapter and the Hindu Mandirs Executive Conference I am indeed proud to be associated with the young and community minded youths of the Surya Narayan Mandir. Each will take the Hindu community to the next level where Hindus will be respected and emulated by the larger American society. It is my firm conviction that the days are not far away when Americans will look to many Hindu American youths for solution to some of the problems in America.

Patanjali Rambrich

VHP America – New York

INTERIM RESULTS OF THE NATIONAL BLOOD DONATION DRIVE

The National Blood Drive Campaign organized by HMEC, an initiative of Vishwa Hindu Parishad of America, has registered a significant success that sets a precedent for future blood drives to come[68]. With the participation of over 79 Hindu Temples at a national level, this major project demanded the arduous efforts of the steering committee members who under the guidance of its' Director, Dr. Rahul Jindal and through team effort, have successfully carried out a tremendous campaign throughout several states in North America. Although, while most of the temples conducted the drive on September 11, 2011, some temples and organizations had to schedule the blood collections on alternate dates, due to prior engagements on that date. As a matter of fact, currently, there are still some blood drives scheduled to take place in the near future.

Phenomenal results have revealed an impressive number of blood units collected (1500 units and counting). For instance, 69 units were collected at the Jalaram Temple in Chicago, Illinois[69].

This project has proven to be a great learning experience for everyone across the board. Here are some of the factors that contributed to this success:

Targeted population was easily reached in person or via individual temples and organizations ways of communicating with members, and it was widely promoted.

There was ample flexibility with scheduling individual blood drives at different locations, making sure that it did not interfere with other religious, and/or major local events—respecting the local temple/ organizations' autonomy in making that decision.

Dissemination of information was done in a simple comprehensive way which included blood drive requirement guidelines; forms and flyer

[68] http://www.youtube.com/watch?v=dSP7tSOw9p0 (Accessed 08/09/2015)
[69] http://hmec.vhp-america.org/ (Accessed 08/09/2015)

templates; and Power Presentation slides. Specific blood drive internet links were included as well as part of the information package.

Dr. Jindal and his colleagues comprising of Dr. Mahesh Manglick, Dr. Abhaya Asthana, Mr. Dhaval Joshipura and Ms. Luz Rodriguez, and took advantage of their vast experience in blood donation drives, and shared their knowledge and expertise with everyone interested. The team responded to everyone's inquiries, and addressed their concerns. We did not only provide encouragement, guidance, and support to everyone by phone or email but he also travelled to be in person at several of the blood donation sites to meet the organizers and to greet the donors himself. Lots of support is one of the crucial factors that made the process easier for the temple organizers who had different degrees of experience in blood donation drives. Some had some experience, and some others had no experience at all. But all, experienced and novices, found a dedicated source of expertise to walk them through all stages from the beginning to the culmination of their local drives. In fact, several of those organizers also shared their experiences and offered the team their feedback, and posted testimony of their experience in their local temple's websites.

Periodic reviews at different stages of development following initial guidelines for deadlines were encouraged but not always totally successful. Also, adequate responses for input and feedback were solicited but there was some reluctance encountered, and even sometimes, it was not possible to get a response.

LESSONS LEARNT AND POTENTIAL SOLUTIONS

i. Establishing specific committees: Long distance massive projects are not easily coordinated. Committees must be created, namely, a Strategic Planning Steering Committee, Local Organizing Committees and sub-committees, as well as Regional Committees if necessary. Each committee/sub-committee must become familiar with the mission, objectives, and guidelines, design a realistic plan of action, which includes a detailed timeline of the project, and the logistics involved from beginning to end. All committees should report to the

Steering Committee on regular basis. Open communication channels that are easily available and agreed upon by the committees to keep everyone in the loop, must be established to promote participation, and collaboration. Effective flow of communication among committees speeds up decision making and implementation of ideas to meet goals and deadlines successfully. Establishing specific committees fosters a sense of community and service among all members. They help reduce reluctance to any form of change, sharing information, and delegating tasks at a local level. It is also an excellent opportunity for elders of the organizations to encourage the participation of the younger generation to develop leadership under the guidance of the elders in the form of mentorship. Together, both mentors and mentees will work hard knowing that it is for a good cause.

ii. Definition of roles and accountability: Everyone involved must acknowledge their commitment and accountability throughout the whole process right from the early preparation stages. Everyone's role in the project is crucial to the accomplishment of its mission.

iii. Feedback and post-event assessment: Everyone will profit from feedback from those who have worked in the project before as it can be incorporated in the guidelines to be made available, especially to those who are new at it. A post-event assessment/evaluation, feedback and constructive criticism should be a standard requirement in a project of such vast volume as this. Organizers' input becomes crucial in the strategic planning stage of the following event as their recommendations, concerns, ideas, etc. will further enhance their own experience as well as everyone else's.

iv: Temple – organization's promoting on their own web sites: The impact of Internet technology on promoting and recruiting donors is a huge opportunity for every temple, organization, and it is often overlooked. Each local temple and organization should make full use of their own web site to promote their drive.

v: **If it's not you, then name someone else:** If you know, you as an organizer cannot possibly be in person at the site ON the day of the blood drive, please make sure to delegate the task to another member of the Committee, and do not be afraid to share and pass on all of the pertaining information so that the event you have worked so hard on goes on smoothly, even when you are absent from it.

FINALLY, BE VERY CLEAR WITH YOUR MESSAGE

There is a misconception that Indian-Americans cannot donate blood. As you can see from the e-mail exchange with Rajdhani mandir in VA, this is not true.

Subject: RE: Sewa International: Blood Donation Event during April

Dear Rajan ji

Thanks. Approximately, 40% of potential donors will not qualify because of low weight, low blood pressure, anemia and travel to India or a number of African countries and some specific areas in South America. This is because malaria is rampant/endemic there. Even with anti-malarial prophylactic medications, the parasites remain in the liver cells and can transmit infection to potential recipients up to a year later.

The criteria for blood donation is the same across the country and mandated by law, so there is no way we can change it. Despite this fact, our average number of positive donations per mandir is 22 units of blood.

Last year we had participation of 79 mandirs under the umbrella of the HMEC.

Currently, a number of Indian student unions at various colleges and universities are doing their blood donation drives with an average of 42 units at each center.

I am delighted that SEVA International and your mandir are also joining the effort. Once, the date is firmed up, we create a flyer with the eligibility criteria for donors. This is sent by mass e-mail to all in the mandir, well in advance of the actual date. We have templates for all this.

Red Cross comes with a huge van which is self-contained- requires 4 parking spaces. However, they are equally happy to set it up inside. For example, at the BAPS in MD, we had it in the van for the last 2 years, while at Mangal Mandir, we set up the camp in the main hall.

Regards,

Rahul

Date: Sun, 19 Feb 2012 17:35:53 -0500

Subject: Re: Sewa International: Blood Donation Event during April

From: rnarayanan.us@...

To: ramesh@deshpande.name; jindalr@...; rohitdd@...

CC: rameshkhanna98@...; asrivastava@...; ppsetia@...; Shwetarohitd@...; darshan.soni@...

Dear Rameshji, Dr. Jindal and Rohit,

I just spoke with Alok Srivastav of Rajdhani Mandir. Of course, there is no issue with the temple providing the facility for the blood drive. Actually they would prefer doing it in the basement area in the temple rather than in the parking lot. However, there are other issues you need to ponder on. Apparently the last time they did it, several of the local potential donors of Indian origin were disqualified from donating blood because of recent trip to India.

Please consider all these issues and if you still want to firm up the date and time or want to discuss anything further, please contact Mr. Alok Srivastava by email or by phone at 703-736---.

Good luck.

Rajan Narayanan

On Sat, Feb 4, 2012 at 7:33 PM, Ramesh Deshpande <ramesh@...> wrote:

Dear (Sarvashree) Ramesh Khanna and Alok Srivastava:

Ms. Parveen Setia, through Dr. Rajan Narayanan (Executive Director of Life In Yoga Institute) was kind enough to provide your email contacts to enable us request you both to please approach Rajdhani Temple board to allow SEWA International to hold a blood donation event in the campus of Rajdhani Temple on April 8, 2012. What we need from Rajdhani temple is only the location for parking the bloodmobile for a few hours in the forenoon of April 8. The focus this time will be to mobilize blood donors in Virginia, around Rajdhani temple. The volunteers of SEWA International will mobilize blood donors while Dr. Rahul Jindal, who works on the Hindu Mandir Executive's Committee

(HMEC) will help organize the event in conjunction with Ms. Sandy Bourget of Inova. The bloodmobile has all the facilities to conduct the blood donation event -- three donors at a time. No other space, except for the three consecutive parking places for cars, is required. The bloodmobile is self-contained in all respects and it will not make any demands on Rajdhani temple for any of its requirements. Please see the YouTube link below and the attached background documentation. Similar blood donation event will soon be conducted at the Hindu Temple in Adelphi while Durga Temple already conducts such events once in every six months in conjunction with Dr. Jindal.

http://www.youtube.com/watch?v=dSP7tSOw9p0

Let me give you a brief background of myself. I am a World Bank retiree and have been living here in Bethesda for the past about 30 years. I am a volunteer of SEWA as well as of the Life In Yoga Foundation/ Institute which conducts Yoga training and research in the community besides a 3-day workshop for medical professionals as part of Continuing Medical Education (CME) program in conjunction with Howard University Medical College.

SEWA International USA, founded in 2003, is part of a larger movement that started in India in 1989. It is a Hindu faith-based service organization in the U.S. It serves the Humanity irrespective of race, color, religion, gender or nationality consistent with timeless Hindu values of self-less service and ideals. Besides blood donation programs, SEWA conducts in Washington Metro Area, a diwali food drive and donates the collected (dry) food to DC Central Kitchen. We will be starting a few other such programs in coming months.

Dr. Rahul Jindal is a Transplant Surgeon at Walter Reed and Clinical Professor at GWU's Department Medicine. He works with Hindu Temples on this particular program with the goal of demonstrating the local Hindus concern for the broader community in which we live. His coordinates are given below. Please feel free to contact him.

I have your contact numbers and will call you tomorrow afternoon to check if you have any questions.

Many thanks and very best personal regards, Ramesh Deshpande (301) 229 ----

Date: Fri, 3 Feb 2012 07:52:28 -0500

Subject: Sewa International: Blood Donation Event during April

From: ramesh@...

To: jindalr@...

CC: rohitdd@...; Shwetarohitd@...

Dear Dr. Jindal

I have been in touch with Rohit and Shweta Deshpande on the proposed blood donation program to be held in April 2012. We have identified two temples to contact for the location -- the Hindu Temple and Rajdhani temple. I know little about this blood donation program -- its profile, history, progress, etc. Before I contact the two temples, I need to get this background information. Will you please forward relevant documents to me at your convenience? My contact number is 301-229 ----. I have your phone numbers. I can also call at your convenient time.

Thanks and very best regards, Ramesh.

SOLUTION:

We created a flyer for mass e-mail which contains inclusion/exclusion criteria. We found that this helped in avoidable disappointment of volunteers who showed up for donating blood.

Some temple devotees who wanted to donate blood had visited India in the last 1 year so they were clearly excluded.

Blood Donation Drive

GIVE A GIFT OF LIFE TO SOMEONE BY DONATING BLOOD!

WHEN: APRIL 8TH, 2012, 10AM TO 4 PM

WHERE: RAJDHANI TEMPLE, 4525 PLEASANT VALLEY ROAD, CHANTILLY, VA 20151

IN COORDINATION WITH

For an Appointment:

Visit inova.org/donateblood, click on Donate Blood 2x, and use Sponsor Code 7882,

Or call 1-866-BLOODSAVES (1-866-256-6372).

The Inova Blood Donor Services Bloodmobile will be located in the parking lot of the temple.

Event Coordinators:

Dr. Rahul M. Jindal

- ❖ Photo identification is required for all donors.
- ❖ The potential donor must:
  - ➤ Be in good health and feel well on the day of donation.
  - ➤ Have a hemoglobin (red blood cell) level which meets the established FDA standard.
  - ➤ Wait 56 days before giving another donation of whole blood.
  - ➤ Weigh at least 110 lbs.
  - ➤ be at least 17 years old
- ❖ All donors are required to complete a health questionnaire and blood safety form during a confidential interview.
- ❖ You cannot donate blood if you have visited India within last 1 year.
  - ❖ Persons who have hepatitis, HIV or transmittable disease should not donate blood. If you have any doubts call any physician in the temple.
    - ❖ For more information on SEWA International, please visit www.sewausa.org.

IS IT POSSIBLE TO BRIDGE THE GAP?

The national Hindu mandir blood donation drive is merely the beginning; the initial results and the enthusiasm of the many volunteers and mandirs has been commendable. A majority of the mandirs wants to continue holding blood drives in their mandirs; some are doing this twice or thrice a year. Indian student unions, the Hindu Student Council in many US universities have already held blood donation drives in their campuses and will continue to do so in the coming years. Commercial apartment blocks in the largely immigrant communities of Queens, New York, have also held blood donation drives – this was a completely new concept. A section of the Muslim community joined in this effort and so did a number of Sikh Gurudwaras and Jain Derasars. Some mandirs tagged bone marrow donation to the blood donation drive and the spectacular result was very gratifying.

The challenge will be to have two drives in every mandir across the US; early results suggest that this is well within the reach.

We learnt that networking was critical to this program. Empowering the local mandirs and encouraging them by regular telephonic contact or visiting the mandir on the day of the drive was very beneficial in building their confidence. Getting students to join in this effort was a good way to ensure the continued success of this program.

However, we failed to get all mandirs under a common umbrella – some groups of mandirs did have blood drives, but refused to be counted as part of the Hindu mandir national blood donation drive. I believe that this attitude will gradually change over the years as younger second generation Hindu Indians take over the leadership of their mandirs.

If there is one take-home message "Networking and keep plugging away"

CHAPTER 6

Case History 3: Sevak Project In Guyana

The advent of the internet and global travel has increased the expectations of the people in developing countries. Renal Replacement Therapy (RRT) is currently non-existent in most developing countries and is tantamount to a death sentence. There are a number of non-governmental agencies which are providing much needed primary care to developing countries; however, few are engaged in highly specialized surgical and medical care. Since its commencement in 2008, our humanitarian program has carried out 26 kidney transplants and numerous peritoneal dialysis catheter placements and vascular access procedures for hemodialysis. We have also delivered lectures and held press conferences to make local doctors and patients aware of the program[11]. We visit Guyana 3-4 times a year with each visit lasting 5-7 days (26 missions so far).

After the successful launch of a program of RRT, we introduced a program of prevention and early detection of diabetes and hypertension, the main causes of kidney failure in Guyana. This project is called the SEVAK Project (www.sevakproject.org) which empowers a local person living in the village look after the health care of the people in their village. The acronym SEVAK stands for "**S**anitation and Health, **E**ducation in **V**illage communities through improved **A**wareness and **K**nowledge of Prevention/Management of Diseases and Health Promotion". This project is modeled on the Independent Duty Corpsman (IDC) in the US Navy who are high school graduates interested in health care. They are given 12 months of training and then assigned to Marine Corps units or Navy Ships[12]. They provide primary care, look at injuries, manage disasters and also check on the preventive care of sailors along with conducting environmental checks such as humidity, temperature and sanitation.

The SEVAK program comprised of training high school students in clinical skills, such as the monitoring/recording of blood pressure, blood sugar, lifestyle modification education, noting dietary practices, so that they could keep better surveillance on the health of their respective villages. This program currently encompasses seven villages of approximately 1000-1500 people each. The stipulation is that each student resides in the village and therefore, is familiar with the environment and his/her neighbors.

METHODS

SEVAK curriculum: The curriculum was developed from three prior intervention programs in India. It is evidence-based and consisted of a set of power points and reading material, which includes basic anatomy, physiology, pathology and disease processes. The 3-months course concluded by a written and oral test followed by skills testing of mock interviews, use of internet, entry of data in excel spread sheet and finally measurement of BP and blood sugar. Rigorous attempts were made during the training to ensure minimal within and between rater variability for all SEVAKs.

Power Points and hand book: These comprise of: 1. Introduction and basic terminology. 2. Concept of SEVAKs. 3. Hypertension. 4. Diabetes. 5. Cardiovascular System including Basic Life Support. 6. Musculoskeletal System. 7. Pulmonary System. 8. Gastroenterology. 9. Endocrinology. 10. Infectious Diseases. 11. Trauma including transportation of patients and liaison with EMS. 12. Pediatrics. 13. Obstetrics: pregnancy and gestational age, hypertension, eclampsia, diabetes & referral. 14. Gynecology: Bleeding and referral. 15. Nutrition Concepts: requirements, CHO, Fats, Protein & Calories. 16. Exercise; Importance and various concepts. 17. Life Style Modification Education. 18. Immunization: Adult & Child schedules and importance in prevention. 19. Preventive Strategies: Breast, Cervix, Prostate, Lung, Mouth & Stomach Cancers. 20. Preventive Strategies: diabetes, hypertension, CVD and other infectious diseases. 21. Water purification. 22. Sanitation including mosquito prevention, toilets etc. 23. Telemedicine - including the use of laptops. 24. Coordination of care and liaison with different levels of care givers. 25. Data collection and analysis. 26. Life style modification education.

Field work: The students have screened 619 people in the pilot phase. The entire program is to screen 200 people a month until the entire population of seven villages comprising 10,000 people are screened. Each SEVAK works over the weekend outside school hours and monitors and follows the screened families and serves as their health advocate.

Selection of villages and SEVAKS: We have selected seven villages in the remote region of Guyana where there are no medical facilities and they are far from any health center. Each SEVAK resides in the village and is familiar with the people they are screening. In this way, the SEVAKS and the families build trust in each other for the long-term.

Monitoring of results: Pre- and post- evaluation of the training is done by the authors via internet and visits to Guyana. Our team visits Guyana every 3 months to perform kidney transplants and associated clinics. During these visits, we accompany the SEVAKS in the field and monitor their progress. Particular attention is paid to visit the patients who have been diagnosed with hypertension and diabetes. We also reinforce the skills of BP and blood sugar measurement.

Statistical Analysis: The population of Guyana in 2010 census was 752,940[13].To estimate the health indices in overall population of Guyana with the error rate of 4% and confidence level of 95%, the required sample size was 600 people. Chi square test was used to assess statistical significance of difference between categorical variables. T- test, Wilcoxon signed-rank test, ANOVA (Analysis of variance) and Kruksal-Wallis ANOVA test were used for continuous variable depending upon distribution (normal or non-normal) and number of comparison groups. Sample size calculations were done based on assumption of simple random sample. Projected results for population of Guyana were derived by calculating 95% confidence interval around their point estimates. "R" was used for all analysis. R is open source statistical analysis software widely used for data analysis[14].

RESULTS

Population screening: In the pilot phase, we have screened 619 people. The results generated from the sample of 619 people can estimate the health indices in overall population of Guyana with the error rate of 3·94% and confidence level of 95%. The plan is to screen 200 people a month until the entire populations of seven villages comprising 10,000 people are screened in three years.

Results from pilot study: The mean age of the sample population was 42·2 years and 43·6% of them were males. 75·1% were married, 3·1% were singles and 5·3% were widowed. The prevalence of obesity (BMI > 29·99) was 12·4%, whereas 43·6% people were overweight (BMI > 24·99). The prevalence of smoking was 12·1% and of alcohol consumption was 37%. Drug abuse was low at 0·5%. All people (100%) had access to a toilet, of which 83·6% were inside the house and rest were out of house. The purified water (by Reverse Osmosis) was available to 59·3 population, whereas 35·4% used well water for drinking (Table 1).

The overall rate of PAP smear testing was 10·3% in women. However, in age group of 16-45 years, rate of pap-smear testing was only 7·9%. Only 5·7% women had breast exam knowledge (Table 2).

The prevalence of diabetes mellitus was 13·9%. Among diabetics, 33·7% were using insulin, and 86% oral hypoglycemic; 14·1% of diabetics had at feet checkup checked in last one year. 33·7% of diabetics had retinopathy. Only 5·8% of diabetics had dilated eye exam in last one year (Table 3).

Prevalence of hypertension in Guyana was 29·4%. 63·2% of them were overweight and 17% were obese. Among hypertensive patients, the prevalence of smoking was 6·6%, tobacco use was 5·5% and alcohol use was 43·4%. 9·9% patients were unaware about existence of hypertension (Table 3).

Projected results for population of Guyana: The prevalence of smoking·in population of Guyana was estimated to be 10·0 – 17·8%. Alcohol consumption was 33·1 – 40·9% and drug abuse was 0 - 4·9%. Smoking hazard awareness was 67·5 - 75·3 and mouth cancer awareness was 53·2 – 61%. Purified water (by Reverse Osmosis) was available to 55·4% – 63·2% population, whereas 31·5% - 39·3% used well water for drinking. The prevalence of diabetes mellitus was estimated to be 10·0 – 17·8% in overall population and prevalence of hypertension was estimated to be 25·5 – 33·3%. Prevalence of obesity was estimated to be 8·5 - 16·3, whereas 39·7 - 47·5% population was overweight (Table 1 and Figure 1).

DISCUSSION

The SEVAK project in Guyana was initially trialed in Gujarat, India[15]. Balagopal et al.[16] have carried out a prototype program to address the shortfalls in the healthcare needs of the villages. One village per district (n=27) in Gujarat, India, have been chosen to screen the residents for diabetes, hypertension, obesity and monitor those with chronic diseases. The project involves coordinating with the villages and identifying bright individuals with, medical and or non-medical, backgrounds who are interested in the project (one per a village of 1000-1500 population), and then train to be SEVAKs. They have shown that such a program has become self-sustaining as the SEVAKs who live in the village will be able to continue the screening, delivery of care and health education. The major difference between the Indian and Guyanese model is that the SEVAKS in Guyana are still in high school and they work in their villages only during the weekends.

The SEVAKs are also trained in good sanitation practices, safe drinking water, smoking cessation and malaria prevention. SEVAKs maintain a database on the medical problems of the villagers and target the high risk groups for detailed health education and monitoring. They also act as liaison between the patient and his/her physician. They will help ensure that patients on TB, HIV, and Malaria treatment are adherent with their medicines and that patients with diabetes and hypertension come for regular checkups and attend health classes. Pregnant women will be screened for diabetes and they will be encouraged to deliver in a hospital or safe environment to decrease maternal mortality.

Vast populations in developing countries do not have access to basic health care. Numerous efforts by government and NGOs have failed to remove this disparity. It was observed in a recent study that in rural India, non-communicable and chronic diseases are the leading causes of death[17]. It was also observed that this pattern of death is unlikely to be unique to these villages and provided a new insight into the rapid progression of epidemiological transition in rural India. Access to care is marginalized and there were no primary health care centers that could manage chronic diseases. This lacuna made them even more vulnerable to chronic diseases and their complications. Seventy per cent of Indian Population lives in the villages (700 million people). Like India and many other developing countries, Guyana is also undergoing an epidemiological transition with both non-communicable and chronic diseases are the leading causes of death.

We have studied diabetes and hypertension in detail in the sample population of Guyana. In developing countries, burden of diabetic complications are very high compared to developed countries. The reason can be the lack of awareness, frequent hospital visits, routine blood glucose measurement and insufficient eye and feet examinations. We tried to assess all these factors in our study population. Also, additive risk factors like smoking, tobacco use and hypertension complicate the pathophysiology of diabetes. In the sample population, 8% of the diabetics were smokers, 4.7% used tobacco and 43% used alcohol. These characteristics were predominantly seen in males for Guyanese population.

For hypertension, our result showed that almost 10% of the hypertensive patients were previously undiagnosed. Follow up measurements are very important in hypertensive patients. As SEVAKs are from the community itself and as they go themselves to the patient's home, follow up of the patients become very efficient. Like Guyana, many of the developing countries have significant percentage of undiagnosed hypertensive population, shortage of health care facility being the prime reason for it. In such scenario, projects like SEVAK act as a prudent alternative. In other results, 55% of the hypertensive patients have their cholesterol checked up in the past two years. 6.6% of all the hypertensive patients are smokers.

The importance of education and delivery of healthcare to this large base of developing countries in their resource-poor settings becomes an urgent and viable issue. Large-scale efforts to improve general awareness about diabetes, hypertension, cardiovascular disease, its risk factors, and to promote healthy lifestyles are needed to reduce mortality, morbidity and improve quality of life. SEVAK project is one such effort to meet the health care need of the rural population in Guyana. The prime feature of the project is that local community members are trained for primary screening of the diseases, so that remote areas of the country, which are underserved as such, can be benefitted by their own community members.

However, our project has limitations as SEVAKs are high school students; therefore, they need to manage their field work along with their academic study. For example, at the time of school examinations, SEVAKs may not be able to perform their duty efficiently. Also, as they are students, maintenance of their personal motivation is also a challenging task. The government of Guyana, according to a Government Information Agency (GINA) release, launched the CHW (community health workers) training program in 2011 as the first step of medical training in Guyana[18]. The CHWs would be receiving specific skills and knowledge that would enable them to drive the delivery of care in the remote primary health care system, much like the Medex. However, we could not find evidence that this program has continued and there are no published outcomes of this effort.

To raise awareness for better health practices, the Government of India installed "Accredited Social Health Activists", called ASHA workers, beginning in 2005. In Hindi language, the word *ASHA* means hope. The Health Care Program of the Government of India targeted the installation of one ASHA in every village of India, by the year 2012. As many as 25,000 ASHA workers per state were planned. ASHA workers are usually females living in the village they work in. Equipped with familiarity of village environment and personal relationships with the other women of the village, these workers educate pregnant women of the village in healthy pre-natal and post- natal practices. Instead of home based child deliveries by inept and ill-equipped midwives, ASHA workers take the pregnant mothers to an approved hospital for deliveries in modern medical facilities under professional care of physicians and nurses. They are paid Rs.600 or $12 for each case, and the mother is paid Rs.1400 or $28. For immunization of each child, the mother is paid Rs.150 or $3. The monetary payments to ASHA workers for the various responsibilities and tasks fall below the usual standards set for health care workers in the medical profession. There have been public demonstrations by ASHA workers with slogans and banners demanding higher payments for their work. However, there are 2 sides of every story and there are numerous instances in which ASHA workers have had a positive impact[19].

We empowered SEVAKs in Guyana to become health care advocates in their villages. Eventually, we hope to shift the reliance from physicians to motivated students who are likely to stay in their villages for the long-term. Preliminary results and feedback on the SEVAK Project from various stakeholders in both the countries has been encouraging. Future plans for the SEVAK project are to (i) produce a detailed policy paper about the life style, environment, family history and blood pressure and diabetes for the Governments of India and Guyana to inform decision making process and allocation of health care funds and (ii) continuously improve the training program based upon the experience so far and extend the SEVAK to other regions of both India and Guyana.

CONCLUSION

We have shown in our pilot study in Guyana that high school students who reside in the village can be taught the basics of survey techniques and measurement of blood pressure and blood sugar. The seven villages selected in this pilot program are in the remote region of Guyana where there are no medical facilities and they are far from any health center. Each SEVAK resides in the village and is familiar with the people they are screening. To conclude, the IDC concept of the US Navy, that has been tried and tested for many decades, has been modeled and modified to develop the SEVAK program in India and Guyana, South America. The broad capabilities taught through this model produce a very capable type of community health worker that can integrate well into the country's health system. Feedback from various stake holders has been positive.

TABLE 1: Baseline characteristics of sample population and projection to overall population of Guyana (N = 619)

CHARACTERISTICS	SAMPLE POPULATION	PROJECTION FOR OVERALL POPULATION OF GUYANA
Age (years ± SEM)	42·2 ± 0·6	
Sex (%)		
Male	43·6	39·7 - 47·5
Female	56·2	52·3 - 60·1
Marital status (%)		
Divorced	0·5	0 - 4·4
Married	75·1	71·2 – 79
Never been married	14·5	10·6 - 18·4
Single	3·1	0 – 7
Widowed	5·3	1·4 - 9·2
BMI > 24·99 (%)	43·6	39·7 - 47·5
BMI > 29·99 (%)	12·4	8·5 – 16·3
Smoking (%)		

Everyday	6·6	2·7 - 10·5
Some day	5·5	1·6 - 9·4
Not at all	85·5	81·6 - 89·4
Tobacco (%)	9·9	6 - 13·8
Alcohol use (%)	37·0	33·1 - 40·9
Recreational drugs (%)	0·5	0 - 4·4
Diet (%)		
Vegetarian	1·3	0 - 5·2
Non-vegetarian	19·7	15·8 - 23·6
Mix	79·0	75·1 - 82·9
Socio-economic conditions		
Education status (%)		
Grades 1 through 8	38·4	34·5 - 42·3
Grades 9 through 11	46·0	42·1 - 49·9
Grades 12	9·2	5·3 - 13·1
College 1 year to 3 years	1·6	0 - 5·5
College 4 years or more	1·6	0 - 5·5
Post-graduate	0·2	0 - 4·1
No formal education	2·7	0 - 6·6
Income level (%)		
Employed for wages	38·1	34·2 – 42
Homemaker	26·7	22·8 - 30·6
Out of work	6·8	2·9 - 10·7
Retired	4·0	0·1 - 7·9
Self employed	20·4	16·5 - 24·3
Student	1·6	0 - 5·5
Unable to work	1·0	0 - 4·9
Toilet (%)	100	96·1 – 100
In house	83·6	79·7 - 87·5
Out of house	16·3	12·4 - 20·2
Chula (%)	97·7	93·8 – 100
Firewood	1·5	0 - 5·4
Gas	92·1	88·2 – 96
Kerosene	4·2	0·3 - 8·1
Stove	0·6	0 - 4·5

Type of Drinking water		
Reverse osmosis water	59·3	55·4 - 63·2
Tube well	2·3	0 - 6·2
Village tank	3·1	0 – 7
Well	35·4	31·5 - 39·3
Diabetes	13·9	10·0 - 17·8
Hypertension	29·4	25·5 - 33·3

TABLE 2: Prevalence of risk factors of diseases and screening in population of Guyana by age groups and sex (N = 619)

	SAMPLE POPULATION	MALES	FEMALES
Smoking (%)			
All Age groups	12·1	27·0	1·2
Age 16-45	11·2	24·8	0·9
Age 46-70	14·4	31·4	1·7
Age > 70	14·8	25·0	0·0
Alcohol use (%)			
All Age groups	37·1	62·2	17·5
Age 16-45	38·8	66·7	17·8
Age 46-70	36·3	59·8	18·7
Age > 70	18·5	31·3	0·0
Tobacco (%)			
All Age groups	9·9	21·5	0·9
Age 16-45	10·4	22·8	0·9
Age 46-70	8·8	19·6	0·8
Age > 70	11·1	18·8	0·0
BMI > 24·99 (%)			
All Age groups	43·6	40·4	46·3
Age 16-45	40·3	39·5	41·1
Age 46-70	51·2	44·6	56·1
Age > 70	39·6	25·0	34·6
BMI > 29·99 (%)			
All Age groups	12·4	10·0	14·4

Age 16-45	11·1	9·9	12·1
Age 46-70	15·3	10·9	18·7
Age > 70	7·4	6·3	9·1
Smoking hazard knowledge (%)			
All Age groups	71·4	77·4	66·7
Age 16-45	74·2	80·9	69·2
Age 46-70	68·8	76·1	63·4
Age > 70	51·9	50·0	54·5
Mouth cancer awareness (%)			
All Age groups	57·1	53·7	59·8
Age 16-45	63·6	58·0	67·8
Age 46-70	47·0	47·8	46·3
Age > 70	48·0	43·8	54·5
Pap smear (%)			
All Age groups	Na	Na	10·3
Age 16-45	Na	Na	7·9
Age 46-70	Na	Na	13·8
Age > 70	Na	Na	18·2
Breast exam knowledge (%)			
All Age groups	Na	Na	5·7
Age 16-45	Na	Na	6·1
Age 46-70	Na	Na	5·7
Age > 70	Na	Na	0·0

TABLE 3: Characteristics of Diabetes patients in Guyana (N = 86)

	ALL DIABETES PATIENTS	MALES	FEMALES	P VALUE
N	86	38	48	
Age group (%)				0·29
16-45	33·7	42·1	27·1	
46-70	61·6	55·3	66·7	
> 70	4·7	2·6	6·3	·
BMI > 24·99 (%)	70·9	71·1	70·8	0·9

BMI > 29.99 (%)	15.1	10.5	18.8	0.29
Smoker (%)	8.0	18.8	0.0	0.003
Uses Tobacco (%)	4.7	10.5	0.0	0.02
Uses Alcohol (%)	43.0	68.4	22.9	< 0.001
Uses re-creational drugs (%)	0.0	0.0	0.0	
Using insulin (%)	33.7	44.7	25.0	0.15
Using oral hypoglycemic (%)	86.0	78.9	91.7	0.19
Taken DM class (%)	0.0	0.0	0.0	
Frequency of DM visits (%)				0.08
Once a year	43.0	36.8	47.9	
Two times a year	40.7	36.8	43.8	
Three times a year	16.3	26.3	8.3	
Frequency of CBG monitoring (%)				0.25
Everyday	5.8	0.0	10.4	
Few times per week	18.6	21.1	16.7	
Few times per month	37.2	34.2	39.6	
Few times per year	14.0	18.4	10.4	
Never	24.4	26.3	22.9	
Tested for HbA1C (%)				0.56
At least once in past year	18.6	23.7	14.6	
Not in past one year	73.3	68.4	77.1	
Never	8.1	7.9	8.3	
Feet checkup (%)	14.0	10.5	16.7	0.41
Frequency of feet checkup (%)				0.34
Once a year	65.1	73.7	58.3	
Twice a year	15.1	15.8	14.6	
Three times a year	10.5	7.9	12.5	
Four times a year	1.2	0.0	2.1	
Five times a year	8.1	2.6	12.5	
Sore or Irritation (%)	2.3	0.0	4.2	0.2
Eye checkup (%)				0.44

Within past month	5·8	5·3	6·3	
Within past year	14·0	10·5	16·7	
Within past 2 years	12·8	18·4	8·3	
Two years ago	16·3	10·5	20·8	
Never	50·0	55·3	45·8	
Has retinopathy (%)	33·7	39·5	29·2	0·32

TABLE 4: Characteristics of Hypertension patients in Guyana (N = 182)

	ALL HYPERTENSION PATIENTS	MALES	FEMALES	P VALUE
N	182	84	98	
Age				0·36
16-45	39·6	44·0	35·7	
46-70	54·4	48·8	59·2	
> 70	6·0	7·1	5·1	
BMI > 24·99 (%)	63·2	59·5	66·3	0·34
BMI > 29·99 (%)	17·0	15·5	18·4	0·6
Smoker (%)	6·6	14·3	0·0	< 0·001
Uses Tobacco (%)	5·5	11·9	0·0	0·001
Uses Alcohol (%)	43·4	59·5	29·6	< 0·001
Uses re-creational drugs (%)	0·0	0·0	0·0	0·28
Previously told about HTN (%)				0·04
Yes	89·0	95·2	83·7	
No	9·9	4·8	14·3	
Cholesterol checked (%)	73·6	76·2	71·4	0·47
Last cholesterol checkup (%)				0·02
Within past year	27·5	16·7	36·7	
Within past 2 years	27·5	31·0	24·5	
Within past 5 years	24·2	31·0	18·4	

BP checkup frequency (%)			.	0·41
Within past six months	59·3	58·3	60·2	
Within past one year	26·4	29·8	23·5	.
Within past two years	10·4	10·7	10·2	
Within past five years	1·1	1·2	1·0	
More than five years ago	2·2	0·0	4·1	

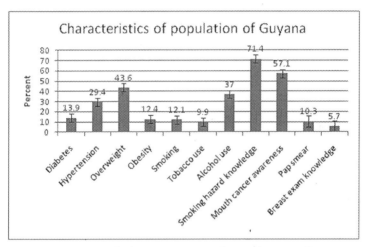

Figure 1: Projected characteristics of population of Guyana

CHAPTER 7

Case History 4: Global Health And Psychology

In order for global health to become a coherent field it will need a multidisciplinary approach. Psychology, both as an independent capacity amongst specialist psychology professionals and as a complementary skill set amongst non-specialist primary care and allied health care workers has the potential to be a key component of the multidisciplinary global health team. Structured and collaborative psychological interventions under controlled conditions have been shown to be effective in treating health disorders in low resource, post conflict and humanitarian situations at home and abroad. However, psychological capacity, has not reached its potential in global health projects, despite initiatives on the part of professional bodies. This is due in part to an absence of undergraduate and postgraduate training pathways which clarify the role of psychology in the field of global health and that equip specialist psychology professionals, non-specialist primary care and allied health care workers with a set of cross disciplinary psychological skills, that are portable across cultures and lend themselves well to vital components such as collaborative health-care and patient engagement. Following the lead of our colleagues in the field of mental health we present what we believe to be amongst the first wave of psychological capacity building pathways for specialist psychology professionals, non-specialist primary care and allied health care workers aimed at enhancing employability and skills needed in preparing to be deployed globally at home and abroad to low resource, post conflict and humanitarian situations.

There is great potential for the integration of psychological perspectives into global health projects particularly with regards to research, scaling up, outcome and promotion of psychological health and prevention of psychological disorders. For example, they could work alongside the global health team on initiatives that prevent the reporting of mental health disorders such as stigma and shame and in helping to overcome the social and economic factors that prevent access to treatment. Similarly, the integration of psychological research into projects concerned with health related behaviours such as compliance, patient engagement, implementing and sustaining change of behaviours which have been highly successful in the western world remains very limited when considered from a global health perspective.

Health psychology works to promote physiological and psychological well-being and help prevent the spread of disease. Therefore, it is well placed to assist the global health team with initiatives such as the Disease Control Priorities Project (DCPP) an ongoing joint research project between the World Bank, National Institutes of Health, World Health Organisation, Population Reference Bureau and the Gates Foundation. The project aims to prioritise disease control across the world particularly in low income countries, post-conflict and humanitarian situations.

This is mainly due to the fact that many of these studies lack the psychosocial and epidemiological data needed to influence policy and attract government funding.

Psychology programs need both undergraduate and postgraduate global health pathways that are accessible to psychologists, medics, nurses and allied health professionals in order to be able to respond to these developments and to the psychological needs of societies and individuals from low resource, humanitarian and post conflict situations at both a national and international level.

Psychology has demonstrated great potential in global projects whereby medical, behavioural, social and emotional components are incorporated into the research design. Psychology has a track record in both controlled intervention trials across a variety of mental health disorders in low resource, post conflict and humanitarian settings and as effective in the treatment of non-mental health conditions involving stress such as bereavement. Psychology has also contributed to establishing collaboration and patient engagement with indigenous populations as part of broader global health projects involving complex health issues such as HIV and malaria as well as overcoming subsequent stigma and shame which can act as barriers to treatment.

In the context of global health initiatives, treatment of mental health issues has been secondary to more overtly life threatening concerns such as infectious disease (e.g. Ebola) or chronic physical health problems (e.g. cardiac disease). Several major global health initiatives have employed psychological sciences to address decision making regarding care, promote adherence and engagement with treatment and facilitate preventative behaviours (e.g. hand washing and use of alcohol based sanitizers) and in dealing with the psychosocial legacy (e.g. fear, panic, social isolation) as well as influencing government policy to ensure that mental health becomes an integral part of the health system in countries such as Sierra Leone and West Africa. The Bill and Melinda Gates Foundation despatched psychologists to Sierra Leone as part of the global health teams to work with family, patients and staff dealing with the stigmatisation and death during the recent Ebola outbreak.

Psychologists deployed with global health teams to Africa and have played a significant role in decreasing rates of malaria. Despite the treatment of choice (e.g. bed nets) having been available for some time, widespread use only increased after the promotion of behaviour change campaigns aimed at all sections of society and government. Similarly global health initiatives relating to more complex risk behaviours such as HIV and AIDS have demonstrated that WHO educational and promotional campaigns aimed at school based behavioural change initiatives.

Given the ongoing and potential intervention for health psychology in global health projects psychology is emerging as a significant contributor to the attainment of the Millennium Development Goals (MDG's). Social psychology also has a particular role to play in promoting gender equality, empowerment of women and in addressing psychosocial factors that present barriers to improving women's status and well-being. For example, research by psychologists in high resource settings has provided insights into male perceptions of domestic violence against women, in so much as men's attitudes to domestic violence lay in the social norms of any given society. Therefore, understanding such norms and bringing about change can impact positively upon domestic violence against women.

In order to reach their global potential psychologists need both the confidence and the skills to navigate psychological competencies that introduce students to diverse experiences requiring them to apply their skills across fast paced, complex and diverse situations, conducting research, scaling up, promotion of well-being and prevention of mental health disorders in low resource, post conflict and humanitarian situations accompanied by mentoring in order that students can make sense of their global experiences.

We have successfully implemented an online course at the University of West London, which may serve as a model for others to follow.

M.Sc. Global Health
SYLLABUS

Term One (September-December, 2014)

• Module 1	Cross Cultural Research Methods and Practice (20 credits)
• Module 2	The Epidemiology and Impact of Mental Disorders (20 credits)
•Module 3	Mental Health, Global Health and Developmental Agenda (20 credits)

Term Two (January-May 2015)

• Module 4	Mental Health Policy, Development and Implementation (20 credits)
• Module 5	Mental Health and Psychosocial Support in Humanitarian Settings (20 credits)
• Module 6	Stigma, Discrimination and Promoting Human Rights (20 credits)

Term Three (June-August 2015)

• Module 7	Dissertation (60 credits)

Curriculum

Year One:

Principles of Global Mental Health: History of Global Mental Health; Disorders; Diagnosis and Classification; Cross Cultural Research Methods and Practice; Global Mental Health and Developmental Agendas; Global Mental Health Resources; Mental Health, Social Development and Security in Humanitarian Settings; Stigma, Discrimination and Promoting Human Rights; Generating Global Commitment for Global Mental Health.

Year Two:

Mental Health Policy, Development and Implementation: Mental Health Policy and Implementation; Scaling Up Services for Mental Health; Child and Adolescent Mental Health; Women's Mental Health; Mental Health; Discrimination and Human Rights; Research Priorities, Capacities and Networks in Global mental Health.

CHAPTER 8

Case History 5: Global Energy Parliament, Kerala, India

JAGAD GURU SWAMI ISA OF KERALA, INDIA, DEVELOPS LIFE FOR TOTAL CONSCIOUSNESS (LTC)

Life for Total Consciousness (LTC) is espoused by Swami Isa who is also the patron of the Global Energy Parliament which had its first conference in Kerala, India, in 2010[70] (1). There are many ashrams in India, some good, some commercial, but only a few achieve an international stature. We describe our personal experience of involvement in one such ashram which started in a small way but has created an international presence by a dedicated group of non-Indians who have settled in Trivandrum, Kerala, India. It started as a small ashram with a few Indians and non-Indian followers, moved into evidence based clinical trial of mind-body medicine and finally into an international organization with branches in US, France and Germany.

Life for Total Consciousness: Life for Total Consciousness (LTC) is a simple but deep-working daily yogic practice evolved by Jagad Guru Swami Isa of Kerala, India. Daily LTC practice can help to receive more spiritual, emotional, intellectual, mental, and physical harmony and happiness. LTC provides the dedicated practitioner with the tools and self-knowledge necessary to attain spiritual empowerment and cosmic realization. LTC is a simple, easy-to-follow system that tunes the physical body, intellect, emotions, ego and consciousness. It works with meditation, sound, simple body positions, breathing exercises and visualization. This meditation can be practiced by everyone, regardless of health, age or time constraints. Swami Isa's system teaches us how to gain new energy rather than lose it, and to balance the negative energies with positive ones. There are several levels of LTC taught by Swamiji, as it is intended to be a life-long course guiding us to ultimate realization.

Benefits: Those who have integrated this practice into their daily lives receive much benefit from it. LTC practitioners report more clarity of thought, more peaceful emotions, higher spiritual awareness, control of addictions, enhanced creativity and charisma, increased concentration, improved studies, and greater body relaxation. Medical

---

[70] http://www.global-energy-parliament.net/ (Accessed 08/09/2015)

science is also finding benefits of daily LTC practice. Informal evaluations by doctors have reported the positive clinical effects of this practice for diabetes, arthritis, asthma, hypertension, addictions, female reproductive problems, memory loss, and psychological disorders. This practice prevents many diseases by increasing immunity, hemoglobin counts, lung strength, and improving general physical health. Even with just thirty minutes of practice, the diastolic blood pressure (which is usually difficult to reduce even using medication) has been reported to drop anywhere from 3 to 10 points.

"Usually within four weeks of practicing LTC my medical patients get impressive results—some can go off medications, too," says Dr. Vijayachandran Nair, a medical doctor in Missouri, USA, who teaches Life for Total Consciousness to his patients with multiple medical problems.

In contrast to many other yogic systems, Life for Total Consciousness is aimed at rejuvenating and refreshing the individual including spiritual growth[71].

The Isa Viswa Prajnana Trust (IVPT) functions under the divine leadership of its Founder and Managing Trustee, His Holiness Jagad Guru Swami Isa. In 2000 the Trust was established as a Registered Charitable Society, situated in Thiruvananthapuram, Kerala (India). Besides popularizing a new social philosophy for human action, the Trust has been engaged in a wide spectrum of social activities listed elsewhere in this document. It has conducted a few international and a large number of national seminars. It runs a research centre, a number of schools and an array of charitable services. The Global Energy Parliament has been created as an international movement for popularizing the new ideas.

All of the Trust's activities are centered round the basic doctrine—the concept of "Total Consciousness". Swamiji's new interpretation to education—"Education for Total Consciousness"—has become very popular in India and is fast getting accepted in other parts of the world.

---

[71] http://www.global-energy-parliament.net/research/geprc-welcome; http://www. ivpt.org/meditation (Accessed 08/09/2015)

The new methodology is envisioned to bring about a true change in the individual and create a new concept of "individual-in-society," where every individual helps in creating a better society.

Main Objectives of the Trust

1. To establish educational institutions that would impart training based on the ideal that "Education is for Total Consciousness" and to develop appropriate modules and teaching aids with a view to bring out perfect teachers for guiding the younger generation through the right track of living and learning.
2. To promote activities that will kindle interest in our ancient culture and make people familiar with the Vedas, Upanishads and Puranas of India and to offer a deeper insight into the wisdom of the Scriptures.
3. To promote devotional-spiritual activities that will help individuals to see into their inner selves and inquire into the mystery of life, sorrow, suffering, death, birth and salvation.
4. To promote research in various areas related to all branches of learning, establish a worldwide research network with a view to bring in universal peace and prosperity.
5. To establish Universal Brotherhood by facilitating the study of universal energy field in relation to man and nature.
6. To promote charitable activities by setting up permanent facilities to reach people in distress.
7. To establish a Yoga Institute to give training in "Life for Total Consciousness" program.
8. To establish a Language Institute to facilitate the study of major world languages with a view to bring in Global harmony.
9. To establish a centre to give training in Information Technology and Business Management.
10. To establish a centre to give training in horticulture and farming.
11. To establish a health care system where Allopathic, Ayurvedam, Homeo, Siddha and alternative medicines will be practiced.

12. To establish libraries and printing and publication divisions to promote learning and research.

Activities

The major activities undertaken by the Trust since its inception are as follows:

(i.)   Establishment of school (Isa Viswa Vidyalayam) - 1998
(ii.)   Veda Conference – 1998
(iii.) 1st National Educational Conference on "Education for Total Consciousness" – 2000
(iv.)   2nd National Educational Conference on "Education for Total Consciousness" – 2001
(v.)   Research Work on Panchabhootha (Swasthi Panchaha Yajnam) – 2001
(vi.)   International Educational Conference on "Education for Total Consciousness" – 2001
(vii.) World Peace Conference (Viswa Santi Sammelanam) – 2003
(viii.) Energy Activation Ceremony (Amba Yaga) – 2005
(ix.)   International Meet (Global Energy Parliament) – 2010
(x.)   Establishment of Research Centre – 2011
(xi.)   Universal Centre for Total Consciousness (Universal University) – Preliminary Measures Completed

HISTORY OF THE UNIQUE ACTIVITIES AND EVENTS CONDUCTED BY THE TRUST SINCE ITS INCEPTION

ESTABLISHMENT OF THE ISA VISWA VIDYALAYAM SCHOOL (1998)

In 1998 the Isa Viswa Prajnana Trust founded the Isa Viswa Vidyalayam, an English Medium School following the C.B.S.E. Syllabus, at Anayara, Trivandrum.

The curriculum of the Isa Viswa Vidyalayam is designed, developed and planned on the basis of H.H. Swami Isa's vision of **Education for Total Consciousness**. The ultimate aim of this institution is to make every child capable of achieving total consciousness, and students learn how to become human beings in the true spirit. It is a complete school for ultimate compassion, concentration and consciousness.

The Isa Viswa Vidyalayam now operates conjunctively as an **Educational Research Centre**, a dedicated wing of the Global Energy Parliament Research Centre (est. 2011). Scientific investigations are being conducted into effects of the Education for Total Consciousness system on the students and the teachers, including gathering data on different components like role of the head of the institution, the atmosphere in the classroom, staff culture, the relation between the school and the parents, society and the school, nation and the school, world and the school, etc. Student and staff bio-energies, as well as other factors in the emotional, intellectual and ego planes are measured over a period of time.

VEDA CONFERENCE (VEDASANGAMAM)--ISALAYAM (1998)

The Isa Viswa Prajnana Trust encourages the study of scientific spirituality, physical and biological sciences, through which the laws of nature are investigated, making use of all modern and scientific methods, in order to develop and propagate a lifestyle in tune with Nature.

The Vedas contain a vast storehouse of knowledge about the Universe, mankind, and Nature, but they are often misleading or mystifying to contemporary audiences, due to their ancient genesis. Therefore, a modern interpretation is necessary in order to impart the correct knowledge contained in the Vedas.

With the aim to propagate a modern and scientific understanding of the Vedas, in May of 1998, the IVPT organized a Veda Conference, under the guidance of H.H. Swami Isa. Renowned scholars of the four Vedas, distinguished educationalists, and dignitaries participated in the three-day Conference. The theme concept was delivered by H.H. Swami Isa about the source of the Vedas, and the science behind various Vedic rituals. Each of the Vedas was discussed for a half day, after which Upanayana was ceremoniously bestowed upon selected members of the community, men and women, children and elders by H.H. Swami Isa.

Her Highness Gowri Lekshmi Bai of the erstwhile Travancore Royal Family inaugurated the function.

CONFERENCES ON EDUCATION FOR TOTAL CONSCIOUSNESS (2000 & 2001)

With a view to make drastic change in the present system of education, the Trust conducted three important educational conferences (i.e., two at the National Level and the other at International Level) in Trivandrum during the years 2000 and 2001. A large number of educational experts from India and abroad participated in all three conferences. One of the important theme papers presented in the conference was H.H. Swami Isa's vision on education, namely Education for Total Consciousness (ETC). Under the guidance of Swamiji, a Committee headed by Dr. A. Sukumaran Nair, Former Vice Chancellor of Mahatma Gandhi University, completed the methodology and the detailed lesson plans for all levels of education, from Lower Kindergarten (LKG) to higher classes.

A brief report of the Educational Conferences held during the year 2001 is attached hereunder. The following suggestions to improve the present educational systems came out from the discussions held in the Conferences.

Equal importance has to be given to objective and subjective elements, its relation to society, environment, and the universe, so that each individual can develop his or her consciousness. According to the vision, there is no change at all in topics to be taught, only in the methodology of teaching. Each topic is correlated with his or her own experience and he or she knows what the relation is to society, environment, and the universe. There is no need of teaching moral science or ethics separately.

It is not merely a theory, now ETC is being practiced in our school, namely Isa Viswa Vidyalayam. Here methodology is applied from the beginning of LKG to the highest classes. It can be applied even to research level also. In our school, the system is implemented in all classes. The teachers selected to work in Isa Viswa Vidyalayam have been given training in this methodology and they find it very easy to handle the various topics in the classrooms. Students are also given project work according to the topics taught, and thus the student population is attaining immense knowledge of the self and surroundings. This helps each individual to know his or her own place in the society according to his or her traits and merits and surely he or she develops a positive approach to life.

This methodology of teaching has been presented to eminent educational experts through educational conferences. They opined that this is the most suitable method for the present world of education.

EDUCATION FOR TOTAL CONSCIOUSNESS

Education for Total Consciousness (ETC) is a new approach to teaching and learning with its own specialized epistemology. It looks upon the acquisition and integration of knowledge as a two-fold process, which comprises of the internalization of knowledge of two kinds – the objective and the subjective aspects of knowledge. The objective aspect of knowledge refers to ideational, descriptive knowledge of the physical world. The objective aspect deals with knowledge that is external to the learner, and treats the learner as one different from his physical and biological environment. The subjective aspect of knowledge refers to knowledge with its major focus on the knower and his learning mechanism that looks inward, one which connects the learner with the aspects he has learnt. Education becomes complete only when the objective and subjective aspects of knowledge get meaning fully integrated. This would imply the use of teaching-learning methods, giving equal importance to both the above aspects of learning.

Education for Total Consciousness
from the Isa Viswa Prajnana Trust

The Education for Total Consciousness emblem denotes the integration of knowledge in the objective and subjective levels that leads to Total Consciousness.

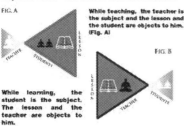

FIG. A

While teaching, the teacher is the subject and the lesson and the student are objects to him. (Fig. A)

FIG. B

While learning, the student is the subject. The lesson and the teacher are objects to him.

Here the knowledge imparted by the teacher and imbibed by the student remains in the objective plane only. (Fig. B)

FIG. C THE EDUCATION FOR TOTAL CONSCIOUSNESS EMBLEM

This knowledge is to be integrated into the subjective level also. The knowledge in the objective plane and knowledge in the subjective level are blended together. Now knowledge has become total (Fig. C).

That is the state of Consciousness. That is the light of Happiness. The inner Consciousness (denoted by the stars in the chest of both the teacher and the students) and the outer Consciousness (denoted in the figure by the oval outline) sublimes together. That is Total Consciousness.

Under the guidance of His Holiness Jagad Guru Swami Isa, a number of eminent educationalists and other scholars and specialists worked for months to evolve a practical scheme which will translate Swamiji's educational Vision into practice – a new model of education which will help to transmit the curriculum content to achieve the highest learning possible, using the new conceptions about knowledge, and the framework of the deeper learning outcomes. The lopsided development of these factors in contemporary society needs to be corrected if we want to cure the ills of present day society. Education has a key role to play in these lapses.

ETC by definition is an attempt to correct the human tendency to use the negative faculties and replace them by actions which are pure and constructive. ETC is an education which goes beyond the conventional boundaries of cognitive education and helps the human beings to educate their thoughts and minds through a system of introspection and positive mind training.

Swamiji's concept of teaching to achieve Total Consciousness can be illustrated with the help of the following example:

Introducing the lesson unit "Water" to young children, the teacher should introduce the notion that three fourths of the Earth is composed of water, while only one fourth is solid matter. This discussion should then be extended to a consideration of the composition of the human body. The teacher presents the view that like the Earth, the human body is also composed of one fourth of solid matter and three fourths water. This part of teaching is to develop the needed subjective knowledge. The idea is further developed by presenting the fact that what exists in this world outside is what exists within oneself. We can also extend to the learner the idea that all the minerals present in the Earth are there in the human body.

In so doing, we are redirecting the attention of the learner to what is inside the learner to his/her own mental processes. By acquiring this kind of knowledge, the learner is lead to an enlightened perception of himself, from objective to subjective knowledge which will help him to identify himself with the rest of the universe. The process of teaching should be designed as to address the following relationships:

- Knowledge : society interrelationships
- Knowledge : environment interdependence
- Knowledge : universe interdependence

This type of teaching has to be followed by a new kind of evaluation to see whether the higher outcomes of instruction envisaged in the new system have all been achieved.

A number of working models has been developed and tested out by practicing teachers under the close supervision of Swamiji. Many senior educationalists were actively involved. The new system argues for a new system of evaluation. The evaluation currently adopted provides only an incomplete picture of a child's development centered round certain superficial cognitive outcomes. What is required is a deeper development profile which will provide a picture of the acquisitions of outcomes within short learning intervals.

The ultimate aim of the new instructional approach, as explained earlier, is to develop a human being who looks upon him/herself as part of the surroundings, and has developed a love for the entire range of objects in his/her surroundings, both animate and inanimate. The learner becomes one with his/her external and internal being. The learner in this system realizes that s/he is an inseparable part of the whole universe around him/her and has no independent existence of his/her own. His/her learning should lead to a self-realization that humans are a miniature of the surrounding universe and s/he is expected to live as a part of it. The understanding will promote universal love and compassion. The educational model followed by "Education for Total Consciousness" is meant to impart this total and true knowledge that goes deep into one's mind, and transcends the barriers of nationality, religion, language, caste and ethnicity.

SUMMARY

His Holiness Jagad Guru Swami Isa, the Founder of the Trust, stated in His invocation address that the present day education is only object-based. We acquire knowledge through our external senses with and without using external instruments. This is incomplete in the sense that it considers only external aspects and totally neglects the internal understanding process. Dr. A. Sukumaran Nair stressed the importance of the subjective and objective aspects of education. Group discussions followed the presentation of papers. Dr. K. Sivadasan Pillai emphasized the interaction of the students at three levels:

1. Pupil and the Environment
2. Pupil and Society (parents, teachers, fellow beings, animals and habitat)
3. Pupil and the Universe (interaction between them) culminating in education for world peace.

Delegates actively participated in the discussions, and important suggestions emerged from the discussion. Dr. M.R. Thampan, Chairman, Asan Samskarika Smithi gave vote of thanks.

THE GLOBAL ENERGY PARLIAMENT (GEP)

The Global Energy Parliament (GEP) is an international body providing scientific research, recommendations and strategies to ensure a self-sustaining, peaceful existence for human beings and the universe.

The conceptual basis of the GEP is the unifying theory of energy outlined in H.H. Swami Isa's "I Theorem", which explains the makeup of the universe in terms of tiny units of vibration (I particles).

The GEP's mission is to apply this concept to:

- Develop human thought through a comprehensive understanding of the relationship between internal and external energy;

- Promote and develop scientific research on energy;
- Create public awareness about balanced energy and programmes to allow individuals to realise its benefits.

The GEP consists of Members and Ministers who are leaders in their fields. National Energy Parliaments, which themselves draw from Regional and Local levels, also constitute the Global Energy Parliament. This structure allows implementation of the GEP's objectives through:

- Regular sessions of Parliament supported by a fulltime Secretariat;
- Identification and resolution of issues at local, regional and national levels through provision of policy leadership, funding, active research and submission of recommendations to elected governments, intra- and supra-national organisations.

FIRST INTERNATIONAL SESSION OF THE GLOBAL ENERGY PARLIAMENT – MASCOT HOTEL, TRIVANDRUM (2010)

From November 12- 14th 2010 was held the first international meet of the Global Energy Parliament. Under the guidance of H.H. Jagad Guru Swami Isa, founder of the Isa Viswa Prajnana Trust and chaired by Dr. A. Sukumaran Nair, Former Vice Chancellor of Mahatma Gandhi University, this three-day international meet inaugurated a new global movement concerning the science of energy.

Local meetings of the Parliament had been initiated by H.H. Jagad Guru Swami Isa in as early as 2000, held at schools, colleges, and centres in the local area of Trivandrum. It grew to include a chapter in Chennai in 2007, and spread to have national centres in France, Germany, Australia and the United States by 2009.

The first international meet held at the Mascot Hotel, Trivandrum, drew together specialists in all fields of knowledge, hailing from five continents. Seventy-seven people made presentations over the three days. Debates were held on various issues concerning an integrated, scientific vision of energy for the betterment of the world and universe at large.

The theme concept of the Global Energy Parliament, by the name of the "I-Theorem," was presented by H.H. Swami Isa. The theorem systematically lays out the structure of the individual and the universe, down to the finest constituent known to modern science (dark matter), beyond it to red matter, white matter, and a single leg of vibration: the "I", and finally, to the Consciousness from which all this manifests.

On the first and second days, presentations were made over a period of six sessions spanning all fields of knowledge including Science, Medicine, Economics, Law, Environment, etc. The third and final day was devoted to Education. Educationalists presented their views, after which the Students' Energy Parliament was conducted in which fifteen students from state colleges and schools, presented papers.

On the final day, the GEP Energy Award was presented to Prof. K.K. Vasu, and the book "Education for Total Consciousness" by H.H. Jagad Guru Swami Isa was officially released. The Vision Dedication for the Global Energy Parliament was presented to the assembly on 14th November, 2011 by Prof. P.J. Kurien, MP.

ASHRAM DEVELOPS AN EVIDENCED BASED APPROACH

27 Jan 2012 16:23:48 +0530

Subject: Message for LTC Research Project

From: mira@...

To: jindalr@...

Dear Dr. Jindal,

We'll be officially inaugurating the LTC study which you kindly wrote and initiated during your visit with us. If you have any message for the doctors, students or public, we would be very happy to convey / publish it.

The pre-screening of the LTC students has been done by us at the ashram. We have about 12 committed students (+ or - 2). Not all of the students are enrolled in college -- most are either looking for work (just graduated) or employed. Hope we can adjust the Protocol for this, as the Pilot Project?

We would like you to introduce you to the main doctor appointed by Ananthapuri Hospital to oversee the medical and neurological tests. His name is Dr. Anil Kumar, Neurophysician, and his phone is: +91 9446-- ---- email: aniltvtvm@...

I've told him you may like to discuss with him about the project, tests, etc. He's planning to do EEG on Sundays and some other medical tests -- he can tell you which ones.

Thanks very much for writing the protocol and helping to initiate this important research project.

Mira

Global Energy Parliament
Organized by the Isa Viswa Prajnana Trust
Trivandrum, Kerala - India
W: www.global-energy-parliament...
P: +91 (0471) 274- - - -

Dear Dr. Jindal,

We'll be officially inaugurating the LTC study and class Tomorrow at 11 a.m. If you have any message for the doctors, students or public, we would be very happy to convey / publish it.

The pre-screening of the LTC students has been done by us at the ashram. We have about 12 committed students (+ or - 2). Not all of the students are enrolled in college -- most are either looking for work (just graduated) or employed. Hope we can adjust the Protocol for this, as the Pilot Project?

We would like you to introduce you to the main doctor appointed by Ananthapuri Hospital to oversee the medical and neurological tests. His name is Dr. Anil Kumar, Neurophysician, and his phone is: +91 9446-- ---- email: aniltvtvm@...

I've told him you may like to discuss with him about the project, tests, etc. He's planning to do EEG on Sundays and some other medical tests -- he can tell you which ones.

Thanks very much,

Mira
Global Energy Parliament
Organized by the Isa Viswa Prajnana Trust
Trivandrum, Kerala - India
W: www.global-energy-parliament...
P: +91 (0471) 274 ----

Mira:

I spoke to a few ethicists here. The payment to and from the participant is governed by local country standards and norms. Just document how much payment was made or given.

I hope this is useful.

Thanks

Rahul M. Jindal, MD, PhD, MBA

Good morning Dr. Jindal,

The meeting was postponed for next week ... some emergency at the hospital. I thought I wrote you an email, if not, sorry!

It's proposed for Tuesday, same time. Hope it will work this time. Will you be free then?

No more news from Mayur since I wrote with some materials he asked for. Recruitment is one agenda item for the meeting. Actually, what do you want Mayur to do?

If we do recruit more, I was wondering when they should enter. And just to confirm, they should be non-university subjects for now to match the current participants, correct?

Thanks,

Mira

On 11 February 2012 08:30, Rahul M. Jindal
<jindalr@...> wrote:

Mira:

I hope your meeting with the physicians went well. Were you able to recruit more students?

Thanks

Dear Dr. Jindal,

Dr. Jayaram, the Psychiatrist, visited today so we could talk in detail more about the tests they conducted. They got most, if not all, of the basic biographical and medical details on the form you wrote.

In addition, they administered the Hospital Anxiety Depression Scale, and the Hamilton Anxiety scale, and a Quality of Life Scale (they don't remember the name at present).

They did not do BMI. They did not do an IQ test. They did not do the CTI.

They asked me for the Ravens and the Constructive Thinking Inventory. I searched a long time on the web but could not find a free version of Ravens or CTI. Could you please ask someone to send us a copy?

On Tuesday they hope to have had the Statistician work up their notes so that we have a clear idea of what we have and what is missing.

Thanks very much,

Mira

Mira:

1. They could still do BMI which is simply height and weight to see the effect on these parameters - especially obesity which is becoming a problem even in India.

2. If they have done the other scales, they can omit CTI.

3. It would be good if they can do the IQ test as it would give an additional parameter in addition to academic achievement.

http://www.iqtest.com/prep.html

Can you re-write the protocol and Performa with the tests actually performed so that we are all on the same page!

Thanks

Rahul

THE STUDY

TITLE: A PILOT STUDY TO ASSESS THE EFFECT OF LTC ON BODY FUNCTIONS

Project Leader: RM Jindal, MD, PhD, MBA, Clinical Professor, Department of Medicine, George Washington University, Washington, DC, USA

Staff:
Dr. Anil Kumar, Neurophysician, Ananthapuri Hospital, Trivandrum, Kerala, India
Dr. S. Jayaram, Clinical Psychiatrist, Ananthapuri Hospital
Dr. Reema Aby, Clinical Psychologist, Ananthapuri Hospital
[Statistician], Ananthapuri Hospital

INTRODUCTION: Anecdotal evidence has suggested that Life for Total Consciousness (LTC) reduces stress and other psychological disorders; improves physical and mental health, including the reduction of cardiovascular risk factors such as high blood pressure and negative health behaviors, enhances intellectual development, and develops full brain potential. This pilot project will evaluate the effects of LTC practice on brain, behavior, and health simultaneously.

PROJECT OVERVIEW
Thirty students (over the age of 18 yrs) will learn the LTC program during the 6 months project. The research will evaluate the health and educational outcomes of LTC practice in these students. Informed consent will be taken. The end point will be 6 months for this pilot study.

OUTCOME ASSESSMENT
Over the course of the study, the 30 participating students will be measured at baseline, three months and again after six months of practice of LTC technique.

Standard measures for all students in the study will include blood pressure, blood count, blood sugar, urine analysis, pulmonary function, health behaviors (smoking, alcohol, and substance usage), psychological stress, emotional intelligence, and practical intelligence.

In addition, we will evaluate: 1) neurophysiological integration, using EEG brainwave coherence measures, 2) cognitive intelligence, and 3) yogic self-measures of physical body, intellect, emotions and ego.

Health Measures

Blood Pressure: Students' blood pressure at each assessment will be measured three times with a mercury sphygmomanometer after five minutes resting without practicing any formal relaxation technique. Three readings will be taken one minute apart. The latter two will be averaged and taken as the clinic mean for that visit.

Blood and Urine Tests: Students' hemoglobin, total and differential white blood cell counts, blood sugar, as well as a urine screen will be measured on a weekly basis.

Pulmonary Function Tests: Lung strength will be assessed by standard a pulmonary function test, as regular practice of breathing techniques (pranayama) is believed to improve lung strength.

Health Behaviors: Smoking, alcohol, and other substance use will be assessed by standard questionnaires used in earlier studies. For alcohol, subjects will be queried by the Weekly drinking Recall (WR) method as to the number of drinks of alcohol consumed during the week prior to completing the questionnaire: 0, 1–4, 5–10, 11–20, and >20 drinks per week. Smoking will be assessed by the number of cigarettes smoked per day, and other substance usage by the number of times per week students engaged in non-prescribed drug use.

General Health Questionnaire: The Beck's Depression Inventory will be used to assess depression and psychological stress, including anger, tension, and other factors related to emotional and physical health.

Emotional Intelligence: The Constructive Thinking Inventory will be used to assess emotional intelligence and general coping skills.

Self-Assessment: Physical, intellectual, emotional and ego health and well-being will be assessed regularly by students using Swami Isa's LTC Questionnaires.

Neurophysiological Integration

i. EEG Coherence: Factors from the Brain Integration Report Card, such as global coherence and power, will be used to assess student neurophysiological integration, which has been associated with development of higher states of consciousness.

ii. Cognitive Intelligence

The Ravens Progressive Matrices test will be used to assess nonverbal cognitive intelligence, or IQ, which has been found to plateau in the 20s.

FUTURE STUDIES: This will include adults followed for a longer period of time (3 years). The cohort in each group will be increased and more rigorous statistic modeling will be carried out. Future groups may include children with attention deficit disorder, alcohol and drug abuse and depression and anxiety.

DATA COLLECTION	ENTRY POINT	3 MONTHS	6 MONTHS	12 MONTHS OR EXIT
Name				
Age/date of birth				
Gender				
BMI				
Address				
Occupation				
Siblings				
Medication use				
Use of alcohol				
Use of Tobacco				
Stressful events in life and family				
Type of neighborhood				

Sharing house/ apartment				
Owner of vehicle				
Sexual orientation				
Sexual partners				
Safe sex behavior				
Police records				
Disciplinary actions				
Death in family				
Family stressors				
Family history of drug or alcohol abuse				
Family income				
Family history of mental disorders				
Family history of Yoga or meditation				
Previous experience of Yoga				
Previous experience of meditation				
Current spiritual practices (i.e., prayer, mantra japa, puja, etc.)				
Pulmonary function test				
Full blood count				
Blood sugar/Cholesterol				
Mean BP				
Urine analysis				
BDI (Assess depression and psychological stress)				
Constructive Thinking Inventory (Assess emotional intelligence and general coping skills)				

Ravens Progressive Matrices test (Assess nonverbal cognitive intelligence)				
SF 12 (Quality of life measure)				
EEG				
Self-Physical				
Self-Intellectual				
Self-Emotional				
Self-Ego				

GEP NETWORKS WITH STUDENTS IN THE US TO INCREASE AWARENESS OF ITS WORK

Dear Mayur,

Thanks for your detailed response.

Dr. Jindal has designed the research study to be for graduate students over 18 years of age. Presently, however, we are not restricting it to students only, because recruitment was difficult.

Please see attached protocol and other materials.

In addition to all of the physical, intellectual, emotional and ego improvements that students receive, we have listed the benefits as follows:

Benefits of the 6-Month Teacher Training Course:

Establish your own daily practice

Become well versed in yogic theory and practice

Understand the science of the self and universe

See medical data on the medical and psychological benefits of your practice

Obtain LTC Teacher Training Certificate

The Ashram website usually has more information on it, but unfortunately we're also trying to fix some bugs with that! When it's up, I'll let you know, and I'll ask your advice about how to advertise on it as well as the GEP homepage.

Thank you!

Mira

On 8 February 2012 19:40, Mayur Patel <mayur2843@...> wrote:

Dear Mira

It is great to hear that Dr. Rahul and Global Energy Parliment team conducting a research on mind/body medicine in Kerala. In order to recruit more participants, we first need to tell our audience on our objectives about our research. What will be the positive outcome from our research? I would say we should conduct a couple of information session to spread out in Kerala. I will help you with creating a Facebook page; however, we need to do some research that how many people using computer and Facebook. I also need to know what the age requirement in this research for participant. We should market our research by Facebook, flyers, radio, and television. Can you send me information about research that we are conducting in Kerala? I will keep in touch with you once I study all the information. Thanks

Sincerely,

Mayur Patel, Rutgers, the State University of New Jersey

GEP GOES GLOBAL

Dear all,

We thank you all very much for making the time to participate in tomorrow's conference call for the Planning Committee of the 3rd Session of the Global Energy Parliament in France. The agenda is below this message.

Attached is a draft of the basic Concept for GEP 2012, which we will be reviewing tomorrow. Please bring any proposals you would like to discuss.

If you will be using Skype for the call, Clara is going to conduct it from her account. Please make sure to "accept" her name as a contact prior to the call, so we can reach you. Clara's ID is: clar…

It would be helpful if everyone please gives us the landline (phone number with country code) where you can be reached, in case there are any technical difficulties from either side.

If you need to confirm the time for your time zone, they are given in a table below the agenda.

We look forward to hearing you tomorrow!

With kind regards,
Mira Purn

CHAPTER 9

Seva Projects In India – Cautionary Lessons

RAHUL M. JINDAL, MD, PH.D.

This interesting advice for scholars visiting India was sent to me by Lyndsay S. Baines, Ph.D. Senior Lecturer Psychology, University of West London, St Mary's Road, West Ealing, London, W5 5RF, which I am including verbatim. It is succinct and timely advice.

I had made two trips to India in the last ten years, with the most recent trip being three years ago, but I had always been travelling with a male, native Indian friend, so had not really had to navigate my way around, deal with the local culture full on, or worry about unwanted attention from men. However, I was well aware that I had to I had to be in the right frame of mind in order to fully appreciate the diversity and richness of my experience.

On the flight to India from the UK, I reflected on what was to come, from the warmth of the people, to the taste of the food; from the adventure of travel to the colorful festivals; from the flowing, feminine clothes to the sunny skies. The single most compelling reason, however, is probably the attitude towards god and spirituality — and how that attitude affects positively almost everything about the culture and atmosphere of India. As I stepped off the airplane with my, '*Safe travel strategies for women in India*' guide tucked into my backpack, I was well aware that you cannot come to India and expect that you will freely be able to do all the things you do at home. You have to accept reality: India is a traditional society in the throes of great change. It is very wise to play it safe, as I had, and wear loose, modest clothes; refrain from overly friendly behavior with unknown men; and be very cautious about moving around at night. If you are confident, you are less likely to attract unwanted attention they say, and I agree. Apparently, rapists look for women they perceive to be easy targets; women who don't look like they will put up a fight. As British, I come from a culture of politeness, but sometimes in India — often, in fact — polite doesn't work. If I feel someone is harassing me for whatever reason, I have become very adept at either becoming very cold and ignoring them, or becoming quickly angry and saying "jaao," loudly, which means "go" in Hindi. I have travelled to Delhi, Agra, Mumbai and Kerala, on overnight trains, in countless auto rickshaws and taxis, and sometimes even on the backs of motorcycles. I have never felt unsafe, but I am cautious and I have come up with a couple of strategies, especially for travel at night. For example, when leaving a bar or restaurant, get someone to walk you to an auto or taxi. Or call someone, and loudly tell them the number of the taxi, so the driver can hear. Plan your travel so you don't arrive in the middle of the night; and try to have someone meet you at the train station or airport. Many hotels and tours offer this service. Always let someone know where you're going, and stay connected to friends and contacts via social media. Carrying a phone is essential for both safety and convenience, I believe, as India is a mobile phone obsessed nation. Everything is done via text message, including train tickets and manicure appointments. You can buy a cheap phone, or get a SIM card for your regular phone, when you get to India. Prepaid rates are very cheap. Just make sure you have a copy of your passport and Indian Visa, and a passport sized photo with you when you go to the store to get the phone or SIM card.

A good way to blend in and protect yourself is to wear Indian clothes. Indian clothes are light, comfortable, inexpensive and appropriate to the climate and the need for modesty. I usually wear the three-piece salwar kameez, or Punjabi suit; or a kurtah and trousers when in India. But wearing Indian clothes is a bit controversial among my Indiophile friends. Some say it just draws more unwanted attention; others say it draws respect and protects you. I am in the second camp. I am a big believer in the "when in Rome" philosophy of travel.

Not only do I wear Indian clothes, but I also tell people I am married to an Indian man and that I live in Delhi. The family is the strongest social structure in India. As the wife of an Indian man, I am perceived as Indian, as part of the society — an insider — and even more importantly, as someone whose movements are probably closely tracked, and who will be missed.

India is a very intuitive country and I often found myself able to second guess the direction of situations and conversations. If you don't feel comfortable, it's up to you to extract yourself from what's happening. **Don't just go along with someone's plans because you're too polite to say no.** Be really careful about who you trust yourself to be alone with, and if you're worried, **search out a family with**

children or a group of women and explain that you'd like to stand near them or with them. Anyone I did this with was more than happy to accommodate – particularly on trains, at stations and at night. Even scoping out the people who look trustworthy is a sensible move, just to feel a bit safer.

CHAPTER 10

Seva Projects In Guyana – Cautionary Lessons

The personality of the philanthropist and local officials can create a major problem as we experienced in our seva project in Guyana. George and the Minister of Health don't see eye to eye: Reconciling private philanthropy with governmental mandates can become a serious liability and lead to the dissolution of the project.

Disenchanted With the Ministry of Health in Guyana-Prominent Philanthropist Turns his Sights on Education[72]

The much anticipated 2nd kidney transplant was conducted at the Public Hospital Georgetown Corporation (PHGC) on January 30, 2009 by a US-led medical team headed by Dr. Rahul Jindal and Dr. Edward Falta. The recipient was former Army Major, Winston George, 47, and the donor was his daughter, Melissa George. Both father and daughter are showing good signs of recovery. Dr. Jindal had also headed the medical team that conducted the 1st kidney transplant in the country on Munesh Mangal, 17 on July 12, 2008. Shortly after Winston George's surgery, Guyana's Minister of Health, announced to the nation and the world that the 2nd kidney transplant was a success. But we, as observers, must never allow the New York based pioneers of this project to go unnoticed, either. It was a non-medical person, Mr George Subraj, together with his Coordinator Mr Lake Persaud, as well as, his New York associates, who broke the proverbial ice and set in motion the right atmosphere for kidney transplants to take place in Guyana. While others, including medical personnel, were skeptical whether such an operation

---

[72] http://www.thewestindiannews.com/?s=Disenchanted+With+the+Ministry+of+Health+in+Guyana-Prominent+Philanthropist+Turns+his+Sights+on+Education

could be successfully performed in Guyana, the US project leader George Subraj had always been optimistic about the outcome. Apart from the significant role played by the medical team, including Dr. Arthur Womble, we also compliment the following NY team members: Mr Tony Subraj, Mr Jaskaran Persaud, and Mr Kawall Totaram.

But success always tends to breed its own enemies. There appeared to have been some kind of conflict in the role and expectation between the New York team and the Ministry of Health. We know, for example, that a regular complaint of the Ministry has been that overseas medical teams tend to interfere with the country's medical policies and protocols. For his part, George Subraj and his associates vehemently rejected this charge. "We respect existing medical policies and protocols, and never attempted to subvert these. All we seek was medical help for needy patients by providing the expertise and resources. We leave the observance of medical protocols to the medical personnel.

Our main task is to put together the team, manage the logistics, such as traveling, accommodation, and publicity, and provide the resources." Lake Persaud notes: "We also ensure that proper after care is provided to patients, including the pursuit of rehabilitative services." For the benefit of readers, it would be recalled that the 2nd kidney transplant surgery, as well as, three others was supposed to have been facilitated by George Subraj and his New York associates, but that did not happen. Instead, it seemed that the Ministry of Health pulled the rug under their feet when they engaged in direct negotiations with the US medical team, without any input from George and his colleagues. The New York team had anticipated that ugly development and sought a meeting with the Minister of Health to work out any differences. Four members of the New York team traveled to Guyana in November 2008 to meet with the Minister to discuss the plan for the 2nd kidney transplant, among other things. To avoid future conflicts, the Minister agreed to issue, within a few days, the New York team with a letter of understanding (LOU) setting out their expected role and function in this process. The New York team left that meeting feeling that everything was back on track. However, after several weeks passed by, and they did not receive the LOU from the Ministry of Health, they began to feel uneasy. All attempts to get further information on the second kidney transplant project were frustrated.

George and Lake decided to have an audience with the President who was passing through New York on his way to Libya. The President assured them that their efforts are appreciated by the Guyana government and encouraged them to continue with the kidney transplant project, even if they have to recruit a new medical team. So, they persevered. The New York team is baffled why they were excluded from the 2nd kidney transplant project since they had an understanding with the Ministry that they would serve as "facilitators" of the kidney project. To unravel, therefore, what had become a mystery to them, George Subraj, Lake Persaud, and Anand Rambharose traveled to Guyana in late January 2009, which happened to coincide with the 2nd kidney transplant surgery there. They received a cold reception from the authorities, and their attempts to have an official meeting with the Ministry of Health did not materialize, either. Despite their humiliation, they were warmly received by the medical team, and they even invited them to lunch.

The NY team asked itself, "How could we serve as facilitators when they didn't provide us with such basic information on the size of the medical team and how long they will stay in Guyana, as well as, the scheduled date of the operation." The New York team just wants some respect. After all, they were the ones to help set the pioneering kidney transplant surgery into motion at a heavy personal and financial cost of over $30,000.

While other groups had taken patients to India for kidney transplant, George thought that it would be a better idea to take the doctors down to Guyana where they could also train local medical personnel to conduct such surgeries in the future; a process that could add sunlight into the lives of hundreds of Guyanese and their families. When asked about their exclusion, George Subraj and Lake Persaud believe that it might relate partly to the question of control, turf battle, and the possible infusion of financial incentives for the medical team that had apparently been negotiated between the Ministry and an international bank.

The announcement following the 2nd kidney transplant surgery that the medical team plans to conduct one such operation every three months, further reinforced their belief in the role of financial incentives. Let's hope that the welfare of patients remains the dominant consideration, and that it does not become a casualty of the monetary incentive.

But the dynamic New York philanthropist, Mr George Subraj, vowed to continue with his mission of helping the needy. While his promise of conducting four more kidney transplant surgeries may not materialize in the present environment, that prospect is not strong enough to stifle his passion for humanitarian work.

Hundreds of groups eagerly seek George's benevolence. Thus, he is currently building a $60,000 state-of-the-art Computer Laboratory at Swami Aksharananda's Saraswati Vidya Niketan High School. The Lab will be equipped with 50 computers, a security system, and necessary infrastructure, and is scheduled to open in August 2009. He is helping to modernize the Hindu Temple at Bel Air, Georgetown, as well as, donating the tiling to the newly constructed Mora Point, Mahaicony Health Clinc. And in New York, he came to the assistance of the Prem Bhakti Mandir of Jamaica, Queens, by donating the $(US)36,000 elevator to this elegant $(US)600,000 monument. Not to mention his patronage of several cultural events, including the annual Holi Sammelan Progam of March 14, 2009. Despite his disenchantment with developments in the kidney transplant project of Guyana, George Subraj and his NY team's commitment to medical outreach will never falter.

George's and Lake's impact will be felt through the famous Guyana Watch (GWI) organization, in which George serves as Vice President. The work of George Subraj, as well as, his business, Zara Realty Corp, is well known in New York, Toronto, Guyana, and elsewhere. Our community has become better because of their remarkable philanthropic work. We commend George and his colleagues for their resilience and for their struggle to help Guyanese and others.

CHAPTER 11

Seva Projects In USA – Cautionary Lessons

SOME TEMPLES GO THEIR OWN WAY

It would seem to an outsider that uniting the relatively small Hindu Indian community in the USA would be easy and painless, but I found out that it was a very complex and time consuming task. I had to deal with big and small egos, as well as, with suspicions of what my interest was, and if there was a payback in doing this. Some sections of the Hindu Indian mandirs wanted to run their own drives and not be under a common tent– defeating the very purpose of "showcasing" the commitment of Hindus and Indians to their new country. Diversity in the Hindu community is as old as India itself.

Re: Seeking your Blessings and Support for 9/11 Hindu Seva day – National Blood Donation Drive

To: Rahul M. Jindal

From: Sadhu (outreach@...)

Sent: Mon 6/06/11 7:44 PM

To: Rahul M. Jindal (jindalr@...)

Good to hear from you. Currently I'm in Chicago and will return to NJ only for one day. Then, we have a Youth Seminar until Sun. So I will be busy till then. I will contact you again next week. I hope you don't mind.

Your team is engaging in a noble initiative, and I'm sure Bhagwan and great sadhus like HH Pramukh Swami Maharaj will bless you.

With prayers,

SADHU

From: "Rahul M. Jindal" <jindalr@...>

Date: Mon, 6 Jun 2011 19:05:54 -0400

To: Swami

Subject: RE: Seeking your Blessings and Support for 9/11 Hindu

Seva day - National Blood Donation Drive

Respected Swami

Jai Swaminarayan.

I would like to personally meet you and seek your blessings regarding the national blood donation drive on 9/11 this year.

I had the privilege of meeting you and Doctor Swamiji in the past. I and my dad have been associated with BAPS organization.

I have been involved in outreach work for many years since I was a medical student (1997-1982) in BJ Medical College, Ahmedabad, Gujarat. My dad was the Dean of BJ Medical College. Drs Dhanani and Bajadia, the world wide Medical Directors of BAPS outreach were my class mates in medical college and we regularly discuss outreach activities on my yearly visits to Ahmedabad.

I have been organizing the Washington, DC, blood donation drive and health fairs for the past few years. At the HMEC last year, we decided to take this concept at a national scale to show our wider involvement in the American community.

With your blessings, we want to make an impact by having the blood donation drive in as many of the 600 mandirs in North America on or about 9/11. Of course, we hope that all the BAPS mandirs will also participate.

I look forward to hearing from you.

Jai Swaminarayan,

Rahul

From: abhaya.asthana@...

To: outreach@...

Date: Mon, 6 Jun 2011 16:40:54 -0500

Subject: Seeking your Blessings and Support for 9/11 Hindu Seva day –

National Blood Donation Drive

Respected Sadhu

Hope all is well with you and Pujya Swami.

As part of the Hindu Seva Day for HMEC this year, a national blood drive is planned on Sept 11 (or thereabouts) with two passionate and energetic physicians behind the idea: Dr Rahul Jindal and Dr Sudershan Pasupuleti. The attached flyers and the announcement below give more details on the project.

Rahul Ji, in fact, has been a dedicated sevak with the B.A.P.S center in the DC area and has done such drives regionally in the past. Similarly, Sudershan Ji, currently the president of the Hindu Temple in Toledo, OH has done extensive seva work and is the coordinator of the Hindu Seva Divas for 2011. We want to do the blood drive on a national scale and for that it would be wonderful if we had the active participation of all the B.A.P.S centers across North America.

We seek your blessing and guidance to make that possible. Rahul Ji will be happy to follow up with you on this with more details.

Jai Swami Narayan.

Abhaya Asthana

HMEC 2011

508-875-

From: abhaya.asthana@...

To: hmec-l@...

Date: Thu, 19 May 2011 14:28:55 -0500

Subject: 9/11 Hindu Seva day - National Blood Donation Drive

Namaskar!

At HMEC 2010 in Houston, we proposed doing a national level blood drive on Sept 11, 2011, the 10th anniversary of the tragic event. We need your help in making this a reality. We urge every temple/organization in North America to conduct this blood drive on the same day to make it a tremendous and impactful seva!

Enclosed is a flyer for this event that you can modify to suit your local publicity needs.

We look forward to your support.

Kind regards,

Contacts:

-Rahul M. Jindal, MD, PhD, MBA

(Coordinator 9/11 Blood Drive)

I received an e-mail from one of our volunteers which is self-explanatory:

Over the last ten months, I have had the pleasure of volunteering on behalf of SAMAR at several local bone marrow registration collection drives. Overall, it has proven to be a wonderful experience. I have had the pleasure of meeting many new people and experiencing, at least in small part, their culture. I have been trained in and become familiar with the process of the bone marrow donor registration, the DNA swab collection, and the database supported. I have learned of the massive need for the drives, the registrants, and the database itself. There has been genuine graciousness and hospitality extended from each hosting temple and, for the most part, from its community.

I have found that, in general, while most are in support of the bone marrow drive initiatives, many are hesitant to immediately sit down and complete the registration process. I feel that there are several underlying issues that account for this. I have found many of the attendees are not aware of the massive need for potential donors to register and join the *Be a Match Registry*. They are not aware of the startling need, especially within their immediate community, for possible potential donors and the critical role they play in saving the life of the individual stricken with any bone or blood related cancer. They are not aware of the latest advancements within the medical field and its technology, with regards to the simplification of the actual bone marrow collection. Overall, the younger members of the community seem much more willing to join the registry over those middle aged and older. They seem much more at ease with the collection of the personal information needed for the database, and with the potential time and effort involved, should they be found to be a potential bone marrow donor for someone. Lastly, they seem quite a bit 'more trusting' of those of us that are registering and collecting the swab samples for the registry.

The 'trust issue' I have encountered, while totally understandable, is frustrating. During the drives, I have noticed a distinct difference in this with my fellow volunteers that are from the South Asian community and me. It is far easier and takes 'less information' from them to get donors to sign up, somewhat of a blind-trust feeling. I have to explain far more just to get them to 'think about it'. My credibility is definitely in question, and while fully understand able, it is very frustrating. I can only hope in time and with continued efforts, this resolves itself. I can't force anyone to trust me and my motivation behind my volunteerism; I can simply have faith that in time it will work itself out. Registering oneself as a donor seems to be a 'no- brainer'. It takes about 20 hours of your time to save the life of another. Being able to fully trust the intentions of those asking you to register and sample and type your DNA, can be an entirely different thought process. Unfortunately with past history, it can be difficult for members of one culture, one community to trust those from another. Hopefully, in time that bridge will be built. In closing, I am honored to be a part of such a needed cause and am fully aware that very often, nothing worthwhile is easily attainable. I believe the first few obstacles in getting potential donors to register can, in time, be eradicated with continued education and awareness, the ladder will take time and faith.

~Jennifer

CHAPTER 12

Seva Projects – Difficulty In Recruiting Subjects

We had planned to recruit 30 students (over the age of 18 yrs.) to learn the LTC program during the 6 months project. The research will evaluate the health and educational outcomes of LTC practice in these students. Informed consent will be taken. The end point will be 6 months for this pilot study. We had thought that a free program in which students will learn meditation and Yoga and also obtain a certificate of competency will attract many college students. Trivandrum is a large metropolis in the Southern Indian state of Kerala with many educational institutions[73] [74]. However, we were sadly mistaken. We have been only able to recruit less than 30% of the subjects required for the study. We attribute this to the changing interests of the students whereby they are no longer interested in learning the ancient arts of India. Another reason was that we were not able to market our program adequately. It was suggested that we create a face book page, which we duly did. We took help of a student who has expertise in marketing via face book[75]:

Dear Mayur,

Thanks for your detailed response.

Dr. Jindal has designed the research study to be for graduate students over 18 years of age. Presently, however, we are not restricting it to students only, because recruitment was difficult.

Please see attached protocol and other materials.

In addition to all of the physical, intellectual, emotional and ego improvements that students receive, we have listed the benefits as follows:

Benefits of the 6-Month Teacher Training Course:

[73] http://trivandrum.gov.in/ (Accessed 08-24-2015)
[74] http://www.corporationoftrivandrum.in/ (Accessed 08-24-2015)
[75] http://www.facebook.com/ (Accessed 08-24-2015)

- Establish your own daily practice
- Become well versed in yogic theory and practice
- Understand the science of the self and universe
- See medical data on the medical and psychological benefits of your practice
- Obtain LTC Teacher Training Certificate

The Ashram website usually has more information on it, but unfortunately we're also trying to fix some bugs with that! When it's up, I'll let you know, and I'll ask your advice about how to advertise on it as well as the GEP homepage.

Thank you!
Mira
On 8 February 2012 19:40, Mayur Patel <mayur2843@...> wrote:

Dear Mira

It is great to hear that Dr. Rahul Jindal and Global Energy Parliament team conducting a research on mind/body medicine in Kerala. In order to recruit more participants we first need to tell our audience on our objectives about our research. What will be the positive outcome from our research? I would say we should conduct a couple of information sessions to spread our message in Kerala. I will help you with creating a Face book page; however, we need to do some research that how many people using computer and Face book. I also need to know what the age requirement in this research for participant. We should market our research by Face book, flyers, radio, and television. Can you send me information about research that we are conducting in Kerala? I will keep in touch with you once I study all the information. Thanks

Sincerely,
Mayur Patel
Rutgers, The State University of New Jersey
Public Health Class of 2013

Bloustein Public Service Association (School Organization)
Vice President

On 7 February 2012 06:34, Rahul M. Jindal <jindalr@...> wrote:
Mayur

We are conducting a research project on mind/body medicine in Kerala. To increase recruitment, I suggested to Mira, local coordinator, that the face book page may be helpful.

The face book page you created for our national blood drive has been very effective. Can you guide Mira on this and how to create a specific page book to increase participation in the project?

Details of the project can be found on the web site:

Global Energy Parliament
Organized by the Isa Viswa Prajnana Trust
Trivandrum, Kerala - India
W: www.global-energy-parliament.net
Perhaps, you can SKYPE with Mira at your convenience.

Thanks
Rahul M. Jindal, MD, PhD, MBA
We also took advice from a marketing expert to increase recruitment.
Ms. L. Rodriguez has a vast experience in recruiting students for a variety of projects in a major university in New York City.
See e-mail below:

Dear Mira,

Since this is an Education and Research "Internship Opportunity" that affords participants a hands-on experience with a certification, yes, regarding the Ayurveda websites/ directories, the recommendation is to send this form and links to the contacts and ask them to post / forward the information to those students who they consider may be interested in the study. From my experience in working with college students, the response from students to participate in Research/Studies is higher when the information comes from faculty/administration they are familiar with-- Pending

Dr. Jindal's approval.

The *Skyscrapercity* is a global forum that has a specific Trivandrum Education and Research Thread where you can post all of the information.

- Kindly follow this link **http://www.skyscrapercity.com/showthread.php?t=723304&page=48#post92996347** it will take you to that specific thread.
- In order to be able to post messages on the SkyscraperCity forums, you must first register **http://www.skyscrapercity.com**
- Once you are registered you can post all of the pertaining information, for instance, the form as suggested (except the response boxes would only apply to the GEP's website).

Trivandrum facebook link (Sorry it did not work before. I tested this once again)

- http://www.facebook.com/thiruvananthapuram
- You are correct Mira, you cannot post directly to their facebook page. Kindly contact them at **trivandrum.facebook@gmail.com** and ask them to post information on their face book page, or let you know how you can do it directly.

Please do not hesitate to let me know how I can help, should you have any further questions.

Kind Regards,
Luz

CHAPTER 13

Reducing Poverty Through Charity Projects

RAHUL M. JINDAL, MD, PH.D.

A variety of efforts are being made to reduce poverty. At the Monterrey Financing for Development Conference in 2002, world leaders pledged "to make concrete efforts towards the target of 0.7%" of their national income in international aid. In today's dollars, that would amount to almost $200 billion each year. In 2005, total aid from the 22 richest countries to the world's developing countries was just $106 billion—a shortfall of $119 billion dollars from the 0.7% promise. On average, the world's richest countries provided just 0.33% of their GNP in official development assistance. The United States provided just 0.22%. The cost of supporting countries to meet the goals would require donors to increase ODA to 0.44% of GNP by 2006 (or $135 billion) and to plan for a scale-up to 0.54% by 2015 (or $195 billion) – well within the bounds of the 0.7% promised in Monterrey. This means that of the combined rich world GNP of approximately $30 trillion dollars, on average just $150 billion a year would be enough to get the world on track to ending extreme poverty throughout the world. These efforts are indeed laudable; however, the end use of these funds remains a challenge. Many government programs are "programmed to fail" for a variety of reasons, the lead cause is rampant corruption and misappropriation of funds at the local level.

Five countries have already met or surpassed the 0.7% target: Denmark, Luxembourg, Netherlands, Norway and Sweden. Five other countries have committed themselves to a timeline to reach this target before 2015: Belgium, Finland, France, Ireland and the United Kingdom. In May of 2005, all members of the European Union (except for those 'new' members who joined after 2002) agreed to meet the target by 2015. This brought the number of rich countries who have already met, or have committed to meet, the 0.7% target by 2015 to seventeen. It is not the flow of funds, but the direction of funds is more important; the priorities have to be decided at the local level. A democratic country, such as India, has a safety mechanism whereby a free press and law courts are able to keep a check on the executive which has the role of distributing the funds flowing from the West.

It is clear that *Better* aid is needed, not just *more* aid. An argument has been made that both the quantity and the quality of development assistance need to increase. Currently, aid is unpredictable, driven by donor objectives, and tied to contractors from donor countries. In low-income countries, only about 24% of bilateral aid actually finances investments on the ground[76]. Public perceptions reflect support for higher levels of aid. When asked what percentage of the federal budget they think goes to foreign aid, Americans' median estimate is 25% of the budget, more than 25 times the actual level. Only 2% of Americans give a correct estimate of 1% of the budget or less. When asked how much of the budget should go to foreign aid, the median response is 10%. Only 13% of Americans believe that the percentage should be 1% or less. Over 60% of Americans believe that contributing 0.7% of national income to meet the Millennium Development Goals is the right thing to do. However, we believe that we need to go one step further, not just *better aid*, but "*accountable aid*". The recipient country or community has to be better stewards of this aid and a set of clear end points have to be set. If these are not met, there should be accountability in terms of "rewards and punishments"

The statistics on poverty are frightening and alarming. More than one billion people in the world live on less than one dollar a day. In total, 2.7 billion struggle to survive on less than two dollars per day. Poverty in the developing world, however, goes far beyond income poverty. It means having to walk more than one mile everyday simply to collect water and firewood; it means suffering diseases that were eradicated from rich countries decades ago. Every year eleven million children die-most under the age of five and more than six million from completely preventable causes like malaria, diarrhea and pneumonia. In some deeply impoverished nations less than half of the children are in primary school and under 20% go to secondary school. Around the world, a total of 114 million children do not get even a basic education and 584 million women are illiterate.

The 10 key recommendations for sector-specific policies and investments discussed in Investing in Development are[1]:

---

[76] http://www.earth.columbia.edu/pages/endofpoverty/oda (Accessed 08/09/2015)

Recommendation 1

Developing country governments should adopt development strategies bold enough to meet the Millennium Development Goal (MDG) targets for 2015. We term them MDG-based poverty reduction strategies. To meet the 2015 deadline, we recommend that all countries have these strategies in place by 2006. Where Poverty Reduction Strategy Papers (PRSPs) already exist, those should be aligned with the MDGs.

Recommendation 2

The MDG-based poverty reduction strategies should anchor the scaling up of public investments, capacity building, domestic resource mobilization, and official development assistance. They should also provide a framework for strengthening governance, promoting human rights, engaging civil society, and promoting the private sector. The MDG-based poverty reduction strategies should:

- Be based on an assessment of investments and policies needed to reach the Goals by 2015.
- Spell out the detailed national investments, policies, and budgets for the coming three to five years.
- Focus on rural productivity, urban productivity, health, education, gender equality, water and sanitation, environmental sustainability, and science, technology, and innovation.
- Focus on women's and girls' health (including reproductive health) and education outcomes, access to economic and political opportunities, right to control assets, and freedom from violence.
- Promote mechanisms for transparent and decentralized governance.
- Include operational strategies for scale-up, such as training and retaining skilled workers.

- Involve civil society organizations in decision making and service delivery, and provide resources for monitoring and evaluation.
- Outline a private sector promotion strategy and an income generation strategy for poor people.
- Be tailored, as appropriate, to the special needs of landlocked, small island developing, least developed, and fragile states.
- Mobilize increased domestic resources by up to four percentage points of GNP by 2015.
- Calculate the need for official development assistance.
- Describe an "exit strategy" to end aid dependency, appropriate to the country's situation.

Recommendation 3

Developing country governments should craft and implement the MDG-based poverty reduction strategies in transparent and inclusive processes, working closely with civil society organizations, the domestic private sector, and international partners.

- Civil society organizations should contribute actively to designing policies, delivering services, and monitoring progress.
- Private sector firms and organizations should contribute actively to policy design, transparency initiatives and, where appropriate, public-private partnerships.

Recommendation 4

International donors should identify at least a dozen MDG "fast-track" countries for a rapid scale-up of official development assistance (ODA) in 2005, recognizing that many countries are already in a position for a massive scale-up on the basis of their good governance and absorptive capacity.

Recommendation 5

Developed and developing countries should jointly launch, in 2005, a group of Quick Win actions to save and improve millions of lives and to promote economic growth. They should also launch a massive effort to build expertise at the community level.

The Quick Wins include but are not limited to:

- Free mass distribution of malaria bed-nets and effective antimalaria medicines for all children in regions of malaria transmission by the end of 2007.
- Ending user fees for primary schools and essential health services, compensated by increased donor aid as necessary, no later than the end of 2006.
- Successful completion of the 3 by 5 campaign to bring 3 million AIDS patients in developing countries onto antiretroviral treatment by the end of 2005.
- Expansion of school meals programs to cover all children in hunger hotspots using locally produced foods by no later than the end of 2006.
- A massive replenishment of soil nutrients for smallholder farmers on lands with nutrient-depleted soils, through free or subsidized distribution of chemical fertilizers and agroforestry, by no later than the end of 2006.

The massive training program of community-based workers should aim to ensure, by 2015, that each local community has:

- Expertise in health, education, agriculture, nutrition, infrastructure, water supply and sanitation, and environmental management.
- Expertise in public sector management.
- Appropriate training to promote gender equality and participation

Recommendation 6

Developing country governments should align national strategies with such regional initiatives as the New Partnership for Africa's Development and the Caribbean Community (and Common Market), and regional groups should receive increased direct donor support for regional projects. Regional development groups should:

- Be supported to identify, plan, and implement high-priority cross-border infrastructure projects (roads, railways, watershed management).
- Receive direct donor support to implement cross-border projects.
- Be encouraged to introduce and implement peer-review mechanisms to promote best practices and good governance.

Recommendation 7

High-income countries should increase official development assistance (ODA) from .0.25 percent of donor GNP in 2003 to around 0.44 percent in 2006 and 0.54 percent in 2015 to support the Millennium Development Goals, particularly in low-income countries, with improved ODA quality (including aid that is harmonized, predictable, and largely in the form of grants-based budget support). Each donor should reach 0.7 percent no later than 2015 to support the Goals and other development assistance priorities. Debt relief should be more extensive and generous.

- ODA should be based on actual needs to meet the Millennium Development Goals and on countries' readiness to use the ODA effectively.
- Criteria for evaluating the sustainability of a country's debt burden must be consistent with the achievement of the Goals.
- Aid should be oriented to support the MDG-based poverty reduction strategy, rather than to support donor-driven projects.
- Donors should measure and report the share of their ODA that supports the actual scale-up of MDG-related investments.

- Middle-income countries should also seek opportunities to become providers of ODA and give technical support to low-income countries.

Recommendation 8

High-income countries should open their markets to developing country exports through the Doha trade round and help Least Developed Countries raise export competitiveness through investments in critical trade-related infrastructure, including electricity, roads, and ports. The Doha Development Agenda should be fulfilled and the Doha Round completed no later than 2006.

Recommendation 9

International donors should mobilize support for global scientific research and development to address special needs of the poor in areas of health, agriculture, natural resource and environmental management, energy, and climate. We estimate the total needs to rise to approximately $7 billion a year by 2015.

Recommendation 10

The UN Secretary-General and the UN Development Group should strengthen the coordination of UN agencies, funds, and programs to support the MDGs, at headquarters and country level. The UN Country Teams should be strengthened and should work closely with the international financial institutions to support the Goals.

- The UN Country Teams should be properly trained, staffed, and funded to support program countries to achieve the Goals.
- The UN Country Team and the international financial institutions (World Bank, International Monetary Fund, regional development banks) should work closely at country level to improve the quality of technical advice.

CHAPTER 14

Social Networks In Management Of Complex Health-Related Projects

Global health initiatives usually require collective business-healthcare professional based partnerships and address health issues and concerns that transcend national borders, irrespective of practices, policies and systems in the host country. Social networks (SNs) formed by organizations like UNICEF, WHO, the World Bank and private corporations, which are working together, have produced innovative financial tools to support these initiatives. The purpose is to find better ways to raise funds, apply resources and develop meaningful alliances among networks working towards a common goal (e.g., delivering vaccines to children in developing countries). Business, social and healthcare networks can amalgamate their skills to prevent illness and relieve suffering, even in the current economic challenges. Social networks, with their ability to foster interdependency, such as kinship, common interest, financial exchange, relationships or common beliefs, knowledge and prestige, are able to operate on many levels, from individual families up to national and global levels. Historically, SNs play a critical role in determining the way problems are solved, organizations are run, and the degree to which both individuals and organizations succeed in achieving their goals. This paper will utilize Social Network Analysis (SNA) as a means to examine three strategic areas to global healthcare delivery: expanding delivery of new or under-utilized healthcare initiatives; achievement of global access to healthcare through private sector partnerships; and the strengthening of research, development and activation of private and political support as a means to empower communities to advocate for policies that will improve their health.

A SN is a complex structure developed by individual players who are connected with one another on a one to one basis. The SNs can be used to understand relationships between individuals, communities, companies or regions. Recently, we have observed a growth in the utilization of SNs amongst global health initiatives, being central to the provision of information on politics, economy, culture, health and educational resources, partnerships and host countries. This paper analyzes the extent to which SNs initiate, support and advocate global healthcare initiatives, inspire public dialogue, and influence healthcare provision. Given worldwide economic and political unrest, complexities of global partnerships, the ever increasing socioeconomic divide, and the spread of infectious diseases, the challenges facing global health providers have never been greater[20][21][22]. Access to data that facilitates an informed, precise delivery of available resources is paramount to the social, economic and psycho-medical well- being of its citizens.

We have seen a growth in the utilization of SNs. These are the digital identification of social structures made up of networks of individuals (or organizations) called nodes, which are tied (connected) by one or more specific type of interdependency, such as friendship, kinship, common interest, financial exchange, dislike or relationships of beliefs, knowledge or prestige. Global health agencies and healthcare workers on the ground have utilized SNs as a means to provide demographic data pertaining to issues ranging from politics, economy, culture, health and education[23].

BACKGROUND INFORMATION

The SNs, once on the ground, can invaluably support global healthcare initiatives as a tool for advocacy. These SNs can take the form of advocacy for improved social services, such as the provision of education, health services and water[24][25]. Social networks can be used to reach large-scale audiences, to reach out to supporters and resources, and to inspire public dialogue with regards to social issues and influence key decision makers. Healthcare workers have sought to hold their ground against the emerging tide of preventable diseases. It is this group who bears the brunt of the daily responsibility for provision of healthcare against competing tides of progress in healthcare and emerging health issues and disease. Yet, behind every diagnosis there is a patient whose family will have to deal with the risk, diagnosis, management and treatment of the disease.

It is important to focus on the individual patient with the disease. Of the eight million cancer deaths that occur throughout the world each year more than half the patients are from low-income countries and, for many, death could have been avoided if early treatment and detection mechanisms had been in place[26]. In addition, millions of patients with untreatable cancer and without access to palliative care are highly likely to die with preventable suffering. Many will be severely financially challenged to meet even the most basic treatment costs.

Social networks focus attention in the global healthcare debate, not only to large global organizations and providers, but also to individual patients. SNs enable global entities and local communities to recognize and plan the importance of acting swiftly and strategically in order to combat the social and economic fallout of preventable disease. Furthermore, the widespread prevalence of disease is more than just a health issue. The social and cultural challenges that accompany them are often founded in the stigma attached to the disease. Progress is stifled by poverty, population growth, climate change all of which contribute to the surge of disease if appropriate intervention is not readily available.

The Guyanese Transplant Initiative did not represent a political group, union stance, philosophy or agenda. The initiative came from a social network representing different educational, professional and racial backgrounds and socio-economic groups. What the members of this SN had in common was the desire to help a young boy in need of life saving surgery, and the vision and communication skills to cultivate social networks and resources amongst the local lay and professional community. Paramount to the initiative was the vision to develop a single surgical mission into the provision of an ongoing comprehensive transplant service that provided intervention, education and hope to renal transplant patients.

The model of funding innovative ways to deliver global healthcare in both developed and developing countries often starts in developed countries by bringing together governments, healthcare professionals and media services[27][28]; all of whom are motivated towards a common goal, that of saving lives and improving health and quality of life.

An example of such a SN initiative is the GAVI Matching Fund. The Matching Funds are funds made available in amount equal to funds available from other sources for a common goal. The Matching Fund impacted global health programs ("GAVI Matching Fund," 2014)[29] by successfully engaging and empowering private institutions such as Anglo American, ARJK Foundation, JP Morgan and the La Caixa Foundation to make significant pledges to immunization programs in developing countries. This is an example of corporations sharing their business skills to positively impact on local and global communities. The impact of corporations sharing their business skills and allowing access to their SNs can extend beyond immunization programs by bringing global health initiatives into larger health communities and exposing them to other essential services.

The Matching Fund is not alone in using innovative financial collaboration to drive global healthcare initiatives. Currently, the "Leading Group on Innovative Financing for Development"[30], which consists of 63 members countries, has become a formidable discussion platform, sharing information and exposing innovative means of raising finance in the form of transaction taxes, solidarity levels and other mechanisms in the shape of international forums to help raise global health finance for organizations such as UNITAID[31]. Access to such specialized finance-based skills has resulted in the acceleration of availability and affordability timelines for vaccination programs in developing countries.

Social networks remain crucial to the above-mentioned global healthcare initiatives, which it is vital to sustain, especially in the current global economic climate. Such initiatives save millions of lives and save billions of dollars in healthcare expenses and lost productivity, thereby positively impacting upon a country's economic growth. Indeed, global health is a major component of economic growth in terms of medical savings alone. Rotavirus vaccine, for example, can reduce hospital admissions for diarrhea by nearly half[32].Vaccinations also positively impact children's cognitive development, higher educational attainment, improved labor productivity and increased savings and investments in the local community. Social networks highlight the value of public-private partnerships, skills and social leverage that they contribute to such programs. For example, local authorities, religious and lay organizations have the ability to engage and connect to even the lowest socioeconomic and underserved members of their local communities. Renal transplant teams based at University of Glasgow, United Kingdom, concerned about the low organ donation rates amongst Indians from the Indian subcontinent, partnered with local Hindu temples throughout the west of Scotland to promote awareness of live organ donation through public forums[33]. The private sector's financial skills acumen goes well beyond financial support as they bring vital business skills and powerful advocacy to the equation.

MECHANICS OF SOCIAL NETWORK ANALYSIS AND GLOBAL HEALTH INITIATIVES

Social networks have the capability to facilitate the pooling of collective resources able to reduce health disparities and propel economic development in poor countries. The role of SNs in pooling collective resources and expertise to develop road maps on how best to save lives by targeting healthcare intervention will enable families, communities and countries to guard against mortality and develop preventable healthcare intervention at a local level. These SN roles will be discussed under the headings: expanding delivery of new or under-utilized healthcare initiatives; achievement of global access to healthcare through private sector partnerships; the strengthening of research and development and activation of private and political support as a means to empower communities.

Expanding Delivery of New or Under-Utilized Healthcare Initiatives

Social networking *platforms* have changed the way we manage the delivery of global healthcare in the western world. Social networking *tools* empower patients to make decisions about their treatment and connect patients with support groups, while telemedicine raises awareness of technological advances. Similarly, SNs have been utilized in resource poor countries to engage the host community in better understanding epidemiology, physiology, culture, economics and politics, thereby targeting global health-care interventions to maximum effect.

Social Networks remain active in helping to identify and assess patterns of responses to such initiatives on a local, national and global level. These networks have the capacity to provide insight and facilitate understanding of population health measures, identify patterns of recurring disease/mortality both within and between countries, capture important time trends, and identify problems in access and health inequalities.

The Zambian government's data driven healthcare initiative to address the chronic lack of healthcare workers in rural areas and ensure staff resources were properly targeted, illustrates the role of SNs in implementation of health policy and influence of systemic factors and health system performance within the current social, political and economic climate ("Zambia's data-driven healthcare initiative," 2011)[34]. In Zambia, both maternal mortality and infant mortality fall short of the UN's health related Millennium Development Goals (MDGs). In order to better meet their goals and utilize to their full potential, the health care workforce used SNs as a means to improve data collection to direct healthcare funding where it was needed most. Health staff carried out biosocial analysis throughout Zambia to determine the health services in greatest demand relative to the staffing levels in the area. They then categorized districts in critical, substantial or moderate need and detailed the existing and optimum number of health workers needed and for which specialization. This initiative improved the delivery of services designed to lessen the burden of disease, especially amongst those living in extreme poverty.

Achievement of Global Access to Healthcare through Private Sector Partnerships

A major global healthcare initiative by the World Economic Forum (WEF) has targeted communicable disease (e.g. TB, AIDS/HIV, malaria) in India, China and Malaysia by employing SNs on a local, national and international level to understand weaknesses in delivery of healthcare in these fields and to strengthen these nations' healthcare systems ("The Global Economic Burden of Non-communicable Diseases," 2014)[35]. However, the global agenda of the WEF extends much further to economic development and engages multiple stakeholders and communicating a global healthcare agenda through the networks of government organizations, academia and private organizations. WEF acts as a facilitator of interconnectivity and subsequently a catalyst for change by engaging and forming public-private partnerships to help address global health challenges.

The Strengthening of Research and Development and Activation of Private and Political Support as a Means to Empower Communities

Pharmaceutical companies such as Covidien (http://www.covidien.com/covidien/pages.aspx?page=Home) and Pfizer (www.pfizer.com)[36], with research and development laboratories in India, Europe and Central America, have broadened their focus and their competitive edge by expanding their research agenda globally. Global expansion, aligned with the refinement of existing products and the development of new products and business models have proved profitable for the corporate and academic community. It has also lead to improvement in patient care and extension of healthcare delivery globally.

Global partnerships have been successful in developing new growth platforms leading to innovative advances in endo-mechanical and energy devices, soft tissue repair and vascular therapies, respiratory, monitoring, pharmaceutical and medical supply product lines.

The following five case studies depict the importance and benefits of SN between countries, private organizations, capital markets and other foundations. To cover every region of the world for the delivery of better health care, a strong and efficient SN is required.

CASE STUDIES

Eye Care Program for the Brong Ahafo region

A study[37] was carried out between July 2008 and January 2010 in the Brong Ahafo region of Ghana to assess the impact of various levels of SNs -international, national, regional and district on the health care system in this particular region of Ghana. From January 1996 to

December 2006, the Swiss Red Cross Society was actively involved in an Eye Care Program for the Brong Ahafo region. It remained the main actor and played pivotal role as a bridge between other local levels of SNs in the region. After December 2006, the Swiss Red Cross completely withdrew from the network because of financial problems. Apart from the Swiss Red Cross, six other local level actors also withdrew between 2006 and 2009 for similar reasons.

After the departure of an international organization and the other actors from the network, the Eye Care system of Brong Ahafo region experienced significant changes. The changes were mainly measured in the terms of *Density, Distance* and *Centrality*. Density is a measure of cohesiveness in networks. The dense network means the actors are well connected and the information spreads rapidly among the actors. The density value for 2006 network was 0.127 with 325 ties, while it was 0.057 with 145 ties for 2009 network. Distance corresponds to the number of links that separate two actors. If all actors were directly connected to one another, the average distance would be 1 and information diffusion would be expected to be fast. The mean distance for 2006 network was 2.424 and for the 2009 network increased to 2.893. This means there was a delay in transfer of information in 2009 network as compared to 2006.

Centrality is defined as the number of direct ties an actor has with another actor compared with total number of direct ties. The network centralization index was 27% in 2006. There were four actors who had strong direct links. The network centralization index was 37% in 2009 with only one actor having strong direct links. This meant that the sources of information in 2006 network were comparatively more than in the 2009 network.

However, the 2009 network made the hospital managers the main point of contact for the eye care activities. All information concerning eye care was then channeled through these managers instead of higher-level actors in 2006 network. Therefore, the managers became more aware about the ongoing eye care activities in their districts. The new structure was less resilient and inferior as compared to the previous one in responding to shocks, circulation of information and knowledge across the scales and implementation of solutions. The study also suggested that international organizations have significant impact on creating links and connection between actors at different levels in the organization.

The Matching Fund

The Matching Fund ("GAVI Matching Fund," 2014)[17] networked its way to raise awareness and empower private individuals and companies to impact upon global health programs like Global Alliance for Vaccine and Immunization (GAVI) Alliance. The GAVI is an organization created by public-private partnership with the goal of increasing availability of life saving vaccines to children of developing countries. The focus of GAVI is to increase the availability of immunization by collaborative work of World Health Organization (WHO), United Nations Children's Fund (UNICEF), the World Bank, donor governments, governments of developing countries, financial institutions, research organizations and the pharmaceutical industry. GAVI's latest public-private partnership is the matching fund. It is designed to generate $260 million by the end of year 2015, of which $130 million is to be provided by the U.K. Department of International Development and the Bill and Melinda Gates Foundation. The matching fund of the other $130 million will be provided by companies including Absolute Return for Kids (ARK), Anglo American plc., Children's Investment Fund Foundation (CIFF), Comic Relief, Dutch Postcode Lottery, "la Caixa", LDS Charities, J.P. Morgan, Lions Clubs International, and Vodafone. The significance of the joint pledges in healthcare terms pans out to cover the cost of immunizing 511,000 children against pneumococcus in 2012 or 980,000 children against rotavirus. In addition to increasing the funds for immunization, it also incorporates customers, employees, and business partners of the companies and draws more public attention. It brings the technological and organizational capabilities to GAVI. For example, Vodafone is helping to increase the awareness about the immunization campaign by using mobile technologies and Lions Clubs International is sending 1.35 million volunteers to raise funds for GAVI.

This is a clear example of corporations sharing their business skills to positively impact on the health care of local and global communities. Corporations sharing their business skills and allowing access to their social networks can be magnified beyond immunization programs by bringing global health initiatives into larger health communities and exposing them to other essential services.

The Zambian Government's Data Driven Healthcare Initiative

Zambia is a small country in Africa with a population of around 13 million. Its economy has progressed at an average rate of five to six percent of Gross Development Product (GDP) over the last decade. However, as Zambia's Six National Development Plan (SNDP) notes, this financial progress has not translated into better general living conditions for the majority of Zambians[23]. Incidence and prevalence of the diseases like malaria and HIV are high. Maternal and child health care indicators also reflect the requirement for better health care policy and system. Zambia's Health Care System has three levels of hospitals - district hospitals, provincial hospitals and tertiary hospitals (Figure 1). Apart from hospitals, there are Health Posts and Health Centers, which cover the nearby area of their location. Apart from the Ministry of Health, the Churches Health Association of Zambia, parastatal organizations, private clinics and traditional healers provide health care. Due to lack of trained staff, financial problems, transportation issues and waiting time, rural populations do not have easy access to health care facilities. As a result, Zambia, like several other developing countries, is lagging behind United Nation's Millennium Development Goals. One of the major reasons for this is the low number of medical and paramedical personnel in comparison to the population of the country. For example, the doctor population ratio was 1:15,500 and a midwife to population ratio was 1:5,200. There were high rates of vacancies in all health and allied health professional positions in government establishments. To address this issue by evidence based methodology, the Ministry of Health in the Zambian government carried out nationwide surveys. The primary objective of the survey was to determine relative demand of various health and allied health professionals. The demand of types of healthcare workers was further defined according to geographic region. This net deficit of all types of healthcare workers was calculated by comparing demand to available staff. Using this deficit data, the recruitment of different types of healthcare workers were prioritized for different geographic regions. This data driven strategy for recruitment has enabled the healthcare system of Zambia to deliver healthcare services more appropriately and efficiently to the growing population. The Zambian government's data driven healthcare initiative to address the chronic lack of healthcare workers in rural areas and to ensure staff resources were properly targeted, serves to illustrate the role of SNs in implementation of health policy, influence of systemic factors, and health system performance with the current social, political and economic climate.

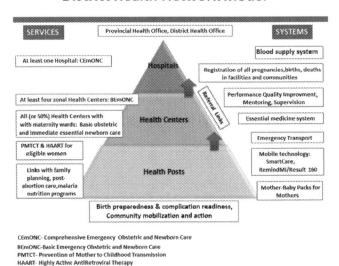

Renal Replacement Therapy in Guyana

Guyana is a small country in Africa. 80% of it is covered by rain forests[38] Water and sanitation sectors are poor in quality and the country ranks poorly on basic health indicators. The population of Guyana is approximately one million and it can be reasonably assumed that there will be approximately 200 new patients who will require a kidney transplant. In Guyana, the burden of chronic kidney disease is significant. Unlike developed countries, average age of presentation is mostly before 40 years. People here were not able to use dialysis service frequently because of financial problems. Moreover, it is politically challenging to manage this issue because of limited national health care budget. Cost of renal transplantation in the United States is approximately $150,000 while in India it is approximately $40,000. In Guyana, annual per capita income is $1,219. So, it is difficult for a person from an average socio economic class in Guyana to get renal replacement therapy[1].

A few years ago, one of a vegetable vendor's sons was diagnosed with kidney failure. She was willing to donate her kidney and appealed to the business community and general public to help her son get a transplant in India and dialysis treatment in Guyana. Mr. George Subraj, a property developer in Queens, New York, came to know about this scenario. Mr. Subraj turned to his SN comprising transplant surgeons from the Walter Reed National Military Medical Center, nephrologists from Drexel University, and Guyanese nurses and physicians. The boy received the life-saving kidney transplant in Guyana without the need to transfer him to another country (Figure 2). Subsequently, several other patients with kidney failure also received a kidney transplant and a dialysis program was established in Guyana. Furthermore, to detect the chronic kidney disease in early stage, a surveillance program has been established in which high school students are taught basic survey techniques and medical interview skills. These students collect health data of the villagers and submit it to a repository using online system under the supervision of US-based physicians. This program can potentially detect the kidney disease at an early stage and help prevent progression by addressing modifiable risk factors like hypertension and diabetes ("SEVAK project," 2014)[77].

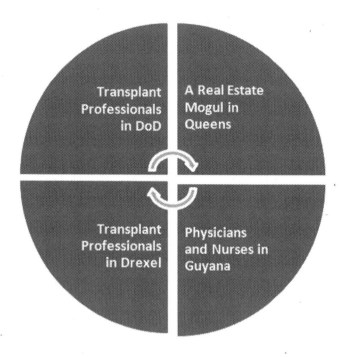

The Leading Group on Innovative Financing for Development

The "Leading Group on Innovative Financing for Development" is a group that connects 64 countries, various institutions, non-government organizations and foundations. ("How the pneumococcal AMC works," 2014; "UNITAID," 2014)[39] The group was founded after the Paris conference on "Innovative Development Financing Mechanism" in 2006, whose purpose was to fight hunger and poverty. Innovative Finance Development Mechanism is a mechanism to raise funds for development with the aim of correcting negative effects of globalization. While Official Development Assistance (ODA) has been the primary source of funding for development, it can be unpredictable. The Innovative Development Financing Mechanisms are stable and

---

[77] http://sevakproject.org/sevakguyana.html (Accessed 08-24-2015)

predictable. There are several major health related development financing mechanisms in existence today like UNITAID, and "Advance Market Commitment for Pneumococcal Vaccines"

UNITAID is based in Geneva and hosted by the WHO. It was established in 2006 by governments of Brazil, Chile, France and the United Kingdom as the "International Drug Purchasing Facility". Later Cyprus, Luxembourg, Spain, Cameroon, Congo, Guinea, Madagascar, Mali and Nigeria became members of UNITAID. Apart from the countries, Civil Society Groups, Non-governmental Organizations and communities also govern it. UNITAID uses innovative financing mechanisms to raise funds for easy availability of diagnostics and treatment for diseases like HIV/AIDS, tuberculosis and malaria in the developing countries. Approximately half of its funds come from a levy on airline tickets with governments and foundations raising the remaining. This organization is based on buyer side, which means it buys healthcare products for the needy developing countries. Because of its significant purchasing power, UNITAID has great impact on the price, speed of production and quality. Other countries, which are not supported by it, also savor the benefits from the UNITAID purchase pattern.

The Pneumococcal Advance Market Commitment (AMC) is a pilot project to make affordable and effective Pneumococcal vaccine available for children in developing countries. The donor countries supply funds to the World Bank according to predetermined terms. The total fund is held by the World Bank on its balance sheet. These assets are paid to GAVI according to AMC terms and conditions. The vaccine manufacturers supply vaccines according to predetermined rates, quantity and duration for which they receive a share of committed AMC funds.

CONCLUSION

Social networks have been highly effective in developing pathways to effective delivery programs and have been a driving force in enabling global health care initiatives. Health initiatives must involve integration, collaboration and support national health policy. Initiatives in developing countries by pharmaceutical companies such as Covidien and Pfizer facilitate integration of global health initiatives into the host community and demonstrate commitment, directly targeting diseases that disproportionally affect developing countries. This leads to evidenced-based decision-making and the development of novel research protocols accelerating medical knowledge and evolving interventions from within the countries where the diseases are endemic.

Physical presence of corporations builds healthcare capacity and not only creates jobs and infrastructure but also facilitates ownership of both the problems and their resolution. Fundamentally, however, global healthcare initiatives are powered by the belief in better healthcare in terms of access and treatment for everyone. Furthermore, every country should have the capacity to determine its own healthcare priorities and the resources to provide sustainable prevention and intervention.

The impact of globalization, the complexities of public-private partnerships, the growing gap between rich and poor, and expanding threats from new and existing diseases are all critical issues that need to be addressed. The developing world also has higher prevalence of cancers related to infectious diseases, especially cervical cancer, which is often detected and treated early in developed countries. Despite the progress made in global health, providers and initiators of global health continue to point to the lack of response from governments who are dealing with global recession and corruption. Frequently, healthcare provision is excessively expensive and in chronic diseases may consume a significant proportion of the national budget as in the case of renal replacement therapy. Consequently, developing countries can easily be left behind, lacking both the capacity to develop new health products and access to affordable healthcare. Saving a woman from dying in childbirth, for example, only to let her die of cervical cancer two years later is indeed shortsighted. This can be prevented by patient-centered leadership.

The true value of SNs is the ability to match public-private partnerships and provide pathways that facilitate leverage with regard to what each group can contribute. For instance, religious organizations often have the credibility to engage with underserved populations in their community. Combined with a private sector contribution, which goes well beyond financial support, organizations bring vital business and powerful advocacy skills to any global healthcare initiative. The combination of innovative finance, advocacy, research and development can impact positively upon a whole range of healthcare developmental challenges over the next decade.

To summarize, a SN with international, national, regional and private sector organizations as its different actors has a significant positive effect on the health care system. It makes the system fast, effective and more resilient to unforeseen shocks.

CHAPTER 15

The Use Of Social Networking Technology In The Promotion And Scaling Up Of Complex Global Health Initiatives

Western medicine has a long tradition of humanitarian service in low resource countries and in crisis and disaster situations. However, advances in social network technology have dramatically changed the manner in which global health services are delivered. A new generation of healthcare professionals, modeled as social entrepreneurs who use collaborative and nonprofit models, has established relationships with healthcare professionals in host countries to actively facilitate early disease detection, and scale up services and research. Oftentimes, technology allows healthcare professionals to contribute to these efforts remotely, without detracting from their routine clinical work. Technology also provides more flexible pathways for global health training in postgraduate education. This article examines the limitations and opportunities of social networking technology, including its use by health care workers as social entrepreneurs, in early disease detection and in scaling up services and research.

Despite the growing momentum on the part of healthcare professionals from high resource countries to form collaborative humanitarian initiatives in low resource and post conflict situations, the majority of populations living in developing countries will not have access to a primary healthcare professional during their lives. The disparities in access to primary healthcare in low resource settings can be attributed to geographical, financial, education and cultural issues, all of which contribute to the global burden of disease and subsequent poor quality of life. When healthcare is needed, but delayed or not obtained, health deteriorates, which in turn leads to loss of income and poverty for an extended family. Such scenarios are common in low resource countries, and the relationship between poverty and access to health care is part of a larger cycle that is the global burden of disease. This article will consider initiatives on the part of government, non-governmental organizations and commercial organizations in improving access to healthcare in low resource settings, using social networking technology to disseminate health care and engage the local population.

The majority of populations in low resource regions of the world have access to a cellphone signal. Collaborative and non-profit organizations such as Medic Mobile (http://medicmobile.org/) were created for the sole purpose of improving access to healthcare in low resource and disconnected communities by using basic mobile communication tools. For example, Medic Mobile has built applications for rural community health workers, caregivers and patients in Malawi using recycled cell phones. Social network technology has transformed global healthcare, especially in remote areas, by facilitating direct interaction with patients, enabling remote training of healthcare workers and supporting research that addresses local health priorities.

To date, there are 481 mentions of Twitter on PubMed, the primary research database for healthcare sciences. These range from monitoring the use of Twitter among cancer patients in Japan[40], and identifying the motivation behind discussions on antibiotics[41], to digital drug safety surveillance[42]. Successful collaboration between healthcare professionals and social networking technology offers the potential to communicate and disseminate information on global health issues, a good example being immunization. India's Pulse Polio Program[43] used social networking technology not only to provide information about the availability of a vaccine for polio, but also to communicate evidence that it can save lives and address the dangers of taking an anti-vaccine stance. This year, three years after the program began, the World Health Organization, declared India a polio free country (Polio Eradication, 2014)[44]. The eradication of polio in India is a testament to social media's capability for data sharing.

Healthcare Professionals as Social Entrepreneurs

Healthcare training programs around the world have recognized the potential and important roles that graduates might play in global health intervention in low resource settings. Global health education has been integrated into existing domestic programs in order that healthcare professions have education in such areas as inter-cultural skills, health policy development, health service planning, resource allocation and ethics, to make appropriate and effective contributions in low resource settings. Healthcare professionals possess many portable skills that equate with an entrepreneurial mindset. One core entrepreneurial skill that healthcare professionals possess is sound clinical judgment. Other skill sets include the ability to experiment and conduct research, make decisions with incomplete information and, in times of uncertainty, to have the courage to recognize when something will not work or should be ended. All of the above skills are likely to encourage local populations, governments and non-profits to invest in innovative ideas.

Touch Surgery[45], a mobile surgical simulator developed by two United Kingdom based surgeons, enables users to practice surgical procedures on their cell phones anywhere in the world, and is a good example of physicians using their entrepreneurial skills in the global health arena. On a larger scale, Orange tele-communications (Tele Health, 2014)[46] has initiated several projects in collaboration with E-Health to provide secure and accessible storage of medical data in low resource settings where access to health-care is poor.

Early Disease Detection

The mobile phone has proven highly efficient in identifying, tracking and communicating outbreaks of communicable diseases in rural areas. Social network technology is able to provide instant data about potential epidemics, decrease the response time, and ultimately save lives. The Real-Time Bio-surveillance Program (RTBP) was launched in India and Sri Lanka to test the potential of using cell phone for health data collection. In its pilot phase, RTBP sought to establish a mobile-based communications system, introduce a computer-based detection system and implement an e-Health based surveillance and notification system[47]. The systems were evaluated over a one-year period, and data from this phase have informed the scale up phase.

Bengtsson, a physician at Karolinska Institute, Sweden, in Collaboration with Children's Hospital Boston, tracks post disaster migration in low resource settings to help first responders find large groups of affected people. Using cell phone data, Bengtsson and colleagues, working in collaboration with Haiti's largest cellular carrier Digicel, showed that by mining anonymized cell phone data, it was possible to track population movements in Haiti during the January

2010 earthquake and the subsequent epidemic of cholera[48]. Bengtsson subsequently used cell phone records to track population movements after the cholera outbreak in Saint Marc and surrounding areas in Haiti[49]. The tracking revealed that many members of the population were moving towards Port au Prince, the largest city in Haiti. These data were invaluable in planning healthcare intervention.

Scaling Up Services

The term scaling up is now widely used in global health literature to describe the process of expanding access, personnel, services, financial support and capacity from pilot projects to meeting the needs of the local population. Scaling up generally involves a considerable increase in the volume of aid, accompanied by health initiatives and financial mechanisms. This has resulted in improvements in health outcomes and some success in large-scale programs. Healthcare entrepreneurs, often at the forefront of such scale ups, have used social network technology to understand health interventions better, strengthen system quality, and deal with the challenges of sustaining scaled up services.

The scaling up of aid volumes for global health began in the late 1990's in response to the HIV/AIDS pandemic and, in particular, in response to the need to make anti-retroviral therapy widely available. The adoption of the Millennium Development Goals (MDG's) in 2000 and debt relief initiatives also helped to increase financial resources needed to fund global health entrepreneurship and social networking technology (Millennium Development Goals, 2014). For example, the Malawi government launched a human resources program via Linkedin and Twitter that increased recruitment of volunteers and nurse tutors[50]. Other examples include international donors who financed the salaries of 2000 additional health workers in Kenya and the introduction of financial, housing, education and other incentives to encourage deployment of Zambian health workers to rural areas[51]. Pre-service training for health workers has been expanded in Ethiopia, Zambia, Mozambique and Uganda using Social Network Technology[52].

Collaborative Research

The use of social networking technology presents researchers with unprecedented opportunities to facilitate collaboration between scientists in high and low resource settings. The Cochrane Collaboration has published work reflecting the potential of social media to disseminate the results of biomedical research and provide up to date clinical information to healthcare providers[53]. Some groups are exploring the use of social media to peer review research, because of the immediacy of interaction and potential cost reductions[54]. There are also lessons to be learned from other knowledge generating, self-correcting communities, such as Wikipedia[78]about the mutually beneficial altruism and status that drives much social networking, and the transparence and accuracy created through visible open review. However the positive innovative uses of social media, while presenting opportunities, are not without their limitations and drawbacks. Social media are open to abuse, as in the case of using Twitter to circumvent traditional regulatory frameworks that control direct consumer advertising by pharmaceutical companies[55]. Unnecessary duplication of research is an issue in developed countries, and competition for funds and publications risks breeding a culture of secrecy among scientists to protect their ideas. However, in developing countries, where resources are scarcer and research results are more critical to save human lives, there should be an even greater demand for a streamlined model of scientific cooperation and setting research agendas.

Ethical Issues in the Use of Social Networking in Medicine

Ethical issues are of prime concern when using social networking technology in health care. There are many ethical principles that are applicable to clinical care and social media. Some of the important principles are confidentiality, privacy protection, solicitation of testimonials and consent. Physicians must be careful about maintaining

---

[78] https://en.wikipedia.org/wiki/Main_Page (Accessed 08-24-2015)

confidentiality of their patients while corresponding with them through social media. The risk of breaching confidentiality is very high compared to conventional face-to-face consultation. Informed consent is as important as it is in real time consultation. Physicians must inform patients about possible treatment options, risk, fees and prognosis. Ultimately, it should be the patient and not the physician who decides the course of treatment. This practice is well recognized in face-to-face to consultation, but can be easily missed in electronic communication. It becomes the physician's moral duty to protect the privacy of patients. In social media networking it is possible to leak patient information unknowingly and, considering the dense nexus of networks in the current era, it does not require much effort to identify a person. Therefore, physicians must be extra vigilant to protect the privacy of their patients. Moreover, practitioners should maintain patient records for legal purpose. Physicians should also be careful about accepting "friend or follow requests" on networking sites. These may lead to the development of alternative relationships, which may not prove healthy for physician or patient. Ethical issues pertaining to location and jurisdiction are also important issues. Physicians must be aware of the laws of other states and jurisdictions to which their online patients belong.

In summary, the important ethical recommendations are as follows: Physicians should avoid using general networking systems like Facebook, Twitter etc. They also should encrypt their conversations with patients. They should make their patients understand which issues should be handled online vs. in-person. Physicians should also avoid writing about their specific patients, and obtain their permission when necessary. They should always share credible information based upon research studies. They should always disclose any financial compensation received. Physicians must avoid anonymity, accurately state their credentials, and mention whether or not they represent an organization. In general they should avoid "friend or follow requests" by their patients[79].

---

[79] http://circ.ahajournals.org/content/127/13/1413.long (Accessed 08-24-2015)

We give several illustrative examples of use of social media under the following six broad headings.

Case Study 1: Primary Care/Medical Care

The Mayo Clinic has used social media technology quite effectively to better health care delivery and information. They have created the Mayo Clinic Center for Social Media (MCCSM) for the application of social media networks to improve health care information. The Mayo Clinic is active on such social media platforms as Twitter, Facebook and YouTube. MCCSM has approximately 836,000 followers on Twitter where it posts updates on various health care topics. Mayo has also started a Social Media Residency, an intensive one-day course that focuses on the strategic use of social media in healthcare. They have produced a book entitled 'Bringing the Social Media Revolution to Health Care',[56] which presents strategic reasons to integrate social media into health care communications. MCCSM also produces educational webinars for its social network members that depict how various forms of social media can impact healthcare. Mayo also provides Social Media Health Care Network accounts. Members of this Social Media Healthcare Network have access to various teaching tools like Learning Modules and Webinars. Moreover, on their website[80], they provide basic information about most diseases for the general population. Readers learn about risk factors, symptoms and possible treatment options for each particular disease. On their Facebook profile, Mayo uploads recent health articles from various sources, answers health related questions, and posts interesting and inspirational medical and surgical cases. Apart from disease and its management, the site also delivers information about healthy lifestyle and preventive measures. According to the list (HCSML- Health Care Social Media List) prepared by Ed Bennet, an advisory board member for MCCSM, there are currently 1,563 health care organizations across the United States actively using one or another

---

[80] mayoclinic.org (Accessed 08-24-2015)

social networking sites[81]. This suggests that social networks have become an essential part of health care organizations. However, the utility of such networks is limited. They sometimes become social forums where people debate one another because of their conflicting views; and the conversation transcends the purpose from what was intended. Moreover, one can use such networks to tarnish the image of the organization and spread misconceptions.

Case Study 2: Health Worker Stability and Security

Physicians are increasingly using social network in their practice. A study by Care Continuum Alliance and QuantiaMD in 2011 researched how clinicians use social media and the views of clinicians about different aspects of social media in health care[82]. According to the 4,000 physicians who participated in the survey, more than 65% used social network platforms for professional purposes. Education was the prime purpose of such networking. They also used social networks for expert advice on patients' conditions, to discuss professional challenges or simply to stay connected. It was evident from the survey that participating physicians were more interested in online "physician-physician interaction" than in "physician-patient interaction." For diagnosis and treatment, over 40 % of the clinicians believed that there was no alternative actually to seeing and examining the patient. Security of online transmitted information is also a concern for physicians. It is likely that more physicians will be open to social media networking when these security concerns are satisfied. According to the report, there are many online patient as well as online physician communities. Physicians believe that these communities have positive effects on the patients, and 40% of the participating physicians have already recommended patient communities to their patients. Half of the physicians were ready to join these communities as a professional guide. However, such communities also have drawbacks.

---

[81] http://network.socialmedia.mayoclinic.org/hcsml-grid/ (Accessed 08-24-2015)
[82] http://www.quantiamd.com/q-qcp/DoctorsPatientSocialMedia.pdf (Accessed 08-24-2015)

For example, some physicians believe that such communities are sources of misinformation and platforms for blaming and complaining about doctors and other health allied bodies. Many such communities become social chat rooms. However, a significant number of clinicians found it possible to interact with their patients online for easy access and better quality care. However, they felt that concerns about privacy, liability and compensation must be addressed first.

Case Study 3: Preventive Medicine/Vaccination

Social networks, like Facebook and Twitter, can significantly contribute to health care initiatives and can be effective tools for research data collection. One such use was demonstrated in a Minnesota study conducted by a research team led by Dr. Erik J. Nelson[57]. These researchers advertised an online survey for Human Papilloma Virus (HPV) Vaccination on Facebook to a targeted locality. Males and females from 18-30 years within a 25 miles radius of Minneapolis participated in the survey; 2,079 individuals responded to the advertisement and 1,003 completed the survey. The study found that 13% of the male respondents and 65.6% of the female respondents had at least one HPV immunization. The data for the entire state were different: 53.8 % for women and 20.8% for male. The corresponding national numbers were: 34.5 % for females and 2.3 % for males. The researchers found this method cost effective and feasible. In addition, this study suggests that local estimates of vaccination rates vary considerably from state and national statistics. This information can direct healthcare resources to particular regions with low vaccination rates.

Case Study 4: Engineering and Environment

Approximately, 8,000 tons of solid waste is generated each day in the Delhi-National Capital Region (NCR) of India. The working condition of waste handlers and traders in India is far from safe. They unknowingly deal with toxins generated from plastics and electronic waste. Chin tan, an NGO based in New Delhi, has formed a network with local organizations like "New Delhi Municipal Council", "Ghaziabad Nagar Nigam", "Safaisena" and "Resident Welfare Association" to set up a solid-waste handling system[83]. This system has replaced conventional waste handling and created greener and safer methods and protocols for cost-effective waste disposal. The organization's other motive is the modification of existing policies for environmental justice and creating green jobs. The NGO strongly believes that rigorous research, consultation, and multi-level dissemination of knowledge are essential to reach this goal. As a result, Chintan has partnered with the Centre for Advanced Studies for India and the University of Pennsylvania to expand its network. Chintan is also planning an "online marketplace" and "an integrated mobile application" to connect waste recyclers and waste generators directly. In three years, they are planning to connect 1600 waste pickers with 200,000 generators and manage 500 tons of Delhi's trash every day[84]. This method will improve the work environment and general living standard of waste recyclers. It will also reduce the time required to dispose waste from its source of origin. Moreover, it is hoped that this endeavor will impact pollution control in this region of India.

Case Study 5: Water and Sanitation

Sanitation is a major issue in developing countries. Waterborne diseases like hepatitis A, typhoid, and infectious diarrhea, all of which are linked to poor sanitation facilities, are prevalent in these countries. The overall health of the community and nation can be enhanced by improving sanitation facilities in these countries. Based in Pune, India, Shelter Associates is an NGO working to improve sanitation in the urban slums of Pune and few other cities in this region of India. The NGO is an integrated network of architects, community workers, analysts and social workers. It has partnered with Baandhni, a group of poor men

---

[83] http://www.chintan-india.org/index.htm (Accessed 08-24-2015)
[84] https://impactchallenge.withgoogle.com/india2013#/chintan (Accessed 08-24-2015)

and women from several cities in Western India[85]. These groups have chosen to work under a single banner (Baandhni) and associate with Shelter Associates to create and maintain profiles of various cities in Maharashtra, compiling the latest information on slums in those cities. One of the prime barriers to urban and rural development in India and other developing countries is lack of detailed knowledge about geography. The Geographical Information System (GIS) is a technique used to analyze data connected to a specific location. The GIS system is designed to generate spatial data about underserved areas to help city planning. This system conducts digital mapping of the urban slum areas with poor sanitation facilities and links it with socio-economic data of the respective area. The data include employment, education and family size. They also include information about infrastructure and facilities such as toilets, water supply, etc. Such maps are composite sources of geographical, demographic and infrastructural information. These maps help identify service gaps and potential areas for improvement in facilities. Shelter Associates will make this map available for partners, government and civil societies[86]. In this way they facilitate governmental efforts to improve sanitation and other essential living facilities.

Case Study 6: Globalization / Economics

Globalization has been the key to development since the era of cultural-revolution. In the modern era, the term globalization is not limited to establishing a franchise or business center in other parts of the world. Information Technology (IT) and Social Network (SN) have expanded and redefined the meaning of globalization. The latest example of this is the "Ice Bucket Challenge" for the Amyotrophic Lateral Sclerosis (ALS) awareness campaign. This challenge has gone viral on social media platforms like Facebook and Twitter[87]. Without

---

[85] http://shelter-associates.org/ (Accessed 08-24-2015)
[86] https://impactchallenge.withgoogle.com/india2013#/shelterassociates (Accessed 08-24-2015)
[87] http://www.nytimes.com/2014/08/18/business/ice-bucket-challenge-has-raised-millions-for-als-association.html?_r=0 (Accessed 08-24-2015)

such well spread social networks, the campaign might not have reached this level of global penetration. Tele-radiology is a healthcare product of information technology and networking, and is gradually becoming popular all over the world. The use of radiological imaging is constantly increasing, while the growth in the number of radiologists has not kept pace with it. Moreover, specialized radiological services are generally restricted to a few larger centers. With the advent of tele-radiology, these limitations have been overcome. Using broadband internet, high speed telephone lines and the latest cloud services, a radiologist sitting in one country can evaluate scans from the other countries. Telepsychiatry is also maturing. With the help of communication equipment, software and high speed internet, psychiatric consultation is accessible through real time video conferencing. The results of the consultation are saved in the patient's medical record electronically. Telepsychiatry reduces long waiting times and cost[88]. Thus, information technology and networking have transformed the world into a compact and connected domain.

---

[88] http://www.dianassociates.com/telepsych.html (Accessed 08-24-2015)

CONCLUSION

Social Network Technology has changed the landscape of global healthcare delivery across low resource settings by giving people who live in isolated rural areas the ability to connect with healthcare systems across the globe. A phone call can compress the time it takes healthcare professionals to assess risks and make decisions for patients. Social Network Technology has enabled healthcare professionals to meet many of the global health challenges in resource-limited areas. Social Network Technology has also changed the way in which healthcare professionals view global health in terms of the ability to impact populations, collect data in real time, and develop intervention strategies that were previously inconceivable. However, the challenges go beyond simply determining the manner in which to reach more people using Social Network Technology. More research is needed to determine how human capacity and resources can keep pace with technology, how Social Network Technology should be used ethically, and how these advances should be integrated into the training curricula of healthcare professionals.

CHAPTER 16

The Growing Phenomenon Of 'Voluntourism'

I and my colleagues are inundated with requests from all levels of
students and others to accompany us on our humanitarian missions.
Some are upfront *"this will be a good networking opportunity"* or *"it will
look good on college essay"* or *"can you write a recommendation immediately
after the mission"*.

An extreme is that a volunteer vacation "looks good on one's CV as
a gap year activity," is a talking point in interviews[89].

Essays for college bound students are competitive and there is an
impression that admission officers are looking for voluntary work as
part of the overall evaluation of the candidate. This has given rise to
voluntourism which combines vacation travel with volunteering at the
destination visited. It's also spawned a new vocabulary: *voluntourist,
ethical holidays, travel philanthropy*, and more. Voluntourism is aligned
with the more established concept of "sustainable tourism," defined by
Sustainable Travel International as "lessening the toll that travel and
tourism takes on the environment and local cultures." Their motto is:
Leave the world a better place[90].

When it's well-organized and thoughtfully planned, the traveler can
indeed use vacation time to great advantage, helping the host country
and gaining many personal benefits. Some of the most obvious pluses
are[91].

- It meets the needs of busy people who want to volunteer and
  travel – with special benefits to families seeking a memorable
  shared experience and to the many adults who prefer taking
  vacation time in the company of others. Given the research
  about Baby Boomers, it seems evident that voluntourism will
  be very popular with them for many years to come.
- Well-managed spurts of volunteer help can be productive for
  many types of projects that need a lot of willing hands. After

[89] http://www.urbandictionary.com/define.php?term=Voluntourism (Accessed
08/09/2015)
[90] www.sustainabletravelinternational.org/documents/op_tp_voluntourism.html
(Accessed 08/09/2015)
[91] http://www.energizeinc.com/hot/2007/07feb.html (Accessed 08/09/2015)

a natural disaster, for example, the enormous clean-up and rebuilding work goes on for years, and a continuous stream of fresh recruits can keep the momentum going.

- Ideally, voluntourism is a people-to-people experience, in which both the helper and the helped become acquainted with one another. Just as Peace Corps or UN Volunteers strives to create cultural exchange and understanding, even brief periods of working together gives everyone involved insight into the world of the "other."
- Positive experiences as a voluntourist can lead to more sustained service, either in return trips to the same country or to more informed and deliberate forms of volunteering back home for international or development causes.

Are There Problems with Voluntourism?

However, many organizations, travel companies and travelers themselves have not understood the value and ethics of voluntourism. A few issues which need to be emphasized with this are:

- How are the volunteering opportunities chosen? Are these real needs and can volunteers truly do something useful in as little as a week?
- Is there an application process or qualifications for volunteers or does the receiving site have to take anyone and everyone who wants to come?

What's the ratio of service to sightseeing?

Rafia Zakaria, a columnist for Dawn, a Pakistan English-language newspaper, wrote an interesting article "*Poverty Is Not a Spectacle*"[92]. She compared voluntourism to hedonism which capitalizes on another Western yearning — the search for life's meaning. She believes that

---

[92] http://www.nytimes.com/roomfordebate/2014/04/29/can-voluntourism-make-a-difference/poverty-as-a-tourist-attraction (Accessed 08-24-2015)

voluntourism treated "receiving communities" as passive objects of the visiting Westerner's quest for *saviordom*. As she has rightly observed that willing (and paying) and often unskilled are led to believe that hapless villages can be transformed by schools built on a two-week trip and diseases eradicated by the digging of wells during spring breaks. I do agree that the photo ops, the hugs with the kids and the meals with the natives are part of this package; the helpers can see and touch those they are saving and take evidence of their new nobility home with them. However, the long-term benefits have to be explored scientifically by outcomes research and compiling the views of the local communities. There is very little evidenced based research on this topic.

Linda Richter[93], a developmental psychologist and the director of the Center of Excellence in Human Development at the University of the Witwatersrand in Johannesburg, South Africa writes that examples of misguided volunteering efforts abound, especially when people want to help AIDS orphans in southern and eastern Africa. Westerners have a yearning to go to orphanages, be it Romania, South Africa, India or elsewhere as it is an "in thing" to do and is seen as the highest form of "saviordom". However, Richter proposes that the better way to help such desperate families is to support them to keep their children at home, where a child can be part of their community for the rest of their lives. Children becoming attached to one volunteer after another in their quest for intimacy and security causes their relationships with other people to be disturbed and can result in a range of adjustment and mental health problems. While children in orphanages long for affection and cling to any adult who responds to them, these short-term relationships are very unhelpful to the child in the longer term.

Amy Ernst[94], a freelance human rights worker and advocate volunteered with victims of sexual violence in the eastern Democratic Republic of Congo and found the experience very rewarding. She found

---

[93] http://www.nytimes.com/roomfordebate/2014/04/29/can-voluntourism-make-a-difference/the-problem-with-a-short-term-presence (Accessed 08-24-2015)
[94] http://www.nytimes.com/roomfordebate/2014/04/29/can-voluntourism-make-a-difference/you-can-help-but-get-support (Accessed 08-24-2015)

that international organizations avoid difficult and controversial areas such as working with victims of sexual violence. Her advice to future voluntourists is that accountability and humility are key, *"if you look hard enough, you will find that all skills are needed; you just need to figure out where and how to apply them in the appropriate context"*.

Voluntourism is a rapidly growing industry, but people interested in international volunteering need to get a realistic grasp on the situation[95]. A sad situation is where a volunteer may unwittingly end up fulfilling a role that a local could have been compensated for, or the volunteer's work might result in a reduction of a paid employee's hours. In many of these cases volunteers are extremely dependent on the host organization's staff, who often end up spending more energy on accommodating the volunteer than he or she is actually worth.

Our organizations believe that if you are deeply interested in volunteering abroad, realize that it is for your own benefit, and that you may not be helping anyone else. Otherwise, wait until you have both the time and skill set to make a valuable contribution. I would also recommend cutting out the middleman. If you wish to volunteer abroad, consider an area where you know there is need, research local organizations and contact them directly. This makes some people nervous, but if there is truly need in the area you are in, there won't be a shortage of opportunities to volunteer. Finally, if you're interested in volunteering and you don't have any experience, consider volunteering locally. This might be unappealing to those who are particularly interested in traveling, but if you don't have any applicable skills that you can transfer, you might be of better use in an environment you're familiar with. If you still want to make an international contribution, consider educating yourself on international causes and fundraising on behalf of one whose mandate resonates with you. The reality is that if you don't have a particular skill set to offer abroad, your money will likely go further than your time, especially when you only have a couple of weeks to spare. Ideally, development and aid work should

---

[95]   http://www.huffingtonpost.com/rudayna-bahubeshi/the-problem-with-voluntourism_b_2712627.html (Accessed 08-24-2015)

be done by country nationals, people that already know the culture, the language, and the nuances of their country. Even more ideally, developing countries should be training and educating people who are actually from specific in-need communities. Far from being "white saviors", if history is any indication, further indiscriminate, unchecked Western meddling can only mean more bad news for the people of the developing world[96]. Finally, there is a need for evidenced based research on the short and long-term benefits of voluntourism.

[96]   http://www.huffingtonpost.com/mario-machado/the-privilege-of-doing-de_b_4832836.html (Accessed 08-24-2015)

CHAPTER 17

Distance Learning

Distance learning (DL) is no longer the new frontier in education and is widely accepted by employers and students. As outlined above, one can clearly see the multi-disciplinary approach can be extremely beneficial to any treatment plan or health issue, locally or globally. Allowing professionals that may already be actively working in their field or specialty to further increase the success of used protocols and treatment plans by broadening their knowledge in areas outside of their initial specialty will be exponentially beneficial to all. DL provides an alternative for them. Additionally, this form of learning may be particularly suitable for developing countries and may be cost effective to students who may not have access to colleges. DL may also be suitable for areas in the world where there are humanitarian crises. I was part of the inception and planning of a unique DL course in global health psychology, an area which has been neglected. I believe that health care professionals who may not be physically able to help the underserved may participate in the many formats of DL now practiced in the West. Social entrepreneurs may subsidize these courses for specific areas of the world, a unique form of seva.

There are well known advantages of DL, however, there are also several disadvantages. The health care professional in the West who may be thinking of participating or funding DL courses for the developing world should keep this in mind.

Advantages and Disadvantages of Distance Learning

Like any kind of educational program, distance learning comes with a host of pros and cons. Before you enroll in any kind of distance learning program, make sure to carefully consider these in order to be sure you'll be getting an education that meets your personal needs, strengths and career goals.

Distance Learning Advantages:

Lots of flexibility: With distance learning courses, students can complete their course work from just about anywhere, provided there's a computer and internet connection. This allows students to work when and where it is more convenient for them without having to squeeze in scheduled classes to an already busy life.

No commuting: Taking a course online can be one way to cut down on costly gas or public transportation. Since students can often work from home to complete their class assignments, both time and money are saved in cutting out the trips to and from class.

Numerous choices for schools: Even if you live in a community with few or no colleges distance learning allows you to choose from a wide variety of schools to complete your education. You may find online schools that specialize in your particular field or one that can provide a great general education. Either way, your options for education will be greatly expanded.

Lowered costs: Prices for online courses are generally cheaper than their on-campus counterparts and you won't have to worry about commuting, moving or getting meal plans on campus, some additional benefits to learning from home.

Learn while working: As distance learning can usually be completed on your own schedule, it is much easier to complete distance learning courses while working than more traditional educational programs. Keeping your job gives you more income, experience and stability while completing your degree giving you less to worry about and more time to focus on your studies.

Distance Learning Disadvantages:

Lack of social interaction: If the classroom environment is what you love most about learning you may want to take a step back and reconsider distance learning. You'll likely get some interaction on chat rooms, discussion boards and through email, but the experience will be quite different than traditional courses.

Format isn't ideal for all learners: Not everyone is an ideal candidate for online learning. If you know you have problems with motivation, procrastination and needs lots of individual attention from an instructor you may want to think long and hard before enrolling in an online learning program.

Some employers don't accept online degrees: While a majority of employers will, there are some who still see a stigma attached to distance learning. Realize that your online degree may not be the ideal tool for some job fields or for future learning.

Requires adaptability to new technologies: If you have never been one to love working with technology you will probably get a lot less out of an online course than your more tech-savvy counterparts. Make sure you feel comfortable working with computers and with online programs before you sign up for a class.

Not all courses required to complete the degree may be offered online: It makes sense that more practical majors like nursing are not offered entirely online, after all, part of the degree is learning to work directly with patients. Find out all the requirements of your degree to see what may need to be completed offline.

Prologue

"I slept and dreamt that life was joy. I awoke and saw that life was service. I acted and behold, service was joy."--- **Rabindranath Tagore**

Our case histories represent a variety of situations across continents. Having initiated and carried these projects from scratch to fruition has given us an insight into the many issues others may face when they initiate their own projects. We experienced frustration at many points in the trajectory of our projects; however, we persevered and perhaps achieved modest success. We should confess that we thought of abandoning and giving up at multiple stages of our projects, however, we were reminded of the beneficiaries and continued against many odds and obstacles. Some of these could have been prevented but others were inevitable.

It could be said that marketing is not for seva projects, but to reach the target audience, as in our case reports, we have to draw them in and engage them in a way that moves them closer to becoming our agent of change. [97]Social media isn't a magical way to gain new business with a few ads and aggressive networking.

Define your audience.

We have to be clear who the target audience is.

---

[97] http://simplymeetups.com/dont-waste-your-marketing-dollars-on-social-media/ (Accessed 08-24-2015)

For example, in the case of our national blood donation drive, we defined our audience as those Indian-Americans who attend the local Hindu temples in the first instance and then move to capture Indian-American businesses and then to student organizations. We did not waste time to target, for example, Chinese-Americans, who also have a low rate of donating blood. We firstly, wanted to make our work with the Indian-American community "a model" which other ethnic communities could use. We believe; it is important to have a narrow defined focus for the initial work.

In Guyana, our focus was narrow – identification and treatment of diseases of the kidney, kidney failure and kidney transplantation. This was motivated by the desire of our benefactor who had many members of his extended family die of kidney failure and the complete absence of dialysis and kidney transplantation in Guyana. We also extended our work to initiate a prospective study of 10,000 people living in rural areas of Guyana with little access to health care facilities. Our work will define the incidence and prevalence of diabetes and hypertension, the two main causes of kidney failure. Moreover, our work will shape health policy as little attention was given to these two important diseases in Guyana.

To recruit college students for the LTC project in Kerala, India, we targeted our facebook page and advertisements towards this group. As recruitment was slow and uneven, we took help from a student in the US and a marketing expert to guide us on ways to increase recruitment.

Our project for "Global Health Psychology" from the University of West London is aimed at network of individuals and organizations that aim to improve services for people living with mental health problems and psychosocial disabilities worldwide, especially in low- and middle-income countries where effective services are often scarce. Two principles are fundamental to the Movement: scientific evidence and human rights[98].

---

[98] http://www.globalmentalhealth.org/about (Accessed 08-24-2015)

Make a compelling offer to capture their attention.

This is critical as in case of the Guyana transplant project, we offered the whole range of treatments from hemodialysis, peritoneal dialysis and eventually kidney transplantation. We made effective use of the local media in all our projects. We used the local press and lobbied the government of Guyana to provide free life-long medications. The press was particularly helpful in spreading the message of life style changes to prevent hypertension, diabetes and kidney failure. We widely publicised the fact that well known team of American physicians was giving their services free of charge and they would also see patients with other medical and surgical conditions.

In case of our campaign to increase the registration for bone marrow transplantation, we publicised the figures that the chances of a South East Asian receiving a bone marrow transplant is 1 in 20,000 vs. 1 in 10 for a Caucasian. We also set up a web site which provided the facts, templates for flyers and contact information of coordinators in temples to facilitate net-working.

For our LTC project in Kerala, India, we advertised the benefits of participation such as, become well versed in yogic theory and practice, understand the science of the self and universe, see medical data on the medical and psychological benefits of your practice and obtain LTC Teacher Training Certificate.

The distance learning (DL) global health psychology course is a unique concept to introduce much needed training in mental health in the developing countries and to workers who go on humanitarian missions. The pros and cons of DL have been much debated and analyzed. However, I look forward to participating as a visiting professor on this course. I also look forward to analyzing the long-term outcomes and feed-back from the students.

Collect the right amount of data and usable customer feedback.

In each of our projects, we collected the data that was necessary to move the prospect to the next step.

In case of our Guyana transplant project, we wrote a series of manuscripts detailing our experience with initiating a peritoneal dialysis program and how we made ethical decisions about which patient to list for transplant. Our data was also presented at a variety of conferences in the USA and other countries. We regularly interviewed the patients and local physicians in Guyana about our services and ways to improve this.

In case of the blood donation drive, we carefully documented and collected data from the various temples and organizations participating in the campaign and eventually created a web site[99] which contained template for flyers, information on the need for blood and bone marrow in South East Asians and pictures of Indian-Americans donating blood.

Test. Analyze. Refine. Repeat.

A high performing marketing process is not typically achieved right out of the gate. Identify bottlenecks in each step of the overall marketing process through testing and simple data analysis. We identified bottle necks in each of our projects.

In case of the Guyana project, we found out early on that the Guyanese physicians at the public hospital[100] were simply not motivated and we moved our mission to a private hospital[101]. This was indeed a drastic step; however it salvaged the program and in the long run was the saving grace. There is a move to expand the transplant program to the government hospital, however, with the caveat that the work ethics need to be vastly improved to provide the best possible care to our patients. We introduced a small charge which would have to be paid by the patient to partially offset the cost of running a private hospital. We also found that patients were more likely to be compliant with follow up and medications if they had to pay this charge.

---

[99] http://hindusgiftoflife.org/ (Accessed 08-24-2015)
[100] https://www.facebook.com/pages/Georgetown-Public-Hospital-Corporation-GPHC/1509032579346095?
(Accessed 08-24-2015)
[101] http://www.drbalwantsinghshospital.com/ (Accessed 08-24-2015)

In case of the blood donation drive, we found that a certain segment of the Hindu temples was not prepared to participate in our cause, so we bypassed them and approached the local temple organizers directly. We decided that in the limited time we had to organize our efforts, time management was important for our volunteers who have full time jobs and other commitments. There is only a certain amount of available time for volunteer activities and rather than focus on changing minds of a small group of intransigent group of people, sometimes, it is best to bypass these.

However, this is not always possible, as many charity projects start serendipitously without a "business plan". The latter is best left to the Ford Foundation[102] and the Gates foundation[103] of this world, which have vast resources and an army of accountants and management consultants for writing business plans. These great foundations have indeed been very successful, however, the case studies we have described are our passion and from the heart.

For a successful seva project, it is important to have passion, commitment and also a marketing process which is innovative to the changing environment in the country – particularly, developing countries which are undergoing enormous changes.

Publish and spread the word of your work.

It is important that your colleagues learn about your seva from conferences, you tube or academic articles. This helps in making them aware of your work and lead to new opportunities of doing seva. An example is given in which a USA surgeon connected us to the Ministry of Health in Djibouti to explore the possibility of initiating a renal replacement therapy program in that country.

---

[102] http://www.fordfound.org/ (Accessed 08-24-2015)
[103] http://www.gatesfoundation.org/Pages/home.aspx (Accessed 08-24-2015)

-----Original Message-----

From: LJ

[mailto: … @mail.mil]

Sent: Monday, June 16, 2014 6:35 AM

To: Jindal, Rahul M CIV US WRNMMC

Subject: kidney transplantation - AFRICA

Dear Dr. Jindal -

Greetings from Djibouti, Africa -

I don't think that we have ever met in person, but I covered for you and Ed Falta a few years ago - I'm a Transplant Surgeon, from Washington University in St. Louis (Barnes / St. Louis Children's), and am currently deployed to Camp Lemonnier, in support of Combined Task Force Horn of Africa (CJTF-HOA). We are located in Djibouti (north of Somalia, west of Yemen). I go and work at one of the Ministry of Health Hospitals a few times a week, and there is an excellent surgeon there who has raised questions about the possibility of kidney transplantation in Djibouti. While I think that this would be extremely difficult, I told him that I knew of an expert who has done this in Guyana.

Do you have any information about how you started the program in Guyana - what was necessary? Limitations? Obstacles? Go-no go points? Financial issues? Issues with ministry of health? Issues with Embassy / DOS? Issues with US military? Other issues? I have read the article that you wrote for the ACS Journal (if you have a copy that you could send, that would be great) - do you have any other written materials (protocols, etc.) that you could forward.

This is only a very, very theoretical inquiry at this point - as I mentioned, I think it is VERY unlikely that this could work in this country, based on my experiences here, but I was asked by their surgeon to at least look into it - and I very much respect him. Anyway, thanks much in advance - hope to meet you in person someday.

V/r

JL

DSS, EMF-Djibouti / CJTF-HOA

On Jun 16, 2014, at 4:44 PM, Jindal, Rahul M CIV US WRNMMC

<Rahul.M.Jindal.ctr@...> wrote:

Hello JL,

Thank you for the inquiry and possibility of a renal replacement program in Somalia. I enclose several of our publications arising from our work in Guyana including power points and the PDF of a book I wrote on this. We have now completed 23 missions to Guyana in which we have done 26 kidney transplants, initiated their first peritoneal dialysis and vascular access program and examined several hundred patients with CKD. More importantly, we have initiated a comprehensive prevention and early detection of non-communicable diseases spear-headed by CAPT Patel (www.sevakproject. org). When I first visited Guyana in 2008, the situation was probably similar to Somalia. There was not even an ultra-sound machine and cholecystectomy (and similar procedures) was all that were done. Initiating the kidney transplant program has raised their standard of health care such as now some cardiac procedures are also done and CT/MRI, etc. have been introduced.

This concept of public-private partnership [PPP] (as described in my PPT and book) could well be applied to other countries. I will be going to India later this year to initiate a similar program. India does have a more sophisticated health care scenario, but the concept of PPP in RRT has not been tried before. Perhaps, you could accompany us on our next mission to Guyana. We now go there 4 times a year. Dr Waller, Corneal Transplant Surgeon is going to introduce corneal transplantation during our next visit in July.

PS: Our colleagues in Drexel University transplant program have developed a hand book and protocols specifically for our program including intake, work up and follow up protocols which I can e-mail you separately.

Thank you for your service and be safe.

Sincerely,

Rahul

-----Original Message-----

From: JL

Sent: Monday, June 16, 2014 11:31 AM

To: Jindal, Rahul M CIV US WRNMMC

Subject: Re: kidney transplantation - AFRICA

Hi Rahul-

Thanks very much for your email and the great attachment. You should be very proud of your accomplishments - really great stuff. One correction - the US military base in Africa is in the country of Djibouti (not Somalia).

I'll pass along your message and great guidance to the surgeon here in Djibouti.

Hope to be able to join you sometime on a mission.

Again, thanks -

V/r

JL

EMF Djibouti

Subject: RE: kidney transplantation - AFRICA

Thank you for the kind words and the correction.

I will be happy to send the Surgeon our low-cost immunosuppression protocols, hand books, modified dialysis fluid protocols and generic medications supply lines from India. In addition, we have set up a SKYPE clinic, FEDEX delivery for cross-match samples to Walter Reed and biopsy specimens to Drexel. I recently addressed the CARICOM countries on this initiative which has enabled some CKD patients from the CARICOM countries to see us in Guyana for kidney biopsies, access procedures and kidney transplants.

Regards,

Rahul

Team work: I would like to emphasize, as I did in the beginning of the book, that we could not achieve anything without the help of dedicated team members many of them gave up their vacations, money and energy to make a difference.

APPENDIX 1, 2 and 3 to SEVAK PROJECT IN GUYANA (CASE HISTORY 3)

SEVAK: HEALTH, DISEASE AND NUTRITIONAL SURVEY

I. DEMOGRAPHICS:
1. Name: _____
2. Address: _____
3. Date of Birth: _____ Age: _____ Mobile No: _____ House No: _____
   MM/DD/YR
4. Total Number of family members in the house: # Adults: ___ # Children: ___
5. Sex: [ ] Female [ ] Male
6. Marital Status:
   a. [ ] Married
   b. [ ] Divorced
   c. [ ] Widowed
   d. [ ] Separated
   e. [ ] Never been married

7. Family Income level (per month):
   a. [ ] < Rs 2,000
   b. [ ] Rs 2,000 – 5,000
   c. [ ] Rs 5,000 – 10,000
   d. [ ] Rs 10,000 – 15,000
   e. [ ]≥ Rs 15,000

8. Employment Status - Are you currently:
   a. [ ] Employed for wages
   b. [ ] Self-employed
   c. [ ] Farmer (If so, do you own land? [] Yes; [] Work as contract work/laborer)
   d. [ ] Homemaker
   e. [ ] Student
   f. [ ] Retired
   g. [ ] Unable to work

9. Educational level: *What is the highest grade or year of school you completed?*
   h. [ ] Grades 1 through 7 (Primary)
   i. [ ] Grades 8 through 10 (Secondary)
   j. [ ] Grades 11 or 12 (Higher Secondary)
   k. [ ] College 1 year to 2 years (Some college)
   l. [ ] College 4 years or more (College graduate)
   m.[ ] Post graduate
   n. [ ] No formal education
   o. [ ] Technical education or Vocational training or more

821442

II. PERSONAL HISTORY

1. Do you have any allergies?
If yes, list them: _____

2. Smoking
a.[ ] Everyday
b.[ ] Some days
c.[ ] Not at all

3. Do you use: (Check all that apply)
[ ] Chewing tobacco/Paan   [ ] Cigarettes   [ ] Bidis
[ ] Smokeless tobacco   [ ] Hookah   [ ] Gutka
[ ] Tobacco paste

4. On average, about how many cigarettes/bidis/Paan/Gutka/chewing tobacco/ smokeless tobacco day do you use now? Number: _____

5. How long have you been using these tobacco products? Years: ____ Months: ____

6. Do you know you can get lung or mouth cancer from smoking or chewing tobacco?
a. [ ] Yes   b. [ ] No

7. Drinking Alcohol: Considering all types of alcoholic beverages, how many times during the past month did you have 5 or more drinks on occasion?
None: ____ Once: ____ Twice: ____ 3-5 times: ____ 6-9 times: ____ 10 or more times: ____

8. How long have you been using alcoholic beverages? Years: ____ Months: ____

9. Drug Abuse: *Have you ever consumed anything such as Aphim, Opium, Ganza or Chorus?* a. [ ] Yes   b. [ ] No

10. Diet - Are you: a. [ ] Vegetarian   b. [ ] Non-vegetarian

11. What type of food do you typically consume? (Check all that apply)
[ ] Home cooked   [ ] Restaurant food   [ ] Fast-food   [ ] Snacks
Has the doctor told you to avoid sugar, salt, oil, etc. *(i.e., do you have any dietary restriction for health reasons)?* a. [ ] Yes b. [ ] No (If yes, please specify: _____)

12. Dietary Habits: (For interviewers = N for never, **S** for sometimes, **O** for often, or **A** for always)
How often do you

a.	Choose a diet low in fat, saturated fat, and cholesterol	N	S	O	A
b.	Limit use of sugars, sodas, and sweets?	N	S	O	A
c.	Eat 5-6 roti/ idli/ nan or 4 cups of rice per day	N	S	O	A
d.	Eat 1-2 medium size fruits each day?	N	S	O	A
e.	Eat 3-5 cups of cooked vegetables each day?	N	S	O	A
f.	Eat 1-2 cups of milk, buttermilk, or curd each day	N	S	O	A

g. Eat 2-3 cups of dal, rajma, soya bean, and nuts   N   S   O   A

h. Or consume meat/fish/eggs each day?

i. Read labels to identify calories, nutrients, fats, and   N   S   O   A
   sodium content in packaged food?

j. Eat breakfast?   N   S   O   A

13. Knowledge of Diseases: *Which of the following do you think are risk factors for diabetes?*
Check all that apply:

[ ] Being overweight   [ ] Being over the age for 45

[ ] Lack of exercise   [ ] Having a baby weighing over 9lbs

[ ] Obesity   [ ] Having a family member with diabetes

[ ] Excessive fat or calorie intake

14. Which of the following do you think are risk factors for cardiovascular disease-- heart attack, stroke, etc.? (Check all that apply):

[ ] High cholesterol   [ ] Obesity   [ ] Getting older

[ ] Heart disease among family members   [ ] Diabetes   [ ] Lack of exercise

[ ] Eating high fat foods   [ ] Smoking   [ ] Being male

[ ] Stress   [ ] Menopause

III. FAMILY HISTORY:
Did any member of your family receive treatment (family history of illness) for the following?
Please do not include spouse and his/her family members.

CONDITION	BROTHER	SISTER	FATHER	MOTHER	(GRAND PARENTS/ UNCLES, AUNTS, ETC.)
Diabetes					
Heart attacks before age 50					
High blood pressure					
Stroke					
Kidney dialysis					
Cancer (Please specify what kind)					

Jaundice					
Arthritis					
High Blood Cholesterol					
Psychiatric Illness					

Did any member of your family receive treatment from traditional healers?
a. [ ] Yes   b. [ ] No

Please check the type of doctors typically visited by your family for sickness:
a. [ ] Medical doctors (MBBS/MD)
b. [ ] Homeopathic doctors
c. [ ] Ayurvedic doctors
d. [ ] Religious healers (Sadhus)

IV. MEDICAL HISTORY:
Did a doctor or a nurse ever examine you for any of the following conditions?
Please answer yes or no.
(Read the choices):

CONDITION	YES	NO	NEVER HEARD OF DISEASE	DON'T KNOW/ NOT SURE	REFUSED
High Blood Cholesterol (Fatty substance in blood)					
Breast Cancer					
Cervical Cancer					
Intestine and anal canal (Colo-rectal Cancer)					
Incontinence or urine retention (Prostate Cancer)					
Diabetes					
Heart Disease					
High Blood Pressure					
Psychiatric Illness					
Arthritis					
Tuberculosis					
Kidney problems					
Thyroid problems					

Jaundice					
Back ache					
Anemia					

DIABETES QUESTIONS:
1. Have you ever been told by a doctor that you have diabetes?
a. [ ] Yes   b. [ ] No

(If female) Told only during pregnancy?
a. [ ] Yes   b. [ ] No

2. How old were you when you were told you have diabetes? Age: _____
3. How many years do you have diabetes? Years: _____
4. Are you now taking insulin?
a. [ ] Yes   b. [ ] No
5. Are you taking diabetes pills?
a. [ ] Yes b. [[ ]] No

List the medications: _____
6. How often do you take your diabetes medications?
a. [ ] Regularly
b. [ ] Take them only when you need it
c. [ ] Take them only when you feel ill
7. Are you experiencing any side effects to the medications?
a. [ ] Yes   b. [ ] No

Please specify: _____
8. About how often do you check your blood for glucose or sugar? Include times when checked by a health professional:
a. [ ] Every day
b. [ ] 2-3 Times per week
c. [ ] 2-3 Times per month
d. [ ] 2-3 Times per year
e. [ ] Never

9. Are you taking any other medications besides your diabetes medications?
a. [ ] Yes   b. [ ] No

Please list the reason: ____
10. Have you ever had any sores or irritations on your feet that took more than four weeks to heal?
a. [ ] Yes   b. [ ] No
11. About how many times in the past 12 months have you seen a doctor, nurse, or other health professional for your diabetes?

a. Number of times: _____ b. [ ] None

12. Has a doctor ever told you that diabetes has affected your eyes or that you had poor vision (retinopathy)?
a. [ ] Yes   b. [ ] No

13. Have you ever taken a course or class in how to manage your diabetes yourself?
a. [ ] Yes   b. [ ] No

14. Do you know anyone who can teach you how to manage your diabetes?
a. [ ] Yes   b. [ ] No

Please specify: _____

BLOOD PRESSURE

1. About how long has it been since you last had your blood pressure taken by a doctor, nurse, or other health professional?
a. [ ] Within the past 6 months (1 to 6 months ago)
b. [ ] Within the past years (6-12 months ago)
c. [ ][] Within the past 2 years (1 to 2 years ago)
d. [ ] Within the past 5 years (2 to 5 years ago)
e. [ ] 5 or more years ago

2. [ ]Have you ever been told by a doctor, nurse of other health professional that you have high blood pressure?
a. [ ] Yes   b. [ ] No à If **No,** skip to question 4.

3. If yes, are you taking any medication for your blood pressure?
a. [ ] Yes   Please list: _____
b. [ ] No

1. Blood cholesterol is a fatty substance (makes the blood thick). Have you ever had your blood cholesterol checked?
a. [ ] Yes   Your cholesterol level is: _____
b. [ ] No

2. If yes, are you taking any medications for your blood cholesterol?
a. [ ] Yes   Please list: _____
b. [ ] No

V. VILLAGE INFORMATION

1. Do you have a toilet?
a. [ ] Yes   b. [ ] No

2. Do you have a Chula?
a. [ ] Gas
b. [ ] Kerosene
c. [ ] Stove
d. [ ] Firewood

3. Does your kitchen have ventilation to the outside (ex- window)?
a. [ ] Yes   b. [ ] No

4.[ ] What kind of drinking water do you have?
a. [ ] Well

b. [ ] Village Tank
c. [ ] Pond
d. [ ] Tube Well
e. [ ] Hand Pump
f. [ ] Stand Pipe
g. [ ] None

5. Do you have RO water or chlorinated water?
a. [ ] Yes   b. [ ] No
MEASUREMENTS
Height:
FT: _____   IN: _____
Weight:
LBS: _____ BMI: _____ Wait Circumference: _____
Blood Pressure: _____
FBS (Fasting Blood Sugar: _____ mg%
VI. DIAGNOSIS:
_____

SIGNATURE

APPENDIX 2: SEVAK CURRICULUM (shown here are first 3 pages of 54. Each section is accompanied by a set of slides)

<u>Table of Contents</u>

11. Infectious Disease
   - Terms
   - Medical Diagnosis and Treatment
12. Trauma
   - Trauma Treatment Guidelines
   - Trauma Assessment
   - Types of Trauma
   - Treatment of Types of Trauma
   - Special Treatment of Pregnant Trauma Patients
   - Burns
   - Electrocution
13. Basic Life Support
14. Pediatrics
   - Evaluation of a newborn
   - Nutritional
   - Medical Diagnosis and Treatment
15. Obstetrics
   - Uncomplicated Pregnancies
   - Complicated Pregnancies
16. Gynecology
   - Uterus
   - Ovary
   - Cervix
   - Vagina
   - Menstrual Disorders
   - Breast
17. Male GU
18. Dermatology
19. EENT
20. Neurological
21. Hematology
22. Orthopedics and Rheumatology
23. Nutrition Concepts
24. Exercise
25. Lifestyle Modification

26. Immunizations
   - Children
27. Preventive Strategies: Breast, Cervix, Prostate, Lung, Mouth, & Stomach Cancers
28. Preventive Strategies: Diabetes, Hypertension, CVD, and other Infectious Diseases
   - Tuberculosis
29. Water Purification
   - Influences on Water Choice
   - Potential Water Sources
   - Water Purification
   - Types of Containers
   - Portable Water Testing
30. Sanitation
   - Flies
   - Fleas
   - Ticks
   - Mites
   - Bedbugs
   - Lice
   - Cockroaches
   - Rodents
   - General Prevention and Control Methods
31. Telemedicine (including use of laptops)
32. Coordination of Care and Liaison
33. Data Collection and Analysis
34. Clinical Rotations only Outpatient
35. Lifestyle Modification Education Demonstration by Students
36. Theoretical and Practical Examination
37. Conclusion

1. INTRODUCTION

Non-communicable and chronic diseases are the leading causes of death as observed in a study in rural India. It was also observed that this pattern of death is unlikely to be unique to these villages and provided a new insight into the rapid progression of epidemiological transition in rural India. Four studies in rural Alamarathupatti, Samiyarpatti and Pillayar Natham in the state of Tamilnadu and another in the village of Karakhadi, in the state of Gujarat showed marginalized access to health care and besides there were no primary health care centers that could manage chronic diseases. This lacuna made them even more vulnerable to chronic diseases and their complications. Seventy per cent of India lives in the villages (700 million people) and the importance of educating and delivery of healthcare to this large base of India in its resource-poor settings becomes an urgent and viable issue. Large-scale efforts to improve general awareness about diabetes, hypertension, cardiovascular disease, its risk factors, and to promote healthy lifestyles, must be undertaken.

According to Srinath Reddy at the present stage of India's health transition, chronic diseases contribute to an estimated 53% of deaths and 44% of disability-adjusted life-years lost and cardiovascular diseases and diabetes are highly prevalent in urban areas. Further, according to the authors, hypertension and dyslipidaemia, although common, are inadequately detected and treated. Demographic and socioeconomic factors are hastening the health transition, with sharp escalation of chronic disease burdens expected over the next 20 years.

There is no organized delivery of health care in rural India. Preventive health care is unavailable in the villages. Clean drinking water is not available to all and the sanitation is not adequate. Immunization though available, does not cover all who need it. In some cases in villages there might be circuit riders, who provide only acute care on the days they come. The second level of care is at the rural health clinic where there are no medicines or the care is at best rudimentary. The third level of care is at the district level where there is the availability of more care but still without the necessary means to provide full basic care. The fourth level of care is in the hospitals located in the cities, which are crowded and provide only acute care. Most of these facilities are financed by the government, which are not well staffed or adequately financed. They do not have any provision for screening or preventive care. Compliance with chronic treatment needs improvement. Life style modification education is not available. Indian villagers work hard in the farms and lose wages when they travel to another town for care. They need local preventive health care and screening for common diseases such as diabetes and hypertension.

In view of the studies done, this is a proposal for a prototype program to address the shortfall in healthcare needs of one village per district (around 27) in Gujarat to deliver diabetes and hypertension care, immunization and educational intervention using individuals, with medical or nonmedical backgrounds who are interested in the project. Such a program will become self-sustaining as the peer educators who live in the village will be able to continue the delivery of care and health education.

APPENDIX 3: Power Points and hand book

These comprise of: 1. Introduction and basic terminology. 2. Concept of SEVAKs. 3. Hypertension. 4. Diabetes. 5. Cardiovascular System including Basic Life Support. 6. Musculoskeletal System. 7. Pulmonary System. 8. Gastroenterology. 9. Endocrinology. 10. Infectious Diseases. 11. Trauma including transportation of patients and liaison with EMS. 12. Pediatrics. 13. Obstetrics: pregnancy and gestational age, hypertension, eclampsia, diabetes & referral. 14. Gynecology: Bleeding and referral. 15. Nutrition Concepts: requirements, CHO, Fats, Protein & Calories. 16. Exercise; Importance and various concepts. 17. Life Style Modification Education. 18. Immunization: Adult & Child schedules and importance in prevention. 19. Preventive Strategies: Breast, Cervix, Prostate, Lung, Mouth & Stomach Cancers. 20. Preventive Strategies: diabetes, hypertension, CVD and other infectious diseases. 21. Water purification. 22. Sanitation including mosquito prevention, toilets etc. 23. Telemedicine - including the use of laptops. 24. Coordination of care and liaison with different levels of care givers. 25. Data collection and analysis. 26. Life style modification education demonstration by the students.

APPENDIX 4: Some letters I received on the subject.

Dear Dr. Jindal,

Here is what I encountered during the 25 years I chose to volunteer. Prior to having my children, most of the time I spent volunteering pretty much involved the typical 'fundraising for a cause' events, 'walk-a-thons', 5K Runs, food drives, and yes, even the dreaded car washes. Most were sponsored through work, so I was simply on the 'being a participant/ able bodied aide', side. I did not really deal with the administrational side of the events. Only thing I really remember is that most of those that were signed up to attend, rarely did. After having the kids, I did quickly become involved with all of the organizations that they were involved with, the Girl Scouts, local Boys & Girls Clubs, and their schools, those types of things. In the last decade, I spent a lot of time volunteering Sports Injury Massage at sporting events, mostly pre and post issues with the athletes, both amateur and pro.

Through the years, I learned two major things regarding volunteerism, charity work, and those needed through all phases. With all of the clubs, organizations, and groups, the one common thread; all always seemed to have a need for fundraising for one thing or another. I guess just like everything else, funds are always short and in demand. Given my creative side and background in art, I was able to come up with 'not so typical' solutions for the organization(s) when they needed to raise fair amounts of money. I, just like everyone else, was simply not interested in spending my Saturday washing cars for a couple hundred bucks. A few of these organizations needed into the six figures and car washes were simply not going be able to generate those kinds of funds. Many already had exhausted the local and federal governments for any grants and subsidies that were available. Very quickly, I learned the admin side of fundraising and the roles of the volunteers that were so crucial to its success. One key element I found across the board, regardless of what group or charity was in need, people simply wanted new ideas, new events. No one is interested in buying wrapping paper, or cookies, or wasting countless hours to earn a little over a dollar per hour washing cars or selling cookies. But, everyone is up for a Vegas Style Evening- auctions, dinner, DJ, tables and dealers, per say. I found we could generate, if done properly, over 50,000 a night, and that was basically only utilizing the parents of the kids involved. In the next few years, I would have the 'boards' of these organization(s) build in 'however many of these functions' were needed to match the funds that were going to be needed. (i.e. At the time of 'sign-up', the parents knew in advance that along with the small session fee, they were going to have to sell 'x' number of tickets). This allowed for people outside of the organization(s) parents to participate and spend, which truly raised the level of 'funds' quite nicely. Most of the parents are tapped out financially anyway. I noticed this seemed far more preferred and no one was 'nickel and dimed' to death. Now, once I had these events in place, many local business would donate year after year. It was easy to organize, the file was already prepared. I asked for things in a way that would ensure more business for them and because they knew in advance this would be a bi-annual or seasonal request, we wouldn't be hounding them every month or so, they were happy to participate (ie, they would offer a 50$ gift card, I would ask for two 20$ and one 10$. This would enable that those individuals would also spend cash of their own when cashing in the gift card. Win-Win for both businesses get a deduction and a future sale, I get what I need for the event). Another key element I was made aware of, it was far easier to get locals to help locals, a company in New York, wants to help 'New York'. This also stood true for parents. The organizations that have levels, divisions, or teams, the parents were pretty much only interested in helping and supporting their own child's group. It did not matter that in a few short months or years, their child would be in next group, they were all about the 'now'. This was the one constant, year after year, decade after decade. People only seemed to show an interest in 'volunteering' when it directly benefited them at that time. Notice, I said, 'show and interest', not all or even close to all of them did actually help. Unfortunately, for quite some time, our society has become so 'inward focused', that many can't look 'outward' to help others. This is honestly where my 'irritation' with volunteerism and charity work lies, the lack of people who morally see and feel that it is the right thing to do. Through all of the years of my service to the many organizations, the one requirement I had was; they not ask me to attend or receive anything for it. For me, I was there because I wanted to be, they needed the help. I did not want any plaques, or certificates, or truly even "Thank Yous". I realized through the years from watching so many 'volunteer' for the wrong reasons, only people who truly feel the desire to help and give their time and talent.... should offer, should participate. Those that are doing it for their own gain in the end, be it situational or monetary, have no business being involved. If they are not there for the right reasons, they can actually stall and risk the progress that is being made by those who truly want to help, selflessly. Truly, those that didn't really want to help were very often the ones that caused problems within the 'flow' of the charity work, the ones that halted the progress with their drama and problems, the ones that would 'drain from' instead of actually 'giving to'. They very often accept, or even take on a task and then they don't follow through, leaving someone with just a moment's notice to pick up and fill in, or worse, the task unfinished. They very often can't simply do what they need to, what they signed up for, they need total direction and guidance (beyond the training period of course) which only takes another person from their task, therefore, stalling overall progress. I know this is a huge dilemma. Charities and Organizations are always in need of volunteers. I simply honestly feel that when accepting volunteers and work from them, it is best to know and 'feel' their intentions. Volunteers have to feel the desire and need to be present in service, they need to be there for the true benefit of others, and they have to deep down, want to be there. The 'heart being in the right place' issue became ridiculously clear to me in my ladder years. Yes, I saw it and was irritatingly annoyed with it when dealing with the youth groups, but I always had to give in to the aspect of, *'well, it is their children and they are just naturally drawn to their needs'*. However, when involved in the sport massage, many events were amateur athletes and some did involve professional athletes. I remember the day it became clear, we were at event in Baltimore that mixed both amateur and professional athletes. It was a 10 day event, we worked on many 'bodies', yes, the professionals can provide for themselves, the amateurs cannot. It was just the norm for the pros to visit us in the medical area as well. It was actually embarrassing who 'accepted' Dr. McKay's offer to help and who accepted it to meet the athletes. More than half the staff, well....let's just say..... Found reason after reason not to be available to work on the amateur athletes. They were simply there to try to meet the few professionals that might come in for a pre or post event session. They were not volunteering from their heart, for the little guy, they were simply there for their own selfish reasons. To me, that is not volunteerism in any form, it is simply self-promotion and should never come 'into play' when helping others, in any magnitude, at any time.

Sincerely,
Jennifer Fries

Namaste Rahul Ji,

I am honored by your request to provide feedback on your upcoming book. Indeed, it is well-researched and well-written. It contains a lot of useful information, your journey, experience, successes and challenges. With acknowledging the participation of so many individuals and institutions, you are showing true leadership, nobility and commitment to inspire others.

A few points for your consideration:

1. Additional examples of Seva projects in India (J K Yog; Ekal Vidhyalaya, Ritambara Devi and many more - perhaps, Abhaya Ji can provide specifics on these and some more). Coverage on ASHA for women can be reduced!

2. Also, there are a number of Indian organizations who are engaged in Sava in the US as well (Once again, I will seek Abhaya Ji's assistance).

3. There is a lot of poverty in the Western hemisphere as well and not just in Eastern.
4. Include the details on the website: www.hindusgiftoflife.org and Dhiren Makwana's contribution.

Clearly, the book is a culmination of many years of dedication and making a real difference in the lives of so many people. I treasure my friendship with you.

Warmly,
Sant Gupta

Dear Dr. Jindal,

Thank you for sharing with me the contents of this fine book and presentations on your Guyana visit and India training mission. I take my hat off to you and I am very grateful for all that you do in making this world a better place for all of us. With your kind permission, May I share your information and email address with Debasis Choudhuri of World Health Academy of California who are engaged with hospitals in Kolkata trying to bring in specialists from the US for technology transfer? Thank you for asking. Greenheart Medical University in Guyana is doing well slow but steadily. All the graduates have passed their boards and completed their internships and are in practice now. During my illness I could not travel to Guyana, so I transferred the leadership to David Koil Pillai, President of Transworld Education of Pune, India. I continue to serve as the Dean Emeritus. I wish you all the best and look forward to hearing from you.

With best regards,
Reza Chowdhury
Dean, Greenheart School of Medicine, Guyana, South America

Dear Dr. Rahul Jindal,

It was an immense pleasure in meeting and hearing your projects at the Atlanta Global health summit. Thank you for agreeing in supporting my meager effort to improve few most desired projects in Bangladesh.

I will appreciate if you support in establishing the cadaveric donor program and also during your visit help the surgeons to improve their technique. We can write the project with your input and submit it to the Dhaka Institutions. You can also send me the video or other details brochure which can be distributed to them early on as a beginning of the effort and connecting them.

I will ask also for the need of cornea. Your work in organizing Guyana's people in NY and getting their support for the whole program is exemplary. I think a short summary of that program can be very inspiring and can be used to encourage other communities in USA.

Best wishes,
Ziauddin Ahmed, MD,
Nephrologist, Drexel School of Medicine, Philadelphia.

REFERENCES

1   Jindal RM, Falta EM, Baines LS, Elster EA. (2011). Health policy for renal replacement therapy in developing countries. Journal of Healthcare, Sciences and Humanities,1: 41.

2   The story of first kidney transplant in Guyana, South America, and lessons learnt for other developing countries, by Rahul M. Jindal. Publisher: iUniverse, 2009.

3   Babakhani A, Guy SR, Falta EM, Elster EA, Jindal TR, Jindal RM. (2013). Surgeons bring RRT to patients in Guyana. Bull Am Coll Surg,98:17.

4   Altieri M, Jindal TR, Patel M, et al. (2013). Report of the first peritoneal dialysis program in Guyana, South America. Perit Dial Int,33:116.

5   15 kidney transplants since programme started in 2008. (http://www.guyanatimesgy.com/2013/04/10/15-kidney-transplants-since-programme-started-in-2008/). Accessed 08/09/2015.

6   Historic kidney transplant completed in seven hours –'new hope' patient being monitored. (http://www.stabroeknews.com/2008/archives/07/13/historic-kidney-transplant-completed-in-seven-hours/). Accessed 08/09/2015.

7   Pueschel M. (2013). DoD Medical Outreach Efforts in Central America Building Partnerships, Stability. (http://intlhealth.dhhq.health.mil/newsandreleases/news/news_latest_news/13-07-10/DoD_Medical_Outreach_Efforts_in_Central_America_Building_Partnerships_Stability.aspx?id=?id=()). Accessed 08/09/2015.

8   Importance of 'Eye Bank' amplified by visiting ophthalmologist. (http://www.kaieteurnewsonline.com/2014/03/23/importance-of-eye-bank-amplified-by-visiting-ophthalmologist/). Accessed 08/09/2015.

9   Sevak Project: Improving access to case in rural India. (http://sevakproject.org/sevakguyana.html). Accessed 08/09/2015.

10   Waller SG, Altieri MS, Jindal RM. (2015). Surgeons develop visionary plan to bring corneal transplants to developing countries. Bull Am Coll Surg,100:22.

11   Guy SR, Womble AL, Jindal TR, et al. (2013). Ethical dilemmas in patient selection for a new kidney transplant program in Guyana, South America. Transplant Proc, 45, 102.

12   Johnson V. A brief history of the U.S. Navy Independent Duty Corpsman (http://navymedicinemagazine.navylive.dodlive.mil/2014/12/08/a-brief-history-of-the-u-s-navy-independent-duty-corpsman/). Accessed 08/09/2015.

13   Demographics of Guyana and Guyanese people. (https://en.wikipedia.org/wiki/Guyana). Accessed 08/09/2015.

14   R: A Language and Environment for Statistical Computing. Vienna, Austria: R Foundation for Statistical Computing; 2013.

15   Jindal RM, Salifu MO, Patel TG, Misra R (2012). Prevalence of diabetic nephropathy in an underserved rural community. Indian J Nephrol, 22:484.

16   Balagopal P, Kamalamma N, Patel TG, Misra R (2012). A community based participatory diabetes prevention and management intervention in rural India using community health workers. Diabetes Educ, 38:822.

17   Joshi R, Cardona M, Iyengar S, et al. (2006). Chronic diseases now a leading cause of death in rural India – Mortality data from the Andhra Pradesh Rural Health Initiative. Int J Epidemiol, 35:1522.

18   Twenty eight community health workers commence medical training. (http://www.stabroeknews.com/2011/archives/10/14/twenty-eight-community-health-workers-commence-medical-training%C2%A0/). Accessed 08/09/2015.

19   National Health Mission. About Accredited Social Health Activist (ASHA). (http://www.nrhm.gov.in/communitisation/asha/about-asha.html). Accessed 08/09/2015.

20   Cheeseman SE (2012). Communication and collaboration technologies. Neonatal Netw, 31, 115.

21   Chunara R, Andrews JR, Brownstein JS (2012). Social and news media enable estimation of epidemiological patterns early in the 2010 Haitian cholera outbreak. Am J Trop Med Hyg, 86, 39.

22   Geissbuhler A, Kimura M, Kulikowski CA, et al. (2011). Confluence of disciplines in health informatics: an international perspective. Methods Inf Med, 50, 545.

23   Toure K, Sankore R, Kuruvilla S, Scolaro E, Bustreo F, Osotimehin B. (2012). Positioning women's and children's health in African union policy-making: a policy analysis. Global Health, 8, 3.

24   Bloom DE. (2011). The value of vaccination. Adv Exp Med Biol, 697, 1-8.

25   Ozawa S, Stack ML, Bishai DM, et al. (2011). During the 'decade of vaccines,' the lives of 6.4 million children valued at $231 billion could be saved. Health Aff (Millwood), 30, 1010.

26   Murray CJ, Lopez AD. (1997). Mortality by cause for eight regions of the world: Global Burden of Disease Study. Lancet, 349, 1269.

27   Brown TM, Cueto M, Fee E. (2006). The World Health Organization and the transition from "international" to "global" public health. Am J Public Health, 96, 62.

28   Stack M L, Ozawa S, Bishai DM, et al. (2011). Estimated economic benefits during the 'decade of vaccines' include treatment savings, gains in labor productivity. Health Aff (Millwood), 30, 1021.

29   GAVI Matching Fund. (2014) (www.gavialliance.org/funding/give-to-gavi/gavi-matching-fund). Accessed 08/09/2015.

30   Leading Group on Innovative Financing for Development. (2014) (http://www.leadinggroup.org/rubrique20.html), Accessed 08/09/2015.

31   UNITAID. (2014) (http://www.unitaid.eu/en/who/about-unitaid). Accessed 08/09/2015.

32 Danovaro-Holliday M C, Wood AL, Le Baron CW. (2002). Rotavirus vaccine and the news media, 1987-2001. JAMA, 287, 1455.

33 Baines LS, Joseph JT, Jindal RM. (2002). A public forum to promote organ donation amongst Asians: the Scottish initiative. Transpl Int, 15, 124.

34 Zambia's data-driven healthcare initiative. (2011) (http://www.theguardian.com/global-health-workers/zambia-s-data-driven-healthcare-initiative). Accessed 08/09/2015.

35 Global Economic Burden of Non-communicable Diseases. (2014) (http://www.weforum.org/reports/global-economic-burden-non-communicable-diseases). Accessed 08/09/2015.

36 http://www.covidien.com/covidien/pages.aspx?page=Home and Pfizer www.pfizer.com Accessed 08/09/2015.

37 Blanchet K, James P. (2013). The role of social networks in the governance of health systems: the case of eye care systems in Ghana. Health Policy Plan, 28, 143-156.

38 Guyana. (http://rainforests.mongabay.com/20guyana.htm). Accessed 08/09/2015.

39 How the pneumococcal AMC works. (2014) (http://www.gavialliance.org/funding/pneumococcal-amc/how-the-pneumococcal-amc-works/). Accessed 08/09/2015.

40 Tsuya ASY, Tanaka A, Narimatsu H. (2014). Do Cancer patients tweet? Examining the twitter use of cancer patients in Japan. J Med Internet Res, 16, e137.

41 Dyar OJ, C.-S. E, Holmes AH. (2014). What makes people talk about antibiotics on social media? A retrospective analysis on twitter use. J Antimicrob Chemother.

42 Freifeld CC, Brownstein JS, Menone CM, et al. (2014). Digital drug safety surveillance: monitoring pharmaceutical products in twitter. Drug Saf, 37, 343.

43 India Polio Fact Sheet. (2012). (http://www.polioeradication.org/Portals/0/Document/InfectedCountries/India/PolioIndiaFactSheet.pdf). Accessed 08/09/2015.

44 Polio Eradication. (2014). (http://www.unicef.org/health/india_61293.html). Accessed 08/09/2015.

45 Touch Surgery. (2014). (http://www.touchsurgery.com/). Accessed 08/09/2015.

46 Tele Health. (2014). (http://healthcare.orange.com/eng/discover-e-health). Accessed 08/09/2015.

47 Sampath WGC. (2010). Real-Time biosurveillance pilot programme in Sri Lanka: Lessons learned. Sri Lanka Journal of Bio-Medical Informatics, 1,139.

48 Bengtsson L, Lu X, Thorson A, Garfield R, von Schreeb J. (2011). Improved response to disasters and outbreaks by tracking population movements with mobile phone network data: a post-earthquake geospatial study in Haiti. PLoS Med, 8(8), e1001083.

49   Schmidt CW (2014). Trending Now: Using social media to predict and track disease outbreaks. Environ Health Perspect, 120, A31.

50   Palmer D. (2006). Tracking Malawi's human resource crisis. Reprod Health Matters, 14, 27.

51   Yu D, Souteyrand Y, Banda MA, Kaufman J, Perriëns JH. (2008). Investment in HIV/AIDS programs: does it help strengthen health systems in developing countries? Global Health, 4, 8.

52   World Health Organization Maximizing Positive Synergies Collaborative Group, et al. (2009). An assessment of interactions between global health initiatives and country health systems. The Lancet, 373, 2137.

53   Sud V, Ejaz K, Fedorowicz Z, Mathew ME, Sharma A. (2011). Cochrane: spreading the message of research to students and juniors. [Editorial]. Cochrane Database Syst Rev (8), ED000026.

54   Gibson M. (2014). The Growing Role of "Post-Publication Peer Review" and Social Media. (http://www.gbsi.org/blog/2014/01/growing-role-post-publication-peerreview-Social). Accessed 08/09/2015.

55   Use social media to strengthen health systems. (2014). (http://www.scidev.net/global/health/opinion/use-social-media-to-strengthen-health-systems.html). Accessed 08/09/2015.

56   Mayo Clinic Center for Social Media (2012). Bringing the social media revolution to health-care, Publisher: Mayo Foundation for Medical Education and Research, ISBN-13: 978-1893005877.

57   Nelson EJ, Hughes J, Oakes JM, Pankow JS, Kulasingam SL. (2014). Estimation of Geographic Variation in Human Papillomavirus Vaccine Uptake in Men and Women: An Online Survey Using Facebook Recruitment. J Med Internet Res 2014,16:e198.

ABOUT THE AUTHOR

Dr. Rahul M. Jindal is currently a Transplant Surgeon at the Walter Reed National Military Medical Center and Professor of Surgery and Global Health at Uniformed Services University, Bethesda, Maryland. Dr. Jindal is a visiting professor in several universities in India and the U.K.

Jindal is the author of over 150 manuscripts; has been funded by the National Institute of Health. Jindal's research work and publications have been cited in text books and have been accompanied by editorials. Jindal has played a crucial role on the medical team that conducted ground-breaking surgery at Walter Reed AMC on Thanksgiving Day in 2009. A 21-year old senior airman, Tre Porfirio was shot three times by an insurgent in Afghanistan; he received the first ever pancreas islet cell transplant after trauma.

Dr. Jindal setup the first comprehensive kidney dialysis and transplant program in Guyana, South America. His team visits Guyana 4 times a year and has performed numerous surgical procedures. Recently, Jindal's team added corneal transplant program to their existing work in Guyana. Jindal endowed a scholarship (Rahul M. Jindal travel fellowship) which will enable selected final year medical students to carry out electives in medical schools in India. He is the Co-Chair of SEVAK Program (www.sevakproject.org) in which his team trains high school students in good preventative measures and diagnosis of diabetes and hypertension in India and Guyana where there are no medical facilities. Jindal narrated the Guyana experience in his book "The story of the first kidney transplant in Guyana, South America, and lessons learnt for other developing countries (Publisher: iUniverse, 2009. ISBN: 9-78144-017387-5).

In addition to his clinical activities, Dr. Jindal earned a PhD in Social Psychology from the Middlesex University, London, for his work on improving quality of life in patients with kidney failure and kidney transplants. Based on his experience in working with psycho-social issues in this group of patients, Dr. Jindal co-authored a book entitled "The Struggle for Life: A Psychological Perspective of Kidney Disease and Transplantation, (Publisher: Praeger, Westport, CT, USA, 2003, ISBN: 0-86569-323-4"

Dr. Jindal recently received the Leadership Award by the "International Leadership Foundation" Washington, DC, 2013. He also received the Outstanding American by choice award by the United States Citizenship and Immigration Services, 2013. Governor of Maryland appointed Jindal as Commissioner, Office on Service and Volunteerism, Maryland (2013) and Commissioner to the Human Rights Commission, Montgomery County, Maryland (2014). Jindal was awarded the Fulbright-Nehru Distinguished Chair to carry out research and teaching in India for 2015-6; and also the Ellis Island Medal of Honor, 2015.

INDEX

flyers   29, 31, 45, 86, 102, 106, 110,
   159, 175, 180, 234-5
Food and Drug Administration
   (FDA)   16
Foote, Barbara   78-80
Ford Foundation   236
Future Group, India   4

G

Ganza   243
Gastroenterology   114, 249, 254
GAVI Matching Fund   194, 200, 262
Geissbuhler A   262
Geographical Information System
   (GIS)   219
George Washington University,
   Washington, DC, USA   153
GEP   145-7, 157-9, 180, 182
GINA   119
Global access to healthcare   197
Global citizenship   5
Global health   xi, 132, 192-3, 210,
   233, 260, 262, 264-5
Globalization   219
GPHC   30, 34, 39-40, 42-4, 54, 235
Guatemala   64
Gujarat   18-19, 117, 173, 252-3
Gujarat, India   19, 117
Gurudwaras   73, 111
Gutka   243
Guyana   x-xi, 13-17, 19-22, 29-41,
   44-7, 50-2, 59-61, 63-4, 115-21,
   166-70, 203, 233-5, 237-9, 259-
   61, 265
Guyana, South America   x-xi, 5, 19,
   59, 121, 259, 261, 265
Guyanese Transplant Initiative   194
GWI   170

H

Haiti   211-12, 263

HCSML   215
Health   13-14, 18, 31-2, 36-41, 62-3,
   83-4, 113, 130, 132-3, 154, 166-
   8, 200-1, 210-11, 215-16, 261-5
Healthcare   47, 62, 193, 196-7, 201,
   210, 212, 215, 261
Healthcare professionals as social
   entrepreneurs   210
Hemodialysis   68
HH Pramukh Swami Maharaj   172
High-income countries   189-90
Hindi   6, 119, 162
Hindu community   100-1, 172
Hindu Mandir Executive Committee
   (HMEC)   71
Hindu temple (Mandir)   73
Hinduism   94-5, 98
Hindus   73-4, 90, 92-9, 101, 109, 172
HIV   16, 20, 68, 81, 117, 130-1, 197,
   201, 205, 212, 264
HLA tissue typing   51
Holi Sammelan Progam   170
Hong Kong   49
Horl et al   47
Hospital Anxiety Depression
   Scale   151
How may I serve you?   vii
Humanitarian   132-3
Hypertension   114, 123, 126, 249,
   251, 254

I

Ice Bucket Challenge   219
Immunization   114, 200, 252, 254
Independent Duty Corpsman (IDC)
   18, 113
India   x-xi, 2-5, 10-11, 18-22, 33-4,
   49-51, 62-4, 90-1, 93-8, 117-21,
   135-7, 162-3, 217-19, 252, 261-3
Indo-Guyanese   59
Infectious   114, 250-1, 254

North American Hindu Temples
National Blood Donation
Campaign 80

O

Official Development Assistance
(ODA) 204
Opium 243

P

Paan 243
Pakistan 65, 224
Pan American Association of Eye
Banks (APABO) 16
Partnerships 197, 261
Patient 50, 249
Persaud, Lakeram 31
Pilot 148-9
Population 115, 118, 130
Population Reference Bureau 130
Poverty 185-6, 224
Poverty reduction strategy 186
Power Points 114, 254
PPP 13-14, 17, 22, 239
PPP corneal transplant mission 17
PPP strategy 22
Prakongsai et al 65
Pre- and post- evaluation of the SEVAK
training 19
Pre-service training for health
workers 212
Prevention 13, 18, 65, 113, 251
Primary care 215
Private sector 187, 197
Problems 224
Promotion 13, 18, 113
PRSPs 186
Punjabi suit 163

Q

Quality of life scale 151
QuantiaMD 216
Quick win 188

R

Ramkissoon, Shankar 100
Rashid et al 66
Ravens Progressive Matrices test
155, 157
Real-Time Bio-surveillance Program
(RTBP) 211
Reconciling private philanthropy with
governmental mandates 166
Red Cross 70, 72, 89, 92, 106, 199
Reliance Foundation 3
Renal replacement therapy (RRT) 113
Renal replacement therapy in
Guyana 203
Resident Welfare Association 218
Resources 50, 133
Reza Chowdhury 259
Ritambara Devi 258
Rotavirus vaccine 195, 263
RRT 13-15, 113, 239, 261
RTBP 211

S

Sabha 85
Sacrifice 11
Sadhu 172, 174
Safe 156, 162
Sanitation 13, 18, 113-14, 218,
251, 254
Sanskrit vii
Satyamev Jayate 3
Scaling up 133, 212
Scriptures 137

World Health Academy of
California 259
World health organization
(WHO) 200
World Peace Conference (Viswa Santi
Sammelanam) 138
World Trade Center (9/11) 80
WRNMMC 237-8, 240

Y

Yoga vii, 107-8, 137, 156, 179

Z

Zambian government's data driven
healthcare initiative 197, 201-2

Printed in the United States
By Bookmasters